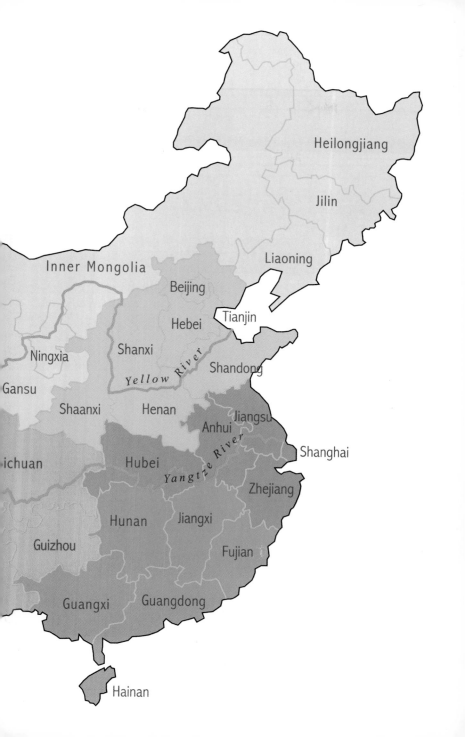

Finding Chinese Food in Los Angeles

FINDING
CHINESE FOOD
 LOS ANGELES

2003

A GUIDE TO CHINESE REGIONAL CUISINES

CARL CHU

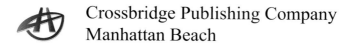

Crossbridge Publishing Company
Manhattan Beach

Finding Chinese Food in Los Angeles
A Guide to Chinese Regional Cuisines
By Carl Chu

Published by
Crossbridge Publishing Company
Box 3555, Manhattan Beach, California 90266
United States of America

Visit our website: http://www.crossbridgepublishing.com

Library of Congress Control Number: 2003091614
ISBN: 1-932296-01-8
First Edition – March 2003

Printed in Taiwan

Disclaimer:

Restaurants come and go all the time. Although every effort is made to provide
the most up-to-date information, any error or omission in this book is wholly
unintentional, and both the author and publisher assume no liability for the
reader's loss, injury, or inconvenience resulting from using information
contained herein.

TABLE OF CONTENTS

PREFACE

The primary impetus in writing this book is to explore the fascinating world of Chinese regional cuisines. Over the past decade, the Chinese food scene in Los Angeles has changed dramatically – particularly in the San Gabriel Valley, where many Chinese immigrants have come and settled. Commensurate with China's vastness, Chinese food is comprised of many different regional styles of cooking. Variations are so diverse that even the Chinese themselves cannot possibly be familiar with them all.

At some time during the research for this book, it became obvious that this was bound to be more than a restaurant guide. In order to gain an insight to the uniqueness of each Chinese regional cuisine, the historical- and social forces shaping these cuisines need to be explored. Thus, this book takes tremendous steps to examine, in more or less detail, the background contexts that make Chinese food such a great culinary tradition. At the same time, the book provides entertaining- and practical information for anyone interested in discovering Los Angeles's Chinese food scene for themselves.

For a long time, the different varieties of Chinese regional cuisines remained untenable to most Americans, because of language- and geographical barriers. The concept of Chinese regional cuisines even seemed superfluous, because for over one hundred years, a solid stereotype of "Chinese food" was shaped by the dominance of Guangdong immigrants in America. Even today, the availability of Chinese regional cuisines is still murky beyond the limits of Chinese takeout restaurants that haunt the main streets of America.

Yet, despite the cultural gaps of the past, the universe of Chinese regional cuisines has come closer than ever within reach. This is especially the case in Los Angeles, where authentic dishes from almost all corners of China are easily accessible. For anyone willing to search them out and giving them a try, the variety of Chinese regional cuisines in Los Angeles is unmatched anywhere else in North America. Without qualification, the colorful Chinese food scene in Los Angeles is among the best in the world, and it adds another unique facet to the city's dynamic social fabric.

APPROACHING CHINESE REGIONAL CUISINES

The best way to begin exploring Chinese regional cuisines is by first adopting some knowledge of their unique characteristics. Each of the four Chinese regional styles, as are presently discussed, are quite distinct: a quick glance through the menus will immediately reveal representative dishes that set one regional style apart from the others. It is the goal of this book to provide insightful knowledge about these cooking styles. Hopefully, by doing so, the longstanding stereotype of Chinese food as a monolithic takeout fodder will be forever changed.

That having said, the information presented in this book is by no means the boundaries by which Chinese regional cuisines are confined. Chefs are constantly reinventing themselves, and in the name of *haute cuisine*, innovative dishes are being created at breakneck speed. Borrowing from foreign ideas, unusual ingredients, and new uses of familiar techniques, Chinese regional cuisines in Los Angeles often defy old traditions. Discovering and sampling new regional dishes has always been part of the fun in appreciating food. Happily, the abundance of high quality local ingredients in Los Angeles helps provide the means by which Chinese regional cuisines transcend the barriers of tradition back home. Altogether, the collection of traditional- and innovative restaurants makes up much of the excitement over the Chinese food scene in Los Angeles.

A NOTE ON DISH DESCRIPTIONS

Many dishes mentioned in this book carry colloquial Chinese names. Some are translated literally from their Chinese names, such as "Pockmark-face Lady's Tofu." Others are left in their phonetic forms, such as "*Dongbo* Pork."

Colloquial names in Chinese dishes are often witty, but for people unfamiliar with Chinese culture, these names reveal very little about the food themselves. Translating Chinese names is also problematic, because no two restaurants describe the same dish the same way. Chinese restaurants compound the problem by frequently giving dubious translations for the dishes. For example, a famous dish from Sichuan – "Pockmark-face Lady's Tofu" – is variously translated as "Spicy Tofu with Minced Beef," "Sichuan-style Tofu," or the mundane "Tofu in Hot Sauce." Wildly different descriptions for the same dish confuse people encountering them for the first time. Others are turned off from trying these dishes simply because they have no clear notion of what to expect.

This book maintains the integrity of Chinese colloquial names whenever possible, either by mentioning them in their Mandarin pronunciations, or by giving them literal translations from their Chinese names. This is followed by detailed descriptions that will not only tell the story behind the dishes' names, but also reveal some interesting facts about them as well.

On the other hand, most Chinese dish names are unremarkably the synopsis of the ingredients that are contained therein. These descriptive names are simply translated into English.

In either case, whether the dish has a colloquial- or descriptive name, the reader can use this book as a reference; when ordering dishes at a restaurant, they can attempt the Mandarin pronunciations, point to the Chinese characters, or describe the dishes to the staff.

INTRODUCTION

Quite simply, Los Angeles has some of the best Chinese food in the world, yet this fact does not seem to get around much. Perhaps this is because most of Los Angeles's Chinese restaurants are located far away from the fashionable Westside, where powerbrokers and trendsetters create interminable influences on local tastes and perceptions. Things outside of the Westside's sphere of influence tend to be overlooked, and in a metropolitan area that spans over 4,000 square-miles, that means a lot about Los Angeles routinely gets ignored.

The term "*San Gabriel Valley*" does not inspire much feeling or emotion in people, even from *Angelenos* who live in and around it. More likely, mentioning it will just produce some unflattering images of middle-America suburbia: crossed with congested freeways, and shaded under a constant pall of smog. Yet, the reality in the San Gabriel Valley is something quite astonishing. It is much more than a dusty oasis sitting in the shadows of the San Gabriel Mountains. Thanks to the tremendous inflow of Chinese immigrants over the past 30 years, the San Gabriel Valley is dynamic and exciting – rapidly growing, changing, and redefining itself as one of the crowning jewels of Los Angeles's multifaceted image.

In the 1970s, a Chinese-born Los Angeles developer named Frederic Hsieh began marketing real estate in Monterey Park, 10 miles east of Downtown Los Angeles. Dubbing it the "Chinese Beverly Hills," he sold the idea of overseas investment to the people back in Hongkong and Taiwan. What he showed the Hongkongers and Taiwanese were attractive qualities of American life – gently rolling hills, wide-open spaces, and ample opportunities to make a better life.

The reaction was more than sensational, resulting in a transpacific land-rush that soon transformed the entire San Gabriel Valley into a blazing hotplate of Pan-Asian commerce. By 1987, Monterey Park had a predominantly Chinese population, and it was proclaimed as the first Chinese suburb in America that same year. This distinction is still rare in other U.S. cities today.

Monterey Park, *the "Chinese Beverly Hills," anchors a large and growing Chinese population in the San Gabriel Valley.*

The Chinese settlement in Monterey Park established the first wholesale shift of the Chinese community from Downtown/Chinatown into the suburbs. Prior to the 1970s, the Chinese community in Los Angeles was kept small by immigration quotas, and it remained inside Los Angeles's city limits. Once immigration was liberalized, the Chinese began pouring in from mainland China, Hongkong, Taiwan, and Vietnam. By 1990, the Chinese had outgrown Monterey Park and the surrounding towns in the San Gabriel Valley. Today, a noticeable Chinese "community" is spread out onto a wide swath of suburbia as far as thirty miles away in Diamond Bar.

Expectedly, Chinese restaurants in Los Angeles followed the eastward move to the suburbs. Wide-open spaces in the San Gabriel Valley gave restaurant owners plenty of opportunities to see their dreams come to fruition. Some owners, including top chefs from Hongkong and Taipei, invested their own money to build palatial tributes to Chinese cuisines – large, bright restaurants that come complete with marble façades, brass fixtures, intimate banquet rooms, and tables for hundreds. Others, such as small family restaurants opened by recent immigrants, dot the street corners and strip malls, serving authentic home-cooking that help the homesick recall old memories.

The quality of Chinese food in Los Angeles also changed with the influx of Chinese immigrants. New restaurants started opening with the palates of the Chinese in mind – not that of the Americans. They began serving genuine regional cuisines never seen and heard of before in America. Sichuan cuisine, Islamic-Chinese cuisine, Hongkong-style seafood cuisine, and even the venerable Beijing Duck all made their ways into the Chinese food scene in the San Gabriel Valley.

Today, there are so many restaurants representing almost every corner of China, that even the Chinese themselves cannot possibly be familiar with them all. The tremendous crop of authentic restaurants – and many are of world-class caliber – altered people's longtime perception that the best Chinese food in Los Angeles was in Downtown/Chinatown. These restaurants also broke ranks with the American stereotype, which had long regarded Chinese food as cheap, takeout fodder hardly worth the consideration as *haute cuisine*.

The paradisiacal sandlot that is the San Gabriel Valley doubles as the logical North American beachhead for food fads emerging from the Pacific Rim. An active and spirited dynamism is constantly churning in this corner of the metropolitan area, showcasing both authentic- and trendy examples of Chinese regional cuisines. Within this mix of suburban neighborhoods is a higher concentration of recommendable restaurants than the Westside, and both the quality and variety of the Chinese food there far outshine those found in old-fashioned Chinatowns of San Francisco and New York. Without a doubt, the San Gabriel Valley is the Chinese Food Capital of North America, and as the Chinese community continues to grow there, its food scene will only become more exciting in the future.

This attractive "Chinese food" restaurant in Los Angeles's Chinatown caters mainly to the tourist crowd.

THE CHINESE IN AMERICA

The Guangdong people (Cantonese) were the first Chinese immigrants in America, originally arriving during the heady days of the California Gold Rush. More Guangdong people came to California in 1864, recruited to work on the western half of the Transcontinental Railroad. These people, mostly men, came from the areas surrounding the city of Guangzhou (Canton) in Guangdong province. Thus, they were commonly referred to as the "Cantonese."

Guandong province during the 1850s was a place of overpopulation and poverty. When the dire conditions festered into desperation, the Guangdong people left in droves, aided by local associations that helped them settle in places around the world, reaching as far as the Americas. People from the eastern Guangdong city of Chaozhou and nearby Fujian province migrated to Southeast Asia, while those from and near the city of Guangzhou settled in Hawaii, North America, and the colonies of the British Empire.

Most of the people who migrated to Hawaii and North America settled in Honolulu and San Francisco, giving rise to both cities' historically large Chinese populations. The Guangdong people quickly stamped their original impressions on Honolulu and San Francisco by giving them idyllic Chinese names. Today, the Chinese still call Honolulu "Sandalwood Fragrance Mountain" (*Tanxiangshan*) – for the precious softwood that once grew in abundance there. San Francisco is known as "Old Gold Mountain" (*Joujingshan*) – an obvious allusion to the California Gold Rush. These are the only two U.S. cities with their own Chinese names.

Although the Guangdong people were able to leave in large numbers, emigration from other parts of China never coalesced during the late nineteenth century. The reigning Qing Dynasty had outlawed overseas travel for all Chinese, but Guangdong province, being at the southernmost part of the country and furthest from the Qing's power from Beijing, was amuck with law-defying expatriation. The presence of British colonists in southern China also helped stem Qing's power there. The British, which outlawed slavery throughout its empire in 1833, desperately needed workers to build its worldwide franchise, and the Guangdong people were more than eager to sign on as contract workers ("coolies") for a chance to escape hardship at home.

Wherever they settled, the Guangdong immigrants profoundly affected the world's perception of Chinese culture. Although Guangdong province accounted for merely eight percent of China's population, Guangdong immigrants made up nearly all of the Chinese living overseas. For over a century, they were the sole sources of contact on which the

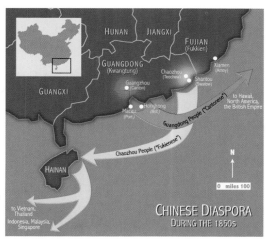

Nearly all of the original Chinese immigrants in America came from Guangdong province.

outside world perceived and stereotyped the Chinese. For one, in the Americas, Europe, and Southeast Asia, people naturally (but mistakenly) assumed that their Guangdong cuisine was the "Chinese food" that represented all of China's various cooking styles.

ANTI-CHINESE MOVEMENTS IN AMERICA

The experience of the Guangdong immigrants in America turned sour soon after their arrival. A series of laws in California between 1850 and 1870 were specifically targeted against them. California's "Foreign Miner's License Tax" (1852) was aimed directly at driving the Chinese out of the lucrative gold mining business. In 1863, Chinese children were barred from attending California's public schools. And San Francisco's "Cubic Space Ordinance" (1867) imposed a minimum amount of living- and working space for each person in the city, in a veiled attempt to close Chinese boarding houses that sheltered newly arrived immigrants.

Anti-Chinese sentiment in the 1870s led to race riots throughout California, including the massacre in October 1871 that lynched 19 Chinese in Los Angeles's Chinatown. The U.S. was barely 100 years old at the time, and although the Chinese population numbered only around 70,000, working class whites felt threatened by the Chinese, who were willing to accept any job for lower pay. Congress, which at the time was tightly contested between Democrats and Republicans, gladly took up the Anti-Chinese cause to curry the working class votes.

In 1882, Congress passed the Chinese Exclusion Act, which prohibited all Chinese immigration to the U.S. It was the first time in American history that an ethnic group was specifically barred from entry into the U.S. Previously, America had maintained an unrestricted immigration policy for everyone. Further, the Chinese Exclusion Act prohibited any Chinese already residing in the U.S. from gaining citizenship.

> *"Whereas, in the opinion of the Government of the United States, the coming of Chinese laborers to this country endangers the good order of certain localities within the territory thereof..."*
>
> **Preamble of the Chinese Exclusion Act, 1882**

The capstone of anti-Chinese legislation in the nineteenth century was laid by the Geary Act, written by a California Democrat and passed Congress in 1891. Among several provisions of the Geary Act was the establishment of the first internal passport system in America, specifically requiring every Chinese person to possess residency papers even when traveling within the U.S. In order to obtain a "certificate of residence," not only must the Chinese person register with the government, they must provide a white person to testify on their behalf in order to satisfy the proof that their claim to residency was legitimate.

LIBERALIZATION OF CHINESE IMMIGRATION POLICY

The Chinese Exclusion Act was repealed in 1943, during World War II when China and the U.S. were allies in their war against the Japanese. However, large-scale Chinese immigration to America did not begin until the passage of the Immigration Act of 1965, which abolished the national quota system. In the roughly eighty years between the Chinese Exclusion Act and Immigration Act, the Chinese population in the U.S. was stagnant. Similarly, America's contact with Chinese culture, including its food, was confined to those of the original Guangdong immigrants.

After 1965, different Chinese groups began arriving in large numbers. First came the Hongkongers and Taiwanese, who were generally wealthy and possessed capital for investments overseas. There were many others who came to America with scant money in their pockets, willingly accepting their pursuit for the American Dream entirely from scratch. In the late 1970s, following the end of the Vietnamese War, many ethnic Chinese of Chaozhou origin (*Chiu Chow*, or *Teochew*) fled racial persecution in Vietnam. Their harrowing plight drew worldwide sympathy as the story of the Vietnamese Boat People. In the 1980s, with the opening of mainland China for trade and travel, people came from Beijing, Shanghai, Sichuan, and all other parts of China. By 1990, the complexions of the Chinese in America had shifted decidedly away from the Guangdong stereotype, and today they reflect, more or less accurately, the diverse panorama of Chinese society as it exists in China.

The Chinese community is well integrated into American society today. Even first generation immigrants in America are no longer bound by certain customs or stereotypes to hold traditionally "Chinese" professions. The old perceptions of Chinese immigrants as cooks, shopkeepers, and laundromat owners are as inaccurate today as a 1955 New York Central timetable. Although a large underground exists to exploit manual immigrant labor, a significant number of Chinese immigrants are ambitious, highly educated professionals who arrive on U.S. shores ready to practice their skills in fields such as medicine, the arts, technology, and trade.

About the only arena in American society still underrepresented by the Chinese is politics. Generally ambivalent to America's political process, the Chinese have a reputation for being docile and passive to movements and changes that affect them. This attitude can be traced, to a certain extent, back to the days of the Chinese Exclusion Act, which expressly barred the Chinese from participating in America's legal- and political institutions. Thus, occasional criticisms of their ambivalence toward America may not be completely fair. However, in an American society that has changed so much since even thirty years ago, the Chinese in the U.S. will have no one to blame but themselves if they do not begin availing themselves more to the exchange of ideas and debates for America's future.

THE CHINESE IN LOS ANGELES

According to the 2000 U.S. Census, there are approximately 330,000 Chinese living in Los Angeles County, making up 3.5 percent of the county's total population. Los Angeles is now the largest Chinese community in North America, and unlike those in other U.S. cities, Los Angeles's Chinese population is not concentrated in any particular neighborhood. The sprawling metropolitan area, with an excellent freeway system and decentralized urban development, makes personal mobility highly accessible and affordable, even for the newly arrived immigrants. No longer bound to traditional inner-city enclaves like Downtown/Chinatown, the Chinese in Los Angeles moved and settled into wherever areas with good schools for their children, and available jobs for themselves.

The San Gabriel Valley is home to the largest number of Chinese people in Los Angeles – an area along a 30-mile stretch of parallel freeways (Interstate 10 and Highway 60) running inland from Monterey Park to Diamond Bar. Another visible concentration of Chinese lives in the upscale Palos Verdes Peninsula – mostly professionals and second- or third-generation Americans. During the 1980s, many middle-class Chinese moved to the middle-priced suburbs of Artesia and Cerritos, midway between Downtown Los Angeles and the Orange County line. That number is dwindling, however, with trends showing more Chinese moving into southern Orange County, particularly to Irvine. Many Chaozhou people – Vietnamese immigrants of Chinese descent – live in the predominantly Vietnamese communities of Westminster and Garden Grove in northern Orange County.

The traditional Chinatown just north of Downtown Los Angeles is no longer a significant part of the Chinese community, which has

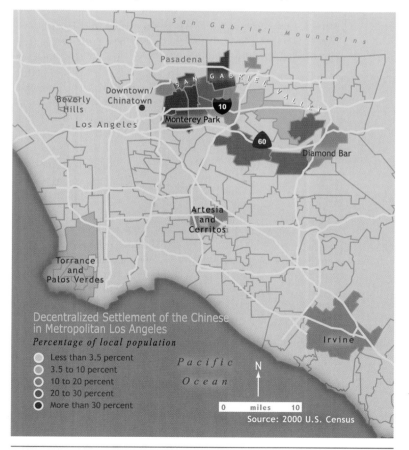

Decentralized Settlement of the Chinese in Metropolitan Los Angeles

Percentage of local population

- Less than 3.5 percent
- 3.5 to 10 percent
- 10 to 20 percent
- 20 to 30 percent
- More than 30 percent

Source: 2000 U.S. Census

moved literally for the wider and greener pastures of the San Gabriel Valley (and beyond). Chinatown is now home to a considerable number of Chaozhou people, giving it more of a Vietnamese atmosphere. Although old Chinese associations and social services continue to serve the Chinatown community, they are mostly catered to an older generation. Otherwise, Chinatown is just a tourist stop that gives only a limited portrayal of the Chinese community that actually exists today.

THE SAN GABRIEL VALLEY

On exceptionally clear days, the San Gabriel Mountains dominate the perspective from any street corner in the valley below. However, the towering, 9,000-foot peaks generally shy behind the murky veil of Los Angeles smog. On the flatlands, Interstate 10 and Highway 60 provide vital lifelines to the locality's pulsating soul. Surrounding the two freeways is an area with a mesmerizing mosaic of churches, temples, teashops, bakeries, acupuncture clinics, supermarkets, beauty parlors, medicine shops, karoake bars, office complexes, travel agents, and restaurants. The suburban cityscape follows the classic southern California archetype – palm-spiked boulevards, strip malls, and

Tree-lined **San Marino** *is forty percent Chinese.*

single-family homes. On the surface, only the colorful swatches of Chinese signs and banners set it apart from the other parts of the metropolitan area.

Yet, though it appears to be dominated by the Chinese, the San Gabriel Valley is in reality far from homogeneous in social makeup. From blue-collar El Monte to million-dollar hilltop homes of Diamond Bar, and from working class Alhambra to the stately mansions of San Marino, the Chinese live side by side with peoples of all ethnic backgrounds, forming a microcosm that reflects, more or less, the overall heartbeat of America.

One thing in common among the Chinese is that they came to America seeking better lives. Regardless of their ethnic origins, regional differences, family backgrounds, and personal wealth, the Chinese migrated 7,000 miles across the Pacific in order to stake a claim on their American Dreams. In the process, they transformed the San Gabriel Valley into sparkling quarters of shopping centers, green parks, and landscaped medians. The city of San Gabriel, an abject mudflat of chain-link, graffiti, and vacancy signs twenty years ago, is now flush with gleaming glass towers and the chiming sounds of cash registers.

Many Chinese have also settled into some of the most prestigious neighborhoods in metropolitan Los Angeles. San Marino, one of the most affluent neighborhoods in Los Angeles County, is forty percent Chinese. Elsewhere, the parking lots of Alhambra, Monterey Park, and Rowland Heights are veritable car shows of late-model imports on any given weekend. Although immigrant life is not without its challenges, hardships, and failures, the success of the Chinese in the San Gabriel Valley is real, and it is not overstated.

CHINESE FOOD AND DRINK

Written history has documented Chinese cooking for over 2,600 years, but most of the regional cuisines seen today date back no more than 600 years. During this "short" but significant span of Chinese history, China went through a series of tumultuous events that saw the decline of the world's once most powerful nation to near extinction. Foreign domination suppressed China for most of those 600 years – first by the Manchus during the Qing Dynasty, and later by western imperialists in the nineteenth century. Interspersed throughout this time were warfare, famines, and political upheavals that dealt a combination of hardship and misery to the Chinese people.

Through them all, Chinese food evolved to embody the experiences of a country that has gone through so much change and trauma. Under foreign dominance, Chinese culture encountered numerous outside influences that were levied upon the people. However, China's longstanding heritage and traditions proved to be more difficult to conquer. Even though they borrowed foreign ideas with liberal ease, Chinese regional cuisines remained uniquely "Chinese" in the ways by which foods are prepared and consumed. It is this distinction – one that draws ideas from others while steadfastly maintaining its traditional character – that makes the entire array of Chinese regional cuisines the top culinary tradition in the world.

Today, Chinese regional cuisines continue to evolve, and in Los Angeles, many are undergoing profound changes in both style and outlook. With the unique blend of local- and imported ingredients available to the chefs, Chinese food in Los Angeles is breaking new ground for authentic flavors, while spearheading a new front of *haute cuisine* with bold and daring new creations.

Skeptics will always be able to say that Los Angeles's Chinese food lacks the true authenticity of the dishes back home. But that is not necessarily a bad thing, nor is it a disparaging thing to say. Benefiting from the agricultural abundance of the surrounding farmlands, and drawing inspiration from the city's dynamic immigrant population, Los Angeles is an unlikely – and unique – showcase for the present and future state of Chinese food.

TEA DRINKING IN CHINESE FOOD

Tea drinking is inseparable from Chinese culture, and it is tied to the everyday life of ordinary people. The Chinese drink tea on any occasion: with friends, at work, on the airplane, *et cetera*, and for the most part, Chinese tea is of no extraordinary quality. It is, to many Chinese, just something to drink instead of plain boiled water. Many people visiting China are surprised to see the Chinese drinking their teas out of mason jars and tannin-stained glasses, but this is, after all, just common practice for a common beverage among common people. It also goes to show how prevalent and unspectacular tea drinking is in China.

Tea gets its name from the Chinese word *cha*. In the old days, tea shipments left for Europe from the port of Xiamen (Amoy) in Fujian (Fukkien) province. There, the local dialect for tea is "*tay*." Summarily, "*tay*" became the word used in areas of the West that received tea shipments by sea, including England, France, and the Netherlands. The English anglicized the term to become "tea" as we know it today. In France and Germany, the word is still *thé* and *Tee* (both pronounced "*tay*"). In the Middle East and Russia, where tea is obtained from overland caravans on the Silk Route, the word is *chai*, similar to the Mandarin pronunciation spoken by the people along the way. Additionally, *cha* is the term used in Japan and Portugal.

Tea drinking plays a special part in the local lifestyles in two unique cities in China. In both Chengdu and Hongkong, tea drinking is elevated to institutionalized art forms, which, practiced in their distinctive ways, exemplify truly colorful aspects of Chinese tea culture.

TEA DRINKING IN CHENGDU

The teahouses of Chengdu, in Sichuan Province, are famous for their ambiance and atmosphere. The most famous and popular teahouses are located along the lake in the city's *Renmin Park*. These teahouses have bamboo tables and chairs set up under the cool shades of trees, providing relaxing spaces for people to sit back, play chess, and people watch. Tea is served in ceramic tea sets called *gaiwancha*, which come with cups set on a saucer and covered with a lid.

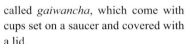

Gaiwancha

Chengdu's tea drinking culture features a unique teacup covered with a lid.

During the Cultural Revolution (1966-76), Chengdu's teahouses were banned because the Communist Party feared that they could foster *counterrevolutionaries* plotting to overthrow Mao Zedong. The paranoia has long since subsided, and today, Chengdu's teahouses are back in vogue.

DIM SUM AND YUM CHA

Tea drinking is also a cultural institution in southern China, where it is the focal point in dim sum/yum cha – the custom of eating snacks and drinking tea for breakfast. Dim sum means "snacks" and yum cha means "drinking tea." Dim sum/yum cha originated in the city of Guangzhou, where busy people ate quick breakfasts consisting of two pastries and a pot of tea before rushing off to work. These were originally modest meals, but in Hongkong they were transformed into lavish parades of intricate snacks, featuring all kinds of pastries, dumplings, and cakes. These dim sum gradually evolved to become artistic showpieces, but the tea drinking part remains unembellished from the old days. The single pot of tea continues to be center to the entire dim sum/yum cha experience.

TEA DRINKING AT CHINESE MEALS

With exception of dim sum/yum cha, the Chinese do not typically drink tea with their meals. They drink tea before- and after the meal, but not during the meal itself. Soup is often considered the "beverage" in ordinary Chinese meals, and it is served at the *end* of the meal to refresh the palates.

Contrarily, serving tea is perfunctory in Chinese restaurants in the U.S. This probably has something to do with the perception that tea is a "Chinese" beverage. Some restaurants charge a nominal fee for hot tea, but most provide it free just as they do for ice water. To request refills of tea, just lift the lid of the teapot and place it at the edge of the table. Waiters understand that an open lid is an empty teapot, and will immediately come to refill it.

THE TEAS OF CHINA

China is one of several great producers of teas in the world, ranking second after India in the tonnage of teas exported. The history of tea cultivation in China extends well before Christ's time, but its development has been slow and sporadic over the centuries. Today, generally better quality teas are grown in India and Taiwan, even though they only started tea cultivation no more than 200 years ago.

The teas of the world fall into one of three general categories: black teas (fully oxidized), oolong teas (partially oxidized), and green teas (unoxidized). India and Sri Lanka (Ceylon) are famous for their black teas. Taiwan is renowned for world-class oolongs. Japan is known for its unique ways of producing and consuming green teas. Only China produces all three types of teas. The variety includes the black tea *Keemun*, the oolong-type *Ti Kuan Yin*, and the green tea *Longjing*.

BLACK (FULLY OXIDIZED) TEAS

The teas popularized by the English and the western world are black teas. Tealeaves are allowed to oxidize fully in the drying and production processes, creating deep, red colors and rich, intense flavors in the brewed tea.

Westerners drink their black teas in a considerably different manner than the Chinese. Westerners prefer a great deal of blending of Indian, Sri Lankan, and Chinese black teas to create multitudes of flavors, which often come with proprietary names such as "Earl Grey," "Irish Breakfast," and even Lipton's perennially consistent teabags. Westerners also prefer adding lemon or milk to control the bitterness and astringency of black teas.

The Chinese prefer drinking varietal black teas *as-is*. That is, blacks teas are unblended and unembellished in any way. Keemun, Pu-er, and Yunnan are major examples of Chinese black teas. The Chinese also like infusing black teas with herbal- or fruit flavors to control the intensity. The Chinese never drink their teas with lemon or milk, unless the teas are served in western-style coffeeshops, or as the *chic nouveau* "Boba Tea."

Keemun
祁門

Grown in the Qimen (Keemun) district of Anhui province, Keemun is by far the most famous black tea from China. Although its quality is overshadowed by more famous black teas from India (like Assam and Darjeeling), Keemun tea has a sweet flavor that is versatile for blending with other varietal teas or herbs. For that reason, most of the Keemun production is blended in one form or another. The best quality Keemun can sometimes be drunk on its own merit as-is.

Yunnan
雲南

This tea from the namesake southwestern province has floral scents and a rich, malty flavor. Yunnan tea is most often blended with other black teas, creating such famous names as Harrod's (a London department store) proprietary *"Assam and Yunnan"* tea. Even when it is drunk on its own, Yunnan tea is best served with milk to tame its high tannin content.

Lapsang Souchong
正山小種

The *Gewürztraminer* of teas is also one that inspires the most polemical emotions in people. Lapsang Souchong's dark, woodsy, and smoky flavors are qualities that people either love or hate, with little middle ground in between. According to legend, Lapsang Souchong was accidentally discovered in Fujian province, where most of it is still grown and produced today. Short on time to dry the tealeaves, tea producers heated them over burning pine and cedar woods. In the process, they discovered the distinctive flavors of Lapsang Souchong were fully infused in the tealeaves.

Pu-er
普洱

A cheap and mediocre-quality black tea from Yunnan, Pu-er tea is popular only in Guangdong province and Hongkong. Pu-er has a very dark, reddish-brown color, and an earthy flavor with unremarkable undertones. A sheer film of natural oils usually appears at the top of the cup, giving the brewed tea an unappealing appearance. However, the love of the Guangdong people for Pu-er tea is unshakable, and its association with dim sum/yum cha is forever etched in the commandments of Chinese food culture. Besides, Pu-er purportedly has grease-cutting qualities that facilitate better digestion of fatty dim sum, justifying its central role as the *cha* in yum cha.

Brick Tea
茶磚

Poor quality Pu-er tea is pressed into bricks for shipment to the non-Han hinterlands of northwestern- and southwestern China, as well as Tibet and Mongolia. After the fall of the Yuan Dynasty, the Mongols took home very few Chinese things with them besides the love for tea. However, the way the Mongolians drink tea is unlike anything that both the eastern- and western cultures are familiar with. The tea

brick is first smashed into pieces, then tossed into a boiling pot of water along with yak butter and salt. The concoction is served hot – tealeaves and floating pieces of fat included – all gulped down for an eye-opening, stunning drink.

OOLONG (PARTIALLY OXIDIZED) TEAS

Partially oxidized teas are golden-brown in color, with mild flavors that fall between those of black- and green teas. However, oolongs have extra dimensions that are quite complex, giving them the kinds of world attention that they deserve. Because of oolong's delicate flavors, much of it, except for the ordinary grades, are left without any blending, flavoring, or scenting. Also, oolongs can be repeatedly steeped without changing the tealeaves, allowing the drinker to savor the different dimensions of the tea each time. However, these complex flavors are often subtle, and are easily conquered by milk. Therefore, oolongs are better drunk without it.

The best oolong teas in the world are grown in central Taiwan, in 3,000-feet-plus elevations near the Tropic of Cancer. These areas are constantly shrouded in cool mists, which is the ideal condition for oolongs. Because of their limited production, oolongs are also some of the world's most expensive teas.

Tung Ting Oolong
凍頂烏龍

Meaning "Frosted Summit," this specialty oolong tea is the most famous tea from Taiwan. Originally grown only on the steep slopes of Tung Ting Shan (Frosted Summit Mountain) in Nantou Prefecture, producers recently began growing Tung Ting Oolong elsewhere throughout central Taiwan. Still, they barely produce enough to meet its demand worldwide. The light, fruity, and flowery scents of Tung Ting Oolong are complemented by a long-lasting, sweet aftertaste. Additionally, the brewed tea has a sparkling body that gives off a slight, refreshing effervescence when sipped.

Ti Kuan Yin
鐵觀音

Grown in Fujian province, on the mainland side of the Taiwan Strait, Ti Kuan Yin is the forebear of Taiwan's oolong tea crop. Ti Kuan Yin, or "Iron Goddess of Mercy," is generally darker than Taiwanese oolongs. It undergoes fifty- to seventy percent oxidization, compared to forty percent for Taiwanese oolongs. While most of the Ti Kuan Yins are only of moderate quality, some of the best have dimensions similar to Tung Ting Oolong, with a more full-bodied taste. Justifiably, prices sometimes reach upwards of $200 per pound.

Pouchong
包種

The foothills outside Taipei, in northern Taiwan, are dotted with small tea plantations that produce the only Pouchong teas in the world. Pouchong, which is only ten percent oxidized, is lighter in flavor than all other oolongs, but with dimensions that are not nearly as complex. Pouchong can be found both on its own as an ordinary tea, or scented into flavored teas. Most Taiwanese productions of jasmine tea are made from Pouchong as well.

GREEN (UNOXIDIZED) TEAS

When tealeaves are steamed, dried, and roasted without allowing them to undergo any oxidation, the end product is green tea, which retains most of the tea's natural characteristics – flowery aromas, mellow flavors, and subtle hints of the earth. Although green tea is generally associated with Japanese tea culture, green tea is also the primary type of tea that the Chinese drink.

China grows several famous varieties of green teas. Additionally, China produces a variety of unoxidized teas called "white teas," which are merely dried without going through the customary steaming- and roasting processes. White tea has a pure, natural taste without the added complexities derived from steaming and roasting.

Longjing
龍井

Sometimes called "Dragon Well" by tea marketers, this is the most famous green tea from China. It is grown in Zhejiang province, in the mountains surrounding West Lake outside the city of Hangzhou. Longjing tealeaves are hand rolled into needle-like shapes, and through the roasting process they attain a rich, nutty flavor. The unique flavor of Longjing tea suggests why these tealeaves are a vital cooking ingredient in Jiangzhe cuisine. It is featured in such famous dishes as Shrimp Stir-fried with Longjing Tealeaves.

Gunpowder Tea

Another green tea from Zhejiang province, gunpowder tea gets its name from the shape of the finished tealeaves, which are rolled into grayish-green pellets resembling old-fashioned gunpowder. These teas are usually of low- or moderate quality, possessing earthy and unassuming flavors suitable for ordinary, everyday drinking.

Huangshan Maofeng
黄山毛峰

This green tea, often simply called *Maofeng*, comes from the scenic Yellow Mountains (Huangshan) of southern Anhui province. Huangshan Maofeng tea is quite rare outside China; its quality is still inconsistent after decades of austere communist policies. However, the surroundings of Huangshan, with its mist-shrouded hills and consistently moist conditions, make for ideal growing conditions that could produce world-class teas in the future.

Pi Lo Chun
碧螺春

A very rare green tea from China, Pi Lo Chun (or *Biluochun*) is of considerably higher quality than all other Chinese green teas. Grown in the mountains near Suzhou, one of China's most scenic cities, Pi Lo Chun tea bushes are planted next to apricot, peach, plum, and mandarin orange trees to allow the tealeaves to absorb sublime hints of these fruits. Pi Lo Chun tealeaves are handpicked only in the spring, when the leaves are just beginning to bud. During the drying process, the leaves are rolled into small, green, snail shell-like pellets before roasting. The tea was so enamored by a 17th century Qing Dynasty emperor that he gave it its poetic name, which means "A Spring of Green Snails."

White Down Silver Needles
白毫銀針

All white teas of China, like this one, are grown in Fujian province. The tealeaves are picked only in April, just as the first leaf buds of the season are about to open. The amount of silvery fuzz on the underside of the tealeaves gives the tea its name. When brewed, white tea has a pale yellow color and a clean, mellow flavor. White Down Silver Needles is a "showpiece" tea, meaning that it should be served in a glass teapot or cup, so that the drinker could appreciate the appearance of the tealeaves.

Green Peony
綠牡丹

Also a "showpiece" tea, green peony is more spectacular for its appearance than for the flavors. Nevertheless, it is a visually stunning example in China's broad and varied production of teas. Grown only in Anhui province, Green Peony is made by tying whole, unbroken, and unoxidized tealeaves into a compact bundle, then pressed into a flat disk before drying and roasting. When the disk is steeped, it "blooms" into a flower-like shape resembling a peony flower. As it

is meant to show and impress the drinker, Green Peony should also be served in a glass teapot or cup.

Herbal and Flavored Teas

Coffee producers make flavored coffees from ordinary coffee beans that have no particularly attractive qualities. Tea producers do the same, making herbal- and flavored teas by infusing low quality tealeaves with the scents of flowers and fruits to boost the tea's value. Popular Chinese herbal teas include the flavors of chamomile, chrysanthemum, ginger, gingko, gingsen, hibiscus, jasmine, lychee, and guava.

Jasmine Tea
香片

Jasmine tea is the most popular flavored tea from China. Jasmine flower petals are layered on top of green tealeaves during the drying process, allowing the floral fragrances to be absorbed. Taiwanese jasmine tea uses locally grown Pouchong, which are minimally oxidized for a slightly richer flavor. Average-quality jasmine teas will contain some jasmine petals in the finished product; higher quality jasmine teas contain only the scented tealeaves. The highest quality of jasmine tea is called "Pearl Jasmine," which is scented numerous times to create a very concentrated fragrance in the tealeaves. Sometimes Pearl Jasmine uses rare green- or white teas, such as White Down Silver Needles, as its base.

FINGER-TAPPING AT TEA DRINKING

Keep a sharp eye out next time while having dim sum/yum cha. You may notice that when someone pours tea for their friend, the friend responds by tapping the table next to the teacup with their fingers. Why?

One story claims that the practice originated with a Qing Dynasty emperor, who once traveled into southern China to survey the land and his subjects. Not wanting to be noticed by the peasants, the emperor wore commoner's clothes and refrained from speaking in public – his court attire and northern dialect would have instantly revealed him as a member of the nobility. One evening, while dining in a country inn, the emperor's servant poured him tea. Without speaking, the emperor tapped his fingers on the table as a sign of gratitude. From then on, the emperor and his servant agreed that the finger tapping would be his way of expressing thanks to his servant.

A different explanation for the finger tapping simply attributes this *digital* reflex to the sparing emotions of the Guangdong people. Renowned for their loud and nonstop chatter, they are nevertheless curiously conservative when it comes to expressing their emotions. Rather than belaboring a mid-sentence "*thank you*," they just tap the table. By doing so, the Guangdong people are able to express their gratitude without suffering the self-effacing embarrassment of saying thanks. Meanwhile, the exigencies of the conversation at hand can continue uninterrupted.

Whatever the real story behind the finger-tapping is, responding to someone's friendly gesture of pouring tea by gently tapping two or three fingers instantly exposes you as an insider to Chinese food etiquette, and also as someone who cherishes the bond and kinship among friends.

Boba Tea

波霸奶茶

The name "Boba Tea" has risen from total obscurity fifteen years ago to become a food fad on the verge of worldwide fame today. Like most dishes from Taiwan's colorful street snack culture, the origins of Boba Tea are largely unknown. But if history is a repetition of precedents, Boba Tea was probably created by a street hawker interested in selling something different from the rest. Then, once word of mouth about Boba Tea hit a tone with the locals, it was immediately copied by competing vendors throughout Taipei until it appeared on every street corner. Now, Boba Tea can be found in coffeeshops and beverage kiosks throughout Los Angeles, and its popularity is quickly spreading to other U.S. cities as well.

Boba Tea is the combination of *boba* – chewy starch balls made from yam starch – with iced tea. It is a common misperception that boba is made from tapioca. In reality, it is the yam starch that gives boba its dark brown color and the chewiness resembling gummy candy. The tea part of Boba Tea is just any ordinary type of black tea, sweetened with condensed milk and thickened further with non-dairy creamer. All that is shaken (and stirred) with crushed ice, and then slurped up with a large colorful straw.

Alcoholic Beverages in Chinese Food

The Chinese love alcoholic beverages. Beers, wines and spirits are consumed in large quantities, mostly for their enjoyment with food, but sometimes for the sheer display of masculine showmanship. Alcohol is always drunk at banquets, but it is rarely consumed with everyday meals. More significantly, alcohol is never drunk alone by itself. Drinking alcohol without food is considered a social taboo among the Chinese; it may suggest why alcoholism is far less common in China than it is in western societies.

Beer and Grain-based Alcohol

Beverages made from grains are excellent choices for Chinese food, with beer as the finest example. Beer goes surprisingly well with most Chinese dishes; it is the second most popular beverage in China, after tea. The slightly bitter, malty flavors of beer heighten the flavors of Chinese cooking, and they generally do not clash with even the most delicate elements of certain dishes. The most famous Chinese beer is Tsingtao Beer – a lager-style beer brewed in the former German concession port of the same name (Qingdao). It is made with a local mineral water that gives the beer its own uniqueness and character.

Also popular with the Chinese are rice wines. There are practical rice wines that are really intended for cooking, and then there are other rice wines like *Shaoxing*, which is a potent sherry-type yellow rice wine from Zhejiang province. Shaoxing has an alcohol content of 18 percent, and can be drunk as a beverage or used as a cooking condiment – most often found in Jiangzhe cuisine recipes. A famous example is the Jiangzhe dish called "Drunken Chicken," which entails pieces of boiled chicken marinated in a brine flavored with this type of rice wine.

Kaoliang is a potent category of grain alcohol, distilled from grains such as sorghum and wheat. *Maotai* is the most infamous example of kaoliang liquors. It is 110 proof, with a taste that is acquired: residing somewhere in the range between kitchen cleaner and gasoline. Men like to test and compare their *jiuliang* (alcohol capacity) at banquets by downing glasses of maotai, generally stopping only when their tastebuds no longer taste the food (or worse).

Wines and Wine Drinking

China has cultivated grapes for winemaking for thousands of years,

but its styles and techniques are profoundly different than that of the western tradition. Chinese wines tend to be earthy and acidic, and are usually blended with herbs and/or insects for medicinal uses. Wines from other fruits: plum, lychee, "dragon-eye" (longan), and kiwi fruit round up the extent of Chinese winemaking, all of which is well inferior to the French and Californians.

No matter what the experts say, wines and Chinese food are very difficult to match, and can seem frustratingly incompatible. Chinese dishes tend to be spicier and heavier in flavor, which can easily overpower the flowery subtleties of white wines. On the other hand, heavier red wines have high tannin contents that scream to be tamed by foods like steaks and creamy sauces – both characteristics that Chinese food lacks. Regardless, wines are in *chic*, and more Chinese are drinking them with their meals. Many restaurants have also begun offering wine lists with detailed descriptions, so that people could pair the right wine with the dishes they are ordering.

*A varietal **Cabernet** from Shandong province.*

Red wines notwithstanding, a regular recommendation with Chinese food is white wines made from Gewürztraminer grapes. This Alsacian and German grape variety has unusually spicy (*Gewürz* means "spice" in German) and burnt flavors, which people either like or hate. Gewürztraminer works relatively well with certain Chinese dishes, such as Beijing Duck. Other varietal whites, such as the popular Chardonnay, are less successful with the deep flavors of Chinese dishes. However, they could accompany certain mellow and herb-based Chaozhou-style seafood dishes with relative success.

For practical purposes, drinking red wines with Chinese food is as gauche as wearing Birkenstocks to the senior prom. This is evident in China, Hongkong, and Taiwan, as well as the San Gabriel Valley, where drinking red wines with meals is the current rage. However, the ways by which the Chinese take their red wines tend to hover on the dubious side of judgment and taste. The Chinese insist on drinking red wines like white wines – either chilled or by adding ice cubes directly into the wine. If that is not enough to send purists to the stratosphere, some Chinese also mix in Sprite to make the wine sweeter.

IMPORTED LIQUORS

Imported liquors are, in most cases, held with considerable esteem by the Chinese, especially for the XO cognac – a popularly accepted status symbol. Startlingly, the Chinese often drink an entire bottle of "Extra Old" through the course of a banquet, showing more of their wealth and less of class. Nevertheless, downing XO invariably leaves good impressions upon families, friends, and cognac marketers in France. XO is so prized that even a Guangdong-style cooking sauce is named after it, despite containing not a single drop of it.

Another favorite imported liquor is Johnny Walker, a scotch whiskey that was popularized in China during the Shanghai days of the Roaring 20s. It only recently relinquished some of its prestige and allure, in deference to nothing else but the almighty XO.

Chinese Desserts

Traditional desserts are woefully lacking in Chinese cuisine. True, the Chinese do make sweets and pastries, but they are not the kinds of cakes, tarts, and *crèmes* that the western world is familiar with. The Chinese do not eat sweets as after-dinner desserts, but as in-between-meals snacks instead, often with tea.

One of the reasons why desserts never made much headway into Chinese cuisine is because ordinary people could hardly afford them in the past. In a society that suffered calamities and famines throughout its history, sugar and fat – vital ingredients in making desserts – were exorbitant luxuries for much of the masses. Also, traditional Chinese homes were not equipped with ovens, and only recently were people wealthy enough to install refrigerators. Without ovens and refrigerators, desserts such as cakes and pastries could not be made at home.

The only place where desserts are a notable part of the local cuisine is in Beijing. They owe much of their existence to the imperial influences of the Qing Dynasty (1644-1911). These delicate cakes and pastries are generally steamed – not baked – and they are mostly made from mungbeans, soybeans, and glutinous rice flour instead of wheat flour. Some of Beijing's favorite sweets were longtime favorites of the Emperss Dowager Cixi (1835-1908), such as the Yellow Pea Cake. They were well-kept secrets behind the Forbidden City walls until the Qing's fall in 1911. Only then were the sweets introduced to the ordinary people, eventually becoming popularized as either tea snacks or after-dinner desserts.

A variety of sweets served in dim sum/yum cha includes both traditional Chinese snacks and western-style desserts. Among them, the most famous pastry on the dim sum cart is the Egg Custard Tart – a light pastry with the egg custard baked into a flaky piecrust. Another classic dim dum/yum cha favorite is the White Sugar Rice Cake – a steamed rice cake leavened and slightly fermented with yeast. Both the Egg Custard Tart and White Sugar Rice Cake exhibit profound influences of the Europeans on Guangdong cuisine during the mid-1800s: using eggs, cream, butter, and yeast that are still rare in other parts of Chinese cooking today. Interestingly, the sweet dim sum dishes are never served as desserts in the evening, even though the dim sum/yum cha house and the seafood house are often one and the same.

To the extent of meeting America's sweet tooth, many Chinese restaurants now serve fresh fruit or fortune cookies at the end of the meal. A few restaurants serve a warm sweet red bean soup thickened with tapioca, or a cold "almond tofu soup" – a favorite summertime gelatin snack. Some restaurants have also added traditional sweet snacks to the dessert section of their menus. These include steamed *baozi* filled with sweet red bean paste, glutinous rice ball soup flavored with fermented glutinous rice, and "Eight Treasures Rice" – a

A Time for Chang-e

Mooncakes often come packed in decorative gift boxes. This one depicts Chang-e, a legend that perpetuates the mystique of the Autumn Moon Festival.

Jiangzhe specialty that resembles a rice pudding. Although they are merely sweet dishes, these snacks can pass off as desserts to finish off a Chinese meal with satisfying success.

MOONCAKES FOR THE HOLIDAY

If there is one traditional dessert that defines China, it must be the mooncake, frequently considered the *Fruitcake of the East*. Every year, when August draws autumn closer, the Chinese fidget with a peculiar holiday ritual that has come to resemble a game of musical chairs played with food. Chinese bakeries and supermarket aisles are stockpiled with boxes of mooncakes, which people buy to give to families, friends, colleagues, and bosses.

In the years past, mooncakes were treasured treats that people gladly ate up. Nowadays, however, they are *comida non grata*. Receiving a gift box of mooncakes is like getting the flu; it is quickly passed on to a "friend," who then gives it to someone else. The giving goes on until the Mid-Autumn Festival, and whoever ends up with the mooncakes then has the misfortune of actually having to eat it.

Mooncakes come with a dense filling laden with fat and sugar. In a more health conscious society today, mooncakes no longer enjoy the appeal it once had. Yet, although few people profess a liking for them any longer, the tradition of giving mooncakes continues with unabated zeal. Considering that a typical Chinese family receives five boxes of mooncakes during this holiday, it suggests that mooncakes get a lot of mileage before they are actually eaten.

Mooncakes are the thematic food item to the Mid-Autumn Festival, which occurs on the 15th day of the 8th month of the Chinese lunar calendar. The day marks the occurrence of the full moon closest to the autumnal equinox, signaling the start of what is always hoped will be a full, bountiful harvest.

The Mid-Autumn Festival is also an occasion for families to gather. Parents bring their children out in the evening to view the full moon, and retell the legend of *Chang-e*, a beautiful woman from antiquity. According to folklore, *Chang-e* mischievously drank too much her husband's *Elixir of Life*, and floated away to exile on the moon with her pet rabbit. The image of her and the rabbit are etched on the surface of the moon, which everyone spend hours contemplating from below.

The association of mooncakes with the Mid-Autumn Festival began during the Tang Dynasty, one of several classical periods of Chinese civilization, when Han culture and technologies flourished. Later on, mooncakes also served important and practical roles in times of turmoil. During the Yuan Dynasty, messages hidden inside the mooncakes that read: "*Kill the Mongol Barbarians by the August Moon!*" were distributed to Han insurrectionists, leading to a popular rebellion that restored Chinese sovereignty and ushered in the Ming Dynasty.

Up until only recently, mooncakes were considered luxurious pastries reserved as a once-in-a-year treat. Traditionally, mooncakes were filled with mashed lotus seeds, lard, and sugar, and baked inside a crusty pastry shell. They are shaped like a thick hockey puck, molded in a wooden press carved with decorative patterns. As such, mooncakes once provided a rare indulgence in fats and sugars, interrupting a routine of meager subsistence that otherwise dominated the people's lives during the rest of the year.

Nowadays, when food is plentiful everywhere, mooncakes are the dreaded parcels of gluttony. Despite efforts by bakeries to replace lard with vegetable oil, and by introducing fancy ingredients such as shark's fin, mooncakes are viewed as stodgy throwbacks to a different era. Mooncakes are fast becoming passé, and have become, as the *Wall Street Journal* once wrote, "like Christmas fruitcakes in the U.S."

In spite of the new identity crisis, mooncakes continue to mean big business for Chinese bakeries. There are mooncakes with many different kinds of fillings on the bakery shelf today. Mashed lotus seeds continues to be the most popular filling, and is still the standard-bearer of the Mid-Autumn Festival tradition. Red bean paste is another common filling, as are mashed jujubes and pineapple jam. More recent inventions tend to fringe on the exotic, including fillings of *jinhua ham*, shark's fins, and an assortment of California-grown nuts.

Many mooncakes also have a salted duck egg yolk stuffed in the center. When such a mooncake is sliced in half, the bright orange duck egg is shown like a round moon, symbolizing the association of the Mid-Autumn Festival with the full moon. How the salty duck egg tastes is another matter, especially with a fruity filling like mashed jujubes. However, many Chinese people no longer eat those mooncakes to know, nor do they appear to care.

Around August and September, when mooncake sales hit full stride, Chinese bakeries are stacked to the ceiling with crates of mooncakes.

Mooncakes can be purchased individually, or in decorative gift boxes. Each dense, palm-sized mooncake weighs around two pounds, and costs around $6. A "fancy" mooncake with one or two yolks can cost up to $10 each. A prepackaged box usually contains four mooncakes – plenty to haunt an entire family for several months.

THE DESSERTS OF BEIJING

Beijing's local cuisine has the only true variety of desserts in Chinese food. Unlike western-style desserts, most of Beijing's desserts are steamed. Additionally, they are mainly made from beans and glutinous rice, instead of wheat flour. Most of the desserts also have an imperial heritage, having first been created to please the sweet tooth of the Qing Dynasty nobility.

Donkey Rolling in Dirt
驢打滾

This sticky, chewy bean-flour dumpling is made from millet flour and mungbean flour, filled with a sweet red bean paste. The dumpling is then coated with soybean flour so that it resembles a donkey rolling in dirt – hence its name. Donkeys are an important beast of burden in northern China, as much as water buffaloes are in the south, and they are

respected for the work they do for humans. It is interesting how *truffles* got its name in a similar manner.

(*Truffles, which are chocolate fudge chunks rolled in cocoa powder, resemble the root fungus of the same name that is found under oak trees in France.*)

Yellow Pea Cake
豌豆黄

A favorite of Empress Dowager Cixi, this dessert is regularly featured in the imperial cuisine of Beijing. Mashed peas are combined with the essence of yellow gardenia, a traditional ingredient in Chinese medicine. Doing so turns the color of the peas

to translucent golden yellow. The mash is molded, cooled, and then cut into bite-sized blocks. The finished dessert

is light and fragrant, with the delicate flavor of peas enhanced by the flowery aroma of gardenia.

Haw Cake
山楂糕

Haw is a pear-like fruit with a tart, dry taste. It is often used in traditional medicine because of its believed effect to improve blood circulation. One way of using haw in desserts is to combine it with mungbean flour to make haw cakes. They resemble the yellow pea cake (above) except

that they have a reddish-purple color instead of translucent yellow.

Aiwowo
爱窝窝

Meaining "Love Nest," aiwowo is an ordinary snack found throughout the streets of Beijing. It is especially popular with the Muslim population. The history of aiwowo dates all the way back to the Yuan Dynasty, at a time when Muslims enjoyed greater privileges in China than the native Hans. Aiwowo was also mentioned in the journals of Marco Polo. It is a steamed rice cake shaped into a

conical cup, similar to *wowotou* – a steamed bun made from corn meal. Red bean paste is stuffed in the middle, like a nest (*wowo*).

Mungbean Cake
绿豆糕

Mungbean flour is combined with lard to create this elegant dessert, which is often molded into round- or square pillbox-shaped pieces. The wooden mold used to shape these cakes can be decorated quite elaborately, sometimes bearing the names of the proprietors that make them, or featuring artistic motifs and patterns.

Ear Cake
耳朵眼

Steamed rice cake made from glutinous rice flour is shaped into a hollow disk, like a small donut, and fried until crispy. Powdered sugar is then sprinkled on top. The sticky and chewy texture of the rice cake makes it resemble an ear.

Cold Osmanthus Rice Cake

桂花涼糕

A steamed glutinous rice cake shaped like a sushi roll, this dessert is stuffed with red bean paste, and coated with a sweet syrup  made from osmanthus flower. The result is a simple, fragrant glutinous rice-based pastry.

Eight Treasures Wowotou

八寶窩頭

The typical *wowotou* of northern China was always made from coarse-ground corn meal. Unfortunately, it was not sophisticated enough for the Empress Dowager Cixi, who demanded that her *wowotou* be made from eight different types of fine- and rough grains, among them: corn, millet, sorghum, and barley. Poor Cixi subsisted on this when she was driven out of Beijing by the Western Powers during the Boxer Rebellion (1900).

Elephant's Trunk Cake

象鼻子糕

Steamed glutinous rice cake is stuffed with jujube paste, and covered with roasted white sesame. The shape of the dessert resembles an elephant with a long trunk.

Dragon's Eye

龍眼

A glutinous rice ball is shaped like the longan fruit, which is colloquially called "dragon's eye" in Chinese. It is stuffed with jujube paste in the center to make this dessert really look like a dragon's eye.

Crystallized Lotus Root

江米藕

Lotus root is stuffed with glutinous rice, and cooked in a syrup flavored with osmanthus flower until it is crystallized. The lotus root is then cooled and sliced thinly, cross-section-wise, to display the root's cavities in an interesting starburst pattern.

Black Glutinous Rice Cake

紫米糕

Black glutinous rice is rare used in Chinese cooking. It generally appears in traditional Chinese medicine, but hardly figures in any Chinese regional cuisine. In this unique sweet dessert, steamed grains of black glutinous rice are wrapped around mashed chestnuts. Then they are shaped either into tart-shaped disks or cigar-shaped rolls.

CHINESE VEGETABLES

The Chinese, especially the people outside Guangdong province, use a greater variety of vegetables than is known to Americans. Unfortunately, much of those vegetables are unobtainable outside the localities in which they are grown, because for a long time Guangdong immigrants have influenced the types of Chinese vegetables cultivated in North America. Common vegetables found in Chinese restaurants in the U.S. include: bok choy, ong choy, Napa cabbage, and gai lan. These vegetables, much like how Guangdong cuisine has come to represent Chinese food, are commonly referred simply as "Chinese" or "Oriental" vegetables.

Los Angeles is blessed to have some of the world's most fertile farmlands in its vicinity, supplying it with abundant and high quality produce year-round. Increasingly, these vegetable farms in the San Joaquin Valley, Imperial Valley, and Riverside County have turned to growing *chic* Chinese vegetables that were previously missing on the store shelves: pea tendrils, edible chrysanthemum leaves, and *Pei Tsai*. They not only satisfy the palates of the area's growing number of Chinese immigrants, they also introduce to Americans new and interesting ways of eating vegetables.

Some Chinese supermarkets also import certain produce items directly from Asia: bittermelons, fresh bamboo shoots, Taiwanese cabbage, and fresh lychees. They add to the variety of ingredients available to the Chinese kitchen, and also open new opportunities to create authentic regional dishes that were previously qualified by Guangdong vegetables.

IDENTIFYING CHINESE VEGETABLES

In Chinese restaurants, it is always acceptable to order a simple stir-fry of seasonal greens. Ask the waiter about the kinds of fresh vegetables they have in the kitchen, since these simple dishes will not appear on the menu. Stir-fried vegetables are seasoned with no more than salt, and perhaps some garlic and chili peppers. Many Chinese prefer to order stir-fried vegetables to balance out other more substantial (and fattier) dishes in the meal.

Certain vegetables, such as watercress, have specific uses in the Chinese kitchen. Others have distinct regional associations. As gradually more varieties of Chinese vegetables are cultivated in California, the options for the chefs will only increase – and so will the quality of both authentic and innovative regional dishes.

Bok Choy

Routinely called "Chinese Cabbage," bok choy is the green leaf vegetable most familiar with Americans. It has long, white, crunchy stems with broad, green, crinkly leaves. Bok choy and its smaller version, baby bok choy, are used widely in Guangdong cuisine – in everything from stir-fries to soups.

Ong Choy

Characterized by thick, hollow stems and thin, spinach-like leaves, ong choy has an earthy flavor with an unmistakably rural character. Another name for ong choy, although rarely used in the U.S., is "Water Spinach." Ong choy is generally stir-fried to retain its delightfully crunchy texture. Popular Guangdong flavorings for stir-fried ong choy could be: fermented bean curd, shrimp paste, or just with garlic and salt.

Yu Choy

A green leaf vegetable that resembles gai lan in that it also has yellow flower buds, yu choy has a milder flavor. Also, yu choy stems are more delicate than gai lan, and it can substitute for spinach in many dishes.

Gai Choy

Commonly called "Mustard Cabbage," gai choy has a strong and pungent flavor that many people avoid. However, the overpowering flavors can be tamed by pickling, and this green leaf vegetable enjoys much of its popularity as a Chinese equivalent of *sauerkraut*. Pickled gai choy is used in a large variety of regional dishes; Guangdong people prefer stir-frying fresh gai choy with ginger to make an earthy counter-punch to fatty meat dishes.

Gai Lan

Also called "Chinese Broccoli," this vegetable is similar to rape (rappini) in that it has a slightly bitter and mustardy flavor. A narrow bunch of small yellow flowers grows at the end of a thick, solid stem. Primarily used by the Guangdong people, gai lan is famously served in dim sum/yum cha – simply boiled in water and served with oyster sauce on top.

Napa Cabbage

Napa cabbage has dense, pale-white leaves with broad, thick stems. Also called "Peking Cabbage," this is virtually a staple in northern China during the winter months, when other fresh greens are unobtainable. Napa cabbage is hardy enough to withstand sub-zero temperatures without spoiling, so it can be kept frozen outside from autumn to spring. Napa cabbage can be pickled like gai choy as well, or it could be preserved in ways like Korean *kimchi*.

Shanghai Cabbage

Also called "Green Stem Cabbage," this green leaf vegetable resembles bok choy in appearance, except that it is uniformly green in color, and has milder flavors than its Guangdong cousin. Shanghai cabbage, as the name suggests, is more frequently seen in Jiangzhe and Shanghai cuisines.

Pei Tsai

A greener and smaller variation of Napa cabbage, this green vegetable has delicate leaves with a subtle smoky flavor. Excellent for both stir-fries and soups, pei tsai is very popular in Taiwan and Japan. In most cases, pei tsai are substitutes for bok choy outside Guangdong and Hongkong.

Amaranth Leaves

The Chinese prefer red amaranth leaves, which impart a reddish-purple color when stir-fried. Amaranth leaves are good substitutes for spinach, and have a very high iron content with a slightly smoky flavor.

Chrysanthemum Leaves

Edible chrysanthemum leaves are thin, frond-like greens that are usually blanched first to bring out its brilliant color. It is the favorite cooking vegetable in Mongolian hotpots, enjoyed for its slightly sweet taste and crunchy texture.

Bamboo Shoot

The young, budding shoot of the tall grass plant has the best flavors when it is harvested in the winter. The creamy, mellow flavors and its distinct crunchiness make the bamboo shoot an ideal ingredient in stir-fries and soups. In North America, bamboo shoot is widely available in tin cans. Fresh bamboo shoots can also be found in Chinese supermarkets that receive regular airfreight shipments from Taiwan.

Bittermelon

A southern Chinese produce, bittermelon is a football-shaped gourd demarcated with longitudinal bumps on its surface. The flavor of the bittermelon, as the name suggests, is bitter and an acquired taste for most people. The bittermelon is, additionally, highly nutritious. It is especially popular during the summer for its said ability to bring down the "heat" in certain dishes.

Wintermelon

A large, oblong melon that could grow over twenty pounds, wintermelon is most popularly used in soups, but it can also be stir-fried. When cooked, the wintermelon is sweet in flavor, and so soft that it virtually melts in the mouth.

Luffa

The same melon that becomes the luffa sponge, this gourd is only edible while it is still unripe. Therefore, the best luffas for cooking should be crisp and firm. Luffa melon is commonly stir-fried or served in soups. The Chinese call this vegetable "fibrous melon," because once it ripens, the luffa becomes tough and not comestible.

Celery

Chinese celery is much thinner and flimsier than American celery. Chinese celery has strong, highly aromatic scents that is often used to enhance the flavors of soups. When purchased in bunches, Chinese celery resembles oversized cilantro – with long, thin stalks and flat, green leaves.

Eggplant

Chinese eggplant is long and thin, resembling a cucumber. The flavors are very similar to American- or European eggplant, which has a round, stubby appearance. Because the eggplant can hold its texture well, it is extremely versatile for all types of cooking techniques, from quick stir-fries to slowly simmered casseroles.

Lotus Root

The root of the lotus plant is a tuber with high starch content. When it is cut cross-section-wise, the cavities of the lotus root are displayed in a decorative starburst pattern. Otherwise tasteless, the lotus root is similar to potatoes in that it is often used as a source of starch, providing an added texture to the dishes.

Scallion

Also called "Green Onion," the scallion has a slightly punchy flavor that has become regarded as the most important ingredient in Chinese cooking. Almost no Chinese meal can exist without the scallion. It is used to enhance the dishes' flavors, and provide color contrast for added visual appeal. Scallions are also practical lifesavers. In times of famine, they were often the only vegetable eaten to sustain the people through hunger.

Leek

Often called the "Giant Scallion," leek is the most important flavoring ingredient of northern Chinese cuisine. Leek is more pungent than scallion, with a flavor similar to nira. Thus, it is not surprising that leek and nira are often confused for the other. Leek is used much like scallions in all types of Chinese dishes, and it often works as its substitute in northern China. Moreover, the strong flavors that rhe leek imparts are said to contribute to the legendary bad tempers of the northern Chinese.

Nira

Often marketed as "leek" – although leek is actually a very different vegetable – nira resembles a cross between lawn grass and scallions. Nira has a very pungent flavor, so much so that it is usually cooked with milder ingredients, and rarely used alone. A flowering nira is more desirable (and expensive), adding some sweetness and extra layers of flavors to the pungency of the dish.

Yellow Nira

The same plant as regular nira, but grown away from sunlight, yellow nira gets its distinctive color from the absence of chlorophyll. In addition, because it cannot mature, yellow nira does not flower. Yellow nira is often used *as-is* without many other ingredients, because it is not as pungent as regular nira. A famous yellow nira dish calls for a stir-fry with Beijing Duck and duck fat, which, albeit simple, is the main course in the "One Duck Eaten Three Ways" meal in Beijing Duck restaurants.

Snow Peas

Also called "Sweet Peas," these tender beans are harvested while they are still young and developing in their pods. The unripe peas and their pods have a slightly sweet flavor, and they retain a high degree of crunchiness when stir-fried over high heat.

Pea Tendrils

The young leaves of the pea plant – pinched off the plant with its budding vines intact – are used as a green vegetable. The flavors are sweet, and slightly suggestive of the peas themselves. In order to retain the mellow flavors of the pea tendrils, they must be cooked very quickly – usually stir-fried over high heat or blanched with little additional seasoning.

Pea Sprouts

The seedlings of the pea plant, after they germinate and with just a few pairs of round green leaves, pea sprouts are similar in concept to bean sprouts, and used accordingly in similar ways. A popular dish is stir-frying pea sprouts with shrimp. The sweetness of pea sprouts matches very well with the delicate (but different) kind of sweetness of the shrimp.

Taro

This starchy tuber is similar to potatoes in the ways by which it can be used in the kitchen. Cultivated in warm, subtropical parts of China, taro plays prominently in southern Chinese cuisine. It is commonly used as a substitute for potatoes, and is occasionally eaten as a staple. When cooked, the starches in the taro turn bright purple, providing interesting color contrasts. Taro is also versatile for use in sweet dishes and snacks, used in milk shakes, ice cream, and even sponge cakes.

Water Chestnut

This vegetable is popular in Guangdong-style cooking, used in many kinds of stews and stir-fried dishes. The crunchiness of the water chestnut is retained even after long cooking times, so that it is often added to provide a contrast to the softer textures in slowly cooked dishes.

Watercress

The Chinese call it "European Greens," for the obvious reason that watercress was introduced by Europeans to southern China during the middle of the nineteenth century. Watercress appears mainly in Guangdong-style cooking, and most frequently in soups.

White Radish

Also called "*daikon*" by the Japanese, white radish is a long root vegetable with a pungent flavor. Like carrots, radishes can be found as an ingredient in salads, soups, stir-fries, and stews. Because it is also hardy for growing in cold climates, white radish is frequently found in northern Chinese cuisine. It along with Napa cabbage constitute the two primary vegetables used in Shandong cooking.

CHINESE BANQUETS

Surely a highlight in anyone's Chinese food experience is attending a Chinese-style banquet. These are festive and rowdy occasions in which people eat and drink shamelessly to excess. Banquets are specially staged for celebrations such as holidays, weddings, birthdays, and anniversaries. For the guests, being invited to a banquet is always an honor; for the hosts, pulling off a well-planned banquet undoubtedly leaves good feelings and impressions with families, friends, colleagues, and associates.

Unlike the four different regional cuisines of China, there are only two basic types of Chinese-style banquets: one based on Jiangzhe cuisine and another on Hongkong-style seafood cuisine. Much of the regional characteristics that define other regional cuisines are missing in Chinese banquets. This is because banquet dishes are deliberately made to be mild in flavors, in order to appeal to everyone's palates. A Sichuan banquet, for example, has no spicy dishes at all, and Beijing banquets have little resemblance to the bland edges that usually characterize northern Chinese cuisine.

STYLES OF CHINESE BANQUETS

Traditionally, the de facto Chinese banquet is based on Jiangzhe cuisine – the cooking style of eastern China. For centuries, the Jiangzhe region was the most prosperous and sophisticated area in China, and its cuisine was widely regarded as the *haute cuisine* of China. Many of Jiangzhe's most famous dishes are regularly featured in these banquets, using a colorful combination of meats, vegetables, and exotic ingredients to create spectacular dishes that require a high degree of culinary skill. Seafood such as shark's fin and sea cucumbers are almost always featured as well. Also notable about Jiangzhe's banquet dishes is the amount of intricate knifework that goes into the preparing the dishes, introducing a level of visual appeal uncommon elsewhere in Chinese regional cuisines.

The second style of Chinese banquets is a more recent development. Over the past fifty years, with the rise of Hongkong-style seafood to prominence among Chinese regional cuisines, a new type of banquet consisting almost entirely of seafood dishes became popular. A Hongkong-style seafood banquet features a procession of creatures from the sea: from shark's fin, shrimp, and scallops, to fish, crabs, and abalone – often in the order from the ordinary to the exotic. A single poultry dish – like Beggar's Chicken or Beijing Duck – always comes in the middle to break the "monotony" of wall to wall seafood.

BANQUET ETIQUETTE

In the course of a Chinese-style banquet, dishes are served one at a time, and they become progressively more extravagant as the banquet moves on. There are always ten dishes in a banquet, starting with an appetizer of cold cuts. Then, the banquet moves on to some sort of soup or a second appetizer, followed by shrimp, then poultry, and then a dish of more exotic meats, and so on. Soup is usually skipped in a Hongkong-style seafood banquet.

In a civilization that is no stranger to hardships in life, Chinese banquets were traditionally the ways by which people defiantly taunted at daily reality. The Chinese never eat rice or noodles at a banquet, because these daily staples are symbols of ordinary lives. Banquets are lavish breaks from reality, so foods that suggest frugality and ordinariness have no place in them. Instead, Chinese banquets only feature meats and vegetables, displaying a degree of wealth, fortune, and hedonistic longing regardless of the actual circumstances.

However, as a gesture of humility, a host often chooses to serve a rice- or noodle dish at the conclusion of the banquet. It is considered an insult for the host not to provide enough food for the guests to eat, so a "just-in-case" staples dish, such as stir-fried rice or noodles, is served as "filler" for anyone who may still be hungry at the end. This is the host's self-effacing way of saying that despite all of the showiness and abundance of the banquet's dishes, they could not possibly satisfy everyone.

The etiquette, on behalf of the guests, is to leave this last dish alone. It is also considered an insult for the guests to suggest that the banquet was inadequate in any way. Therefore, the filler should get no more than a cursory pecking. Actually finishing this dish implies that the host had indeed failed to provide enough food for the guests.

The only exception to the last-dish etiquette is the *Longevity Noodles* served only at birthday banquets. These long, hand-pulled noodles are a Shandong cuisine specialty. Starting from a single ball of flour dough, a skilled chef pulls thin strands of noodles up to four feet long by hand. The length of Longevity Noodles symbolizes perseverance and success, and they are generally intended for celebrating the life of an elder person or a well respected guest-of-honor. Longevity Noodles are served in a starchy egg-drop soup, similar to a popular Shandong noodle dish called *Dalu Mian*. Guests eagerly slurp down these noodles with gusto, as a sincere wish for the guest-of-honor's continued health and prosperity.

OTHER BANQUET ETIQUETTE

Chinese banquets begin only after the entry of the guest-of-honor. In a wedding banquet, the guests-of-honor are the groom and the bride. In other celebrations, such as holidays and parties, the guest-of-honor is usually the eldest member of the host's family. In more formal banquets, the guest-of-honor enters the banquet hall with guests standing to their feet under cheers and applause. In those situations, the guest-of-honor often applauds back at the guests in a curious gesture uncommon in western cultures.

All of the tables at a Chinese banquet are round and of uniform size. The center table is reserved for the guest-of-honor, the host, and selected individuals who are the eldest, wealthiest, and most successful among the invited guests. Although all of the tables look the same and are served the same assortment of dishes, a high degree of social stratification takes place at a banquet. Lesser guests are seated at other tables, with their status ranked by the distance from the center table. In some pockets of Chinese society, banquet tables are still segregated by sex.

Banquets are the only occasions in the Chinese diet where alcohol is routinely consumed. The favorite alcoholic beverages in banquets include beer, *maotai*, and *shaoxing*, as well as imported cognac and whiskey. More recently, French wines have come into vogue, with red varieties enjoying enthusiastic patronage.

Drinking alcohol at Chinese banquets is nearly obligatory for men, and much less so for women. Banquets provide an ideal venue for many to size up the competition in regard to masculinity and showmanship. The ability to hold one's alcohol is, to some, a symbol of personal worth and pride.

Alcohol drinking is also a highly socialized affair at a banquet. Not only do they create loud, rowdy scenes, flowing alcohol opens up a side of people typically unseen in the emotionally-reserved Chinese.

CHINESE-STYLE BANQUETS IN LOS ANGELES

Although a majority of Chinese-style banquets in Los Angeles are patterned after Hongkong-style seafood cuisine, a growing number of Jiangzhe restaurants now offer traditional alternatives to Chinese-style banqueting. With everything considered, banquet options are replete with selections for all types of budgets, and banquet rooms range from intimate parties for ten, to wedding feasts for hundreds. With a large variety of venues available, there is a right Chinese-style banquet for every occasion.

Banquet restaurants have specially designed banquet menus that list the ten dishes for the table, along with the price. Seafood banquets – some using exotic creatures such as abalone and shark's fin – can cost well over $1,000 per table. More modest meals featuring barbecued meats and stir-fries can be accomplished for $250 or less. Jiangzhe-style banquets are more sophisticated, and they generally cost more than seafood banquets using similar ingredients. On average, one can expect a Chinese-style banquet in the San Gabriel Valley to cost $400 per table.

Sea Harbour Seafood Restaurant

The newest seafood house in the San Gabriel Valley is also the most sensational by far. Banquet dishes feature abalone from South Africa, as well as rare ginseng from Jilin province in northeastern China. The rest of the banquet menu features *haute cuisine* dishes hovering between innovative and daring. Nothing is commonplace in this extraordinary restaurant, and Sea Harbour is quickly establishing a solid reputation as the top Hongkong-style seafood house in Los Angeles. Commensurate with the quality of the food is the price, with some banquets costing around $2,000 per table.

3939 N. Rosemead Blvd., Rosemead
Phone: (626) 288-3939

Ocean Star Seafood Restaurant

Stepping into this palatial seafood house, one immediately feels the immensity of Ocean Star's stature: it is perched on a two-story strip mall like a bejeweled crown on a satin pillow. The many banquet rooms provide cozy ambience for company parties and family celebrations. Also, a large central hall erupts with the cheers of wedding banquets every weekend. Thanks to the excellent quality of local Pacific catch, Ocean Star's seafood cuisine has been for years one of most celebrated in Los Angeles.

145 N. Atlantic Blvd., #201-203, Monterey Park
Phone: (626) 308-2128

Newport Seafood

Seafood prepared in Chaozhou cuisine's cross-cultural style is simple, affordable, but arguably better than the Hongkong style. It has none of the added gild and pretense, and all of the fresh and spicy flavors of Southeast Asian cooking. Newport Seafood is one such place that focuses on Chaozhou-style seafood, offering ordinary and well-prepared dishes with hints of Thai- and Vietnamese cookings. Appropriately, Newport's banquet menu maintains a humble tilt – featuring practical dishes that are priced around $300 per table.

18441 E. Colima Rd., Rowland Heights
Phone: (626) 839-1239

Mandarin Shanghai Restaurant

This restaurant serves supreme examples of Jiangzhe and Shanghai cooking, and its banquet menu is a welcomed digression from the Hongkong-style seafood that dominate much of the Chinese-style banqueting choices in town. Jiangzhe's banquet cuisine generally features two or three seafood dishes, with the remainder comprised of interesting dishes such as lotus root stuffed with glutinous rice, honey-baked ham, and braised squab. These dishes are also more elaborate and intricate than those found in a seafood banquet. At around $600 per table, Mandarin Shanghai's banquets are in the middle of the spectrum of banquet options available in Los Angeles.

558 Las Tunas Dr., Arcadia
(626) 445-4555

970 N. Broadway, #114, Los Angeles
(213) 625-1195

Rounds of toasts are initiated by tapping chopsticks on the plates, amid a chorus of cheering and hoo-hawing. Anyone can also initiate an individual toast, simply by raising their glass in the other person's presence, and saying a few well-wishing words. Then they exchange a greeting of *"ganbei"* ("cheers," or literally, "dry glass") before both down their drinks. It is polite for the host to walk up to each table to toast all of the guests. Younger guests may pay their respect to the elders by approaching their tables and offering toasts in the same manner. People who do not drink alcohol can have their glasses filled with fruit juice or soft drink instead.

CHINESE BANQUETS IN LOS ANGELES

In much of China, and also in Taiwan, the de facto banquet cuisine is based on Jiangzhe cuisine. Hongkong-style seafood, which only gained popularity in 1960s, plays a minor role in the Chinese banqueting culture. In America, however, where the history of Guangdong immigrants is long established, the representation of banquet styles is reversed. A Chinese banquet in Los Angeles is more likely to be a Hongkong-style seafood banquet, held at many of the area's glittering and palatial seafood houses.

Making arrangements for Chinese banquets is easy, although banquets are not the most economical meals around. There are always ten dishes in a Chinese banquet, and each table seats ten persons. Planning banquets takes into consideration the concept of ten: banquet menus all feature a selection of ten dishes; and quoted prices are for a table of ten persons. Chinese restaurants that serve banquets have special banquet menus that list several banquet choices, featuring pre-selected dishes of varying degrees of extravagance. All the host needs to do is to select the right banquet for the occasion, and specify the number of tables required.

REGIONAL STYLES OF CHINA

The term *Chinese Food* refers to the cooking of the Hans – the ethnic majority that makes up over ninety percent of China's population. The Hans are concentrated in only about half of China's territorial landmass, and China's regional cuisines represent only those areas where the Hans have traditionally dominated. Despite the existence of 55 minority groups in China, Chinese food is solely the custom of the Hans, and shares very little similarity with the traditions of other minorities.

Chinese regional cuisines can be divided into four major styles: Southern, Northern, Western, and Eastern. However, depending on who you ask, there can be as many regional styles as there are pages in the Shanghai phone book. Every village, city, and province has some claims on their own specialties, but generally, all of the Han cooking styles can be categorized into these four major groupings.

Socially speaking (and this applies to Chinese food as well), regional differences in China are more pronounced than they are in the U.S. For example, the northern Beijing dialect (Mandarin) is incomprehensible to a Guangdong person, and vice versa. The lands of northeast China share little economic affinity with Sichuan in the west. Regional identity is routinely bandied with pride among the Hans, who will readily identify themselves as the peoples of their provinces first, and then as Chinese second.

Apropos to Chinese cuisines, regional variations are as diverse as the Hans themselves. However, for a long time the only Chinese food available in America was cast after Guangdong cuisine. That situation is changing in Los Angeles, however, with the San Gabriel Valley riding the crest of a Chinese "Culinary Revolution" currently underway. There, Chinese food is no longer the domain of Moo-shoo Pork and the Two-item Combo. Instead, the local Chinese food scene has been transformed by a host of regional flavors, including the sophisticated cuisine of Shanghai, the Southeast Asian flair of Chaozhou cooking, and the cross-cultural fusion of Hongkong-style coffeehouses.

SOUTHERN CHINA

The cuisine of southern China is represented by the Guangdong style of cooking, with several offshoot cuisines emerging from Guangdong's cooking traditions as the results of historical events over the past 200 years. Southern Chinese cuisine is the youngest of China's four classic regional cooking styles. It is somewhat overrated in importance when compared with other regional cuisines; the long-time dominance of Guangdong immigrants abroad created the misperception that Guangdong cuisine represented all of China. In reality, Guangdong cuisine does not have many famous dishes that it calls its own, nor is it a sophisticated style of cooking. However, it does succeed in combining many western influences to its cooking techniques, more so than any other regional cuisine of China.

Southern Chinese cuisine is, essentially, the Chinese food for beginners. The dishes are very uncomplicated – with light, sweet, and tepid sauces that mainly rely on the fresh flavors of the ingredients for their character. This characteristic is especially important when dealing with the delicate and subtle flavors of seafood, which is popularized by the seafood cuisine of Hongkong. Seafood is also prepared to perfection in the Chaozhou style, which fuses Chinese cooking techniques with Southeast Asian ingredients.

Also considered as southern Chinese cuisine is Hunan cuisine, which is actually a fusion of several Chinese cooking traditions, most notably Guangdong and Sichuan.

Los Angeles enjoys an immense selection of southern Chinese cuisines, from small Guangdong-style barbecue shops to opulently appointed Hongkong-style seafood houses. In addition, recent immigrants have brought in waves of trendy foods to America's shores, enlightening the food scene with the cross-cultural concoctions of Hongkong-style coffeeshops. Moreover, the world-famous tradition of dim sum/yum cha is propelled to the level of *haute cuisine* in Los Angeles, with innovative snack dishes unlike any other dim sum found elsewhere in the U.S.

GUANGDONG CUISINE

"Guangdong cuisine remains light and practical - much less refined than Jiangzhe cuisine, and not as complex in flavor as Sichuan cuisine."

Guangdong (Cantonese) cuisine is the Chinese regional style most familiar to Americans, and it is often perceived simply as "Chinese food." This perception came from America's first Chinese immigrants, who came from the city of Guangzhou (Canton) on the Pearl River Delta near the southern coast of Guangdong province. Guangdong people made up almost all of the Chinese immigrants in America until the 1950s, and they gave many Americans their first and only taste of Chinese food. The dishes found in neighborhood takeout restaurants combine traditional Guangdong cooking techniques with American ingredients. Names such as "Orange-flavor Chicken," "Broccoli Beef," and "Egg Fu-yung" came into America's vocabulary this way.

Guangdong cuisine, in its traditional form, shares only a few similarities with the American version of Chinese food. Among them are Guangdong cuisine's fondness for fresh and light tastes, and preference for sweet- and fruity flavors. Guangdong's dishes are generally prepared very simply – resorting to a lot of stir-frying. This cooking technique uses high heat and short cooking times, which spare the ingredients from breaking down and losing their natural characteristics in the process.

Guangdong's fertile soils and subtropical climate help adorn its landscape with a lush green canopy, cultivated with rice, sugarcanes, oranges, lychees, longan, et cetera. Guangdong's maritime perch provides ample quantities of seafood, and rivers supply the land with irrigation water and plenty of freshwater fish. Guangdong's subtropical climate is unique within China's diverse and vast landscape; its cuisine uses many herbal, medicinal, and seafood ingredients not found elsewhere in China.

Guangdong province has always been an impoverished and unsophisticated place, and its cuisine continues to show predominantly rural characteristics. Centuries of poverty and privation forced the Guangdong people to find use of everything for food: animals like frogs, snakes, and turtles are regulars inside a Guangdong kitchen, as well as all kinds of "exotic" animals not typically eaten in mainstream China. It is said that the Guangdong people will eat just about anything with four legs – except the table – a nearly veritable fact that even the Chinese themselves routinely joke about.

Guangdong's cuisine was largely nondescript and unremarkable until fairly recently. In 1841, British warships forcibly opened Guangzhou to the opium trade. For over a century after that, Guangzhou received not only unlimited quantities of dope from the British, it made substantial contacts with Europeans as well. Consequently, Guangdong cuisine reflects many of the West's influences. For example, Europeans taught Guangdong people how to use western vegetables such as broccoli, tomatoes, and watercress ("European vegetable"), all of which are not found in other regional cuisines. Foreign influences do not belie Guangdong's earthy and rustic characters, however; it remains light and practical – much less refined than Jiangzhe cuisine, and not as complex in flavor than Sichuan cuisine.

VARIATIONS OF THE GUANGDONG COOKING STYLE

A new cuisine emerged from Hongkong over the last fifty years, with marked differences from Guangdong's cooking styles. The differences spring from Hongkong's political and social separation from Guangdong province starting in the 1950s, during which Guangzhou and mainland China stifled under communist rule. Even though Hongkong and Guangzhou are merely 100 miles apart, Hongkong prospered as a free port while Guangzhou stagnated. In its prosperity, Hongkong chefs began creating innovative dishes that made use of the city's access to seafood and foreign ingredients. The resulting seafood cuisine is now considered as *haute cuisine* today. (See chapter on Hongkong-style Seafood House.)

Another variation of Guangdong cooking is Chaozhou cuisine (also known as *Chiu Chow* or *Teochew*). The eastern Guangdong city of Chaozhou, near the border with Fujian province, was the base of Chinese immigration to Southeast Asia, particularly to Thailand and Vietnam. Chaozhou people, as they are called, also settled in places like Penang in Malaysia, Singapore, and Indonesia. Their cooking reflects traditional Fujian and Guangdong cooking techniques, with significant overtones of tropical- and Southeast Asian flavors. Hot and spicy flavors from chili peppers, coupled with fresh herbs like mint leaves and basil, plus the use of fish sauce – an indispensable condiment in Thai- and Vietnamese cuisines – set Chaozhou cooking apart. Seafood also plays a prominent part, prepared even lighter and more delicately than Hongkong's style. (See chapter on Chaozhou Cuisine.)

A third variation of Guangdong cooking is the cuisine of the Hakka people – a mysterious ethnic group long ostracized and persecuted by the Hans. The word *Hakka*, which means "guests," refers to a group of people who originally came from China's north-central deserts. They were removed from their homeland as far back as 800 years ago, during the Song Dynasty (960-1279). From there, the Hakkas were chased south, where they eventually settled in eastern Guangdong province. Later, large numbers of Hakka people migrated to Southeast Asia and Taiwan, during the period of mass migration of the Guangdong people.

Having endured centuries of suffering, the Hakka people have a stereotype for being frugal and hardworking. Their cooking rarely uses fresh seafood, as their difficulties precluded them from enjoying such luxuries. Instead, Hakka cooking is very crude, with lots of pickled vegetables and preserved meats. The food is also oily, with heavier flavors due to the preponderance of preserved ingredients. As yet, there

are no restaurants dedicated to Hakka cuisine in Los Angeles. However, as they are currently very popular in Taipei, Hakka cuisine may soon make its way across the Pacific.

GUANGDONG'S COOKING TECHNIQUES

Stir-frying is the most important cooking technique in Guangdong cuisine. In addition, many different cooking techniques are employed to achieve a wider variety of culinary styles. Some of these techniques are ideal for specific types of ingredients, and some are quite unique to Guangdong cuisine.

Stir-Fry

炒

The most common cooking technique in Guangdong cuisine is stir-frying, which is also popular throughout China. Stir-frying uses high heat and oil to cook food quickly. Ingredients must be cut into small pieces in order to be properly cooked this way.

"Bake"

焗

This is a distinctive Guangdong cooking technique, in which ingredients are coated with starch or flour, fried to a crisp, and then simmered in a soup stock. The starch in the fried pieces thickens the soup into a hearty stew, while helping it absorb all the flavors of the ingredients. Interestingly, many restaurants translate this method as "baking," even though it shares no relationship to the oven-baking technique familiar in the West.

Deep-Fry

泡

Deep-frying in Guangdong cuisine is done over medium heat, so that the ingredients do not overcook prematurely. Deep-frying in the Guangdong tradition is not as artistic and skilled as the Japanese have in making *tempura*, but it is nevertheless a popular method of preparing all sorts of meat- and vegetable dishes. Oftentimes, the deep-fried foods are returned to the wok for an additional stir-fry with a sauce. Otherwise, the sauce is prepared separately, and poured on top of the deep-fried foodjust before serving.

Flash-Cook

灼

The flash cooking method uses very high heat in the wok with little oil to stir-fry foods quickly. This method is similar to a style used in Shandong cuisine, with the difference being that in Guangdong cuisine, a sauce is prepared separately, and then poured over the food. In Shandong cuisine, flavoring is added directly into the wok while the ingredients are being flash-fried.

Sautée & Simmer

扒

A distinct Guangdong cooking style, ingredients are first sautéed in a pan, then stock is added to allow everything to simmer slowly. An example is crab,

first sautéed with green vegetables, is then added with broth to simmer until fully cooked. Starch is added at the end to thicken the broth and end the cooking process.

Simmer

燴

Guangdong-style stews are made from a hearty mix of ingredients, slowly simmered over low heat, and thickened with starch prior to serving. This popular cooking method is often done in an earthenware hotpot, which is served directly from the stove to the table while everything is still bubbling hot inside.

GUANGDONG'S CONDIMENTS AND SAUCES

Guangdong cuisine skillfully uses a variety of sauces, which play a pivotal role in the flavors of its dishes. The main ingredients are generally cooked with very little additional seasoning, so that their natural flavors are not overwhelmed. The way Guangdong cooking manipulates sauces has parallels to French cuisine. In Guangdong cooking, the sauce is often prepared separately from the primary cooking process, and then combined with the food at a later time. The sauces are also light, complementing the flavors of the ingredients rather than altering them. The Guangdong pantry is stocked full of condiments that are used to create these sauces, many of which are not used anywhere else in China.

Lao Chou

老抽

This is a dark soy sauce produced in Guangdong province. It is full-flavored, but with less salt than sheng chou, the lighter type of soy sauce described below. Dark soy sauce actually contains less salt than light soy sauce; the color and flavors of the soy sauce gives it its name. For example, lao chou has deep flavors and a dark caramel color that make it unsuitable for things like sushi. Rather, lao chou is appropriate for all types of stews and stir-fries, where coloration is more important without overpowering the dishes with saltiness.

Sheng Chou

生抽

The light soy sauce has exactly the opposite characteristics of lao chou. It is light in color, and with a much higher salt content. Sheng chou is used in situations where flavoring is more important than imparting coloration to the food. A good example is in steaming fish. The light soy sauce adds flavors without staining the fish to the color of burnt coffee. Guangdong cuisine is the only place in Chinese cooking where soy sauce is expressly differentiated between lao chou and sheng chou. Elsewhere, soy sauce is a general, all-purpose condiment with coloration and saltiness falling somewhere between those of lao chou and sheng chou.

Chu Hou Sauce

柱候醬

Modern condiment producers have successfully marketed this half-and-half mixture of sweet bean paste and sesame paste. Legend has it that a country chef named Leong Chu Hou invented this sauce, which was later named in his honor. Mr. Leong's cat accidentally knocked over a pot of sweet bean paste one day, spilling it

into an urn of sesame paste. Loathing waste, Mr. Leong blended the mess together with sugar and light soy sauce, and came away with an instant classic. A common dish using Chu Hou Sauce is a beef brisket stew simmered with white radishes.

Plum Sauce
梅子醬

Plum sauce is made from dried salted plums. Westerners are familiar with it as "duck sauce," which is used as a dipping sauce for roast duck at Chinese takeouts. The plum sauce has a fruity, tangy flavors that are irresistibly attractive, yet it is rarely used in cooking outside Guangdong province. Besides using it as a dipping sauce, the plum sauce has a variety of uses including adding a tangy dimension to barbecued meats and stir-fried vegetables.

Ketchup
茄汁

Tomato sauce demonstrates Guangdong's distinctive penchant to incorporate fruity flavors to its dishes. In addition, it shows a

degree of western influence in its culinary heritage. Tomatoes are an imported fruit from the West, and are rarely used in other Chinese regional cuisines. Interestingly, the word ketchup, the American stuff on burgers, fries, and meatloaf, is a Cantonese word, derived from *ke-sup*, meaning "tomato juice."

Shrimp Paste
蝦醬

This pungent sauce made of crushed salted shrimp is not for everyone. It looks rather unappetizing – bluish gray in color with a pasty consistency. The flavors are earthy, as expected from any preserved seafood. This is a sauce that is grounded to the essence of peasant cooking. However, skilled chefs frequently turn this thick, humble sauce into heavenly creations, used with steamed fish, flash-cooked beef, and all kinds of stir-fried vegetables.

CATEGORIES OF GUANGDONG DISHES

Guangdong cuisine does not have many famous dishes that resonate throughout China. Rather, it has a large variety of dishes created by throwing together different combinations of ingredients. Thus, it is best to consider Guangdong cuisine in categories such as rice, noodles, and earthenware hotpots. Each category contains a bewildering array of similar dishes, differentiated only by the combination of featured ingredients.

BARBECUES

Barbecue shops are an easily recognizable feature of Guangdong-style restaurants. The shop windows are stocked with roast ducks, boiled chickens, sides of roasted suckling piglet, roasted pork, octopus, et cetera. Barbecue shops are generally located adjacent to the restaurant's dining room, and they serve takeout customers as well. Many barbecue items are important cooking ingredients in Guangdong cooking, so people regularly come in as part of their shopping routine.

Roast Duck
粵式燒鴨

Often confused for Beijing Duck, the Guangdong-style roast duck is likewise ordinary, but without all of the intricate steps in preparing them. Ducks are simply marinated in a brine of salt, sugar, and five-spice, and then roasted over open flames until golden brown. The duck skin does not attain the crispiness that distinguishes the Beijing Duck; the entire duck is chopped into pieces, and can be eaten as an appetizer with a plum dipping sauce. It can also be used as a flavoring ingredient in a variety of stir-fries, soups, or rice- and noodle dishes.

Boiled Chicken
鹽水雞

A whole chicken is boiled in a saltwater brine. There is not much

more to that. Guangdong-style boiled chicken tends to be less fully cooked, so that the bones still retain the bright red color of blood. This way, the chicken meat is firmer to the bite. Boiled chicken is chopped into pieces and eaten either as an appetizer or a main dish. A marinated oil of chopped fresh ginger and scallions is its customary dipping sauce.

Soy Sauce Chicken
豉油雞

Similar to the boiled chicken, soy sauce chicken is boiled – except that soy sauce is added to the brine to provide a pale brown coloration. The presence of soy sauce also presents an altogether different flavor to the chicken. It is also accompanied by a marinated oil of ginger and scallions for dipping.

Charsui Pork
叉燒肉

Often just called "barbecue pork," the name "charsui" suggests the method by which it is cooked: hung from a hook and roasted until golden brown. Sides of pork loin or ribs are marinated with salt, hoisin sauce, and honey, then roasted on a hook over open flames. Charsui pork is also one of the most important ingredients in Guangdong-style home cooking; shoppers regularly stop by the barbecue shop to take a side of it home. Among the versatile uses of charsui pork is the famous steamed bun stuffed with a lickety-sweet filling.

Roast Suckling Piglet
燒乳豬

The entire suckling piglet is often hung and grotesquely displayed in the barbecue case. The piglet is roasted until its skin is golden and crispy from head to tail. Traditionally, the roast piglet was food reserved for special occasions, but the advent of the barbecue shops has made it affordable by selling it in small portions, thus popularizing its use in many household dishes. Bite-sized roast piglet can be stir-fried with seasonal greens to provide extra flavors and textures. It is also found in all sorts of rice- and noodle dishes.

NOODLES

Rice is the primary staple in Guangdong cuisine, but noodles also play a significant part in Guangdong's lineup of dishes. The large variety of noodle dishes presents a confounding challenge for many, because restaurants often translate dish names differently. A *Lo Mein* in one restaurant may be called *Chow Mein* in another. And what a Guangdong-style restaurant calls *Chow Mein* has no equivalent in American-style takeouts.

One can reasonably expect to find five types of noodles in a typical Guangdong-style restaurant.

Chow Mein
炒麵

Chow mein is often misinterpreted as stir-fried noodles. And in many American Chinese takeouts, chow mein is just a stir-fry with no noodles at all. In the authentic Guangdong form, chow mein consists of pan-fried noodles with a sauce on top. It has no equivalent anywhere else. These yellow-colored egg noodles are first steamed, then blanched, and finally fried in a shallow pan. Because chow mein is fried in a large clump, only the outside is crispy, while the noodles inside remain fluffy and *al dente*. Upon serving, chow mein is topped with a sauce made of the featured meats and vegetables, such as fresh seafood, chicken, or tomato beef stew.

Lo Mein
撈麵

Guangdong-style lo mein is a noodle soup with the noodles culled from the soup (*lo* means "culled"). The noodles are served dry with meats and vegetables on top, and the flavorful soup is served separately as an accompanying beverage. Typical lo mein dishes include barbecued meats, beef brisket, and a plain broth with wontons.

Chow Fun

炒粉

Fun is a broad, flat rice noodle popular in Chaozhou cuisine. Chow fun is a stir-fry of *fun* with a selection of meats and vegetables. It is not a pan-fried dish like chow mein. Many chow fun dishes demonstrate a Southeast Asian tilt in flavors, using ingredients such as satay beef, or curry and tomatoes in a combination popularly called "Singapore-style."

Yi-fu Mian (Noodles)

伊府麵

Or commonly called *yi mein*, this noodle originated from Shandong cuisine, the master of noodle making skills in China. These pale white noodles are made from flour, egg whites and oil, which give them a wriggly texture. In Guangdong-style restaurants, all yi-fu noodle dishes, except one, are served in a soup with the featured combination of ingredients on top. The only exception is a plain stir-fry of yi-fu noodles with just scallions only.

Rice Vermicelli

米粉

Like chow fun, rice vermicelli (also called *mifen*, *meefun*, or *beehon*) is a stir-fried rice noodle dish. Rice vermicelli is much thinner than *fun*, and has similarity to Italian angle hair pasta. Often, the choice between *fun* and rice vermicelli is purely based on personal preference. Some people like the flat, broad *fun*, and others like the thin, stringy rice vermicelli.

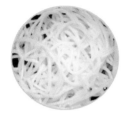

Earthenware Hotpot

沙鍋

A distinctive Guangdong cooking technique, savory stews are slowly simmered in an earthenware hotpot. A hearty mix of ingredients, such as seafood, meatballs, pork ribs, and tofu, are all placed into the pot with with hearty vegetables and cellophane noodles. The earthenware hotpot doubles as the serving vessel, brought from the stove directly to the table while the contents are still bubbling inside. Popular earthenware hotpots include pork spareribs with eggplant, and a fish head stew simmered with Napa cabbage.

OTHER TYPICAL STIR-FRIED DISHES IN GUANGDONG CUISINE

Many of the typical Guangdong-style stir-fries can be found in Chinese takeouts. Many are instantly identifiable by Americans, using familiar meats and ingredients commonly found throughout North America. Some Guangdong dishes are adaptations of other Chinese regional specialties. They were altered to suit the palates of the Guangdong people, which generally prefer light, mild, and uncomplicated flavors.

Beef Brisket in Tomato Sauce
蕃茄牛肉

Tomato is not a common vegetable in Chinese cooking, and beef is not the type of meat commonly eaten in China. The combination of tomatoes and beef gives this dish a western aura, and when it is cooked into a stew, as is in this case, it is often considered as "American-style." This dish is popularly served over plain rice or on chow mein, but can also be served as a main dish in the meal.

Beef Flash-fried with Scallions
蔥爆（蒙古）牛肉

Often called Mongolian Beef, this dish is adapted from the Islamic Chinese cuisine from northern China. As the name suggests, beef is flash-fried with scallions, with very little sauce. The alternative name – Mongolian beef – suggests the dish's origins from the north, adapted for Guangdong palates by using scallions instead of leeks like they do in northern Chinese cooking.

Beef-and-Broccoli
芥蘭牛肉

Although not much more needs to be said about this classic takeout favorite, Beef-and-broccoli in a Guangdong-style restaurant is a different dish because it uses gai lan – also called Chinese broccoli. Otherwise, the dish maintains its traditional takeout form, featuring stir-fried slices of beef in oyster sauce, and topped over a layer of blanched gai lan.

Pork Spareribs with Salt and Pepper
椒鹽排骨

This very popular dish is very uncomplicated – pork spareribs are deep-fried, perhaps coated with flour or starch but generally left unbattered. A dish of salt and black pepper is provided on the side for dipping.

Chicken with Cashews
腰果雞丁

Cashew nuts are indigenous to the Americas, so this dish suggests a multi-cultural dimension to Guangdong-cuisine. Diced chicken is stir-fried in a light soy sauce with crunchy pieces of cashew nuts, making good use of contrasting textures and flavors.

Kungpao (Gongbao) Chicken
宮保雞丁

Kungpao chicken, in its familiar Americanized form, is an adaptation of an adaptation. This dish originally came from Guizhou province, near Sichuan, which is famous for hot and spicy food. A milder, sweeter version of the dish was adapted to better suit Guangdong's palates, which are not accustomed to spicy foods. When Kungpao Chicken traveled with Guangdong immigrants to the U.S., it got a second adaptation, this time with American ingredients such as bell peppers, yellow onions, and often minus the original requites of chili peppers and peanuts altogether. It has very little resemblance to the original from western China.

Sweet-and-sour pork
甜酸肉

Guangdong dishes use a lot of deep-frying, and prefer foods with sweet and fruity flavors. Both characteristics can be found in sweet-and-sour pork. Pork pieces are battered and fried,

then coated with a tart, fruity plum sauce. Chinese takeout restaurants usually use a reddish plum sauce that they buy in large tubs from food warehouses. Authentic Guangdong-style restaurants prefer to make their own plum sauce. Without the food coloring, their plum sauce is golden in color.

GUANGDONG-STYLE RESTAURANTS IN LOS ANGELES

The abundance of Guangdong-style restaurants in Los Angeles is difficult to miss. Endless parades of barbecue shops, seafood houses, and family restaurants help recall the neighborhood food scenes in Guangzhou and Hongkong. Places like the successful Sam Woo chain have fairly predictable menus of typical Guangdong stalwarts such as kungpao chicken and seafood chow mein. Additionally, hundreds of rice- and noodle dishes jockey for space on the voluminous menus of Guangdong-style restaurants. Typically, Guangdong-style restaurants also open early, serving informal dim sum of the so-called "One Pot, Two Items" breakfasts in the morning.

Hakka cuisine is currently enjoying the status as a trendy food item in Taipei, but it has yet caught the attention of people on this side of the Pacific. In the absence of any strictly Hakka-style restaurants in Los Angeles, the only chance to experience examples of Hakka cooking is to find occasional references of famous Hakka dishes on the menus of other Chinese regional restaurants. Among the best-known Hakka dishes are *braised chicken in basil*, *pork belly stewed in preserved vegetables*, and a glutinous rice ball soup served in a meat broth.

Phoenix Inn

There is always a crowd at Phoenix Inn – especially popular with families who flock there for its ample portions and terrific food. Phoenix Inn is somewhat uncharacteristic of typical Guangdong-style restaurants in that it does not have a barbecue shop. Instead, Phoenix Inn makes up for it with an upscale bakery next door. Also interesting is an array of "healthy choice" dishes that are sparing in oil, salt, and free of MSG. The house special, "Phoenix Inn Boneless Chicken" is a cold cuts dish that is truly a gem among all others.

208 E. Valley Boulevard, Alhambra
(626) 299-1238

Fortune B.B.Q. and Dim Sum

This archetypal Guangdong-style restaurant is as authentic as it gets. The regular menu serves up Guangdong favorites like barbecues, rice dishes, noodle dishes, and miscellaneous stir-fries. A built-in bakery and barbecue shop serves dumplings, baozi, and small pastries of the "One Pot, Two Item" breakfast. All around, the florescent lights and dowdy (but clean) surroundings scream pensively for the old days of Guangzhou.

18406 Colima Rd., #A, Rowland Heights
(626) 839-0626

MPV Express

The offspring of the popular MPV Seafood Restaurant nearby, MPV Express serves cafeteria-style Guangdong cuisine, complete with all sorts of barbecued items, dim sum, and typical stir-fries of Chinese takeout fame. The prices are very reasonable; the place is especially popular with *salarypersons* during lunchtime.

429 W. Garvey Ave., Monterey Park
(626) 307-7338

Sam Woo B.B.Q. Restaurant

By far the most successful Guangdong-style eatery franchise in North America, Sam Woo has expanded from its roots in Southern California to places as far away as Toronto. The comprehensive menu of Guandong-style dishes includes all types of rice- and noodle dishes. It also has a well-stocked barbecue shop glowing with roasted ducks, suckling piglets, barbecue pork, and boiled chickens.

514 W. Valley Blvd., Alhambra
(626) 281-0038

19008 Pioneer Blvd., Cerritos
(562) 262-0888

15333 Culver Dr., Ste. 722, Irvine
(949) 262-0888

803 N. Broadway, Los Angeles
(213) 687-7238

18908 E. Gale Ave., Rowland Heights
(626) 572-8418

140 W. Valley Blvd., #107, San Gabriel
(626) 572-8418

and other locations

More restaurants are listed in Appendix I.

SEAFOOD DISHES

Guangdong's seafood staple includes fish, clams, oysters, crabs, scallops, shrimp, and squid. In Guangdong-style restaurants, they tend to be simple stir-fries, or served in an earthenware hotpot. In Hongkong-style seafood houses, seafood dishes are more refined, using more of the rare and exotic ingredients such as shark's fins, swallow's nests, and sea cucumbers.

Stir-fried Squid in Shrimp Sauce
蝦醬鮮魷

Shrimp sauce, or more accurately shrimp paste, needs some getting used to, and many people never do. The pungent scent is offensive to some people, but its earthy tones tell a lot about Guangdong cooking, suggesting the frugality and innovativeness of Guangdong peasants. Shrimp paste is also very salty, so a little bit of it goes a long way in stir-fried dishes of seafood and vegetables, with no need of further flavorings.

Fried Rock Cod Fillet with Corn Sauce
栗米石班

Pieces of rock cod are battered and fried, then coated with a sauce almost right out of a can of cream of corn soup. This is a very typical home-cooking dish, with a light and sweet flavor derived from corn. Although corn is a Native American crop, its pervasive household use suggests a familiarity with this ingredient, as well as the extent of foreign influences on Guangdong cuisine.

HONGKONG-STYLE SEAFOOD HOUSE

"Seafood houses are spread all over the San Gabriel Valley like Cheez Whiz, tempting a wide audience to explore the likes of sautéed shrimp in XO sauce, steamed rock cod, and abalone shabu shabu."

Hongkong-style seafood houses are huge, boisterous places – loud with people's chatter and clanking glasses, and bright under neon lights and sparkling chandeliers. In Hongkong, seafood houses are forthright proclamations of the city's wealth, a conceit it brazenly and shamelessly flaunts.

Evolving from the traditions of Guangdong cuisine, Hongkong's seafood cuisine rose to prominence during a time when Hongkong became separated from its Guangdong cousin. Hongkong was first ceded to Britain as a Crown Colony in 1841, and then the Communist takeover of 1949 sealed it off from the mainland. But as Hongkong flourished on its own, its chefs began experimenting with new dishes that, while mostly holding on to traditional Guangdong cooking techniques, incorporated western influences and all sorts of seafood. The result is a cuisine simple in execution, but unsparing with some of the choiest, rarest, and most expensive ingredients in the world.

Sitting on the South China Sea, Hongkong has access to virtually limitless supplies of seafood. Lobsters, crabs, prawns, and an array of fish are all consumed in great quantities. Rare species and exotic imports add to the colorful mix. In Hongkong, money talks as fast as Chick Hearn in the fourth quarter; as long as the price is right, any imaginable creature could be, and is, eaten.

*The colossal **Jumbo Floating Restaurant** in Hongkong's Aberdeen Harbor defines the city's colorful seafood cuisine.*

Today, Los Angeles and the San Gabriel Valley have some of the best Hongkong-style seafood houses in North America, rivalling Vancouver. Before the Chinese takeover in 1997, many wealthy Hongkongers left for North America, taking their money and professional skills with them. Many famous Hongkong chefs landed in Los Angeles, either on their own volition or were attracted by lucrative contracts. The 1988 arrival of Hui Pui Wing – one of the most celebrated Hongkong chefs at the time – not only brought Harbor Village Restaurant to Monterey Park, it set off a Chinese "Culinary Revolution" that forever changed the landscape of the Chinese food scene in Los Angeles.

Although the original Harbor Village is long gone, Hongkong-style seafood houses are now spread all over the San Gabriel Valley like Cheez Whiz. ABC, NBC, NYC, MPV, Empress Harbor, and Ocean Star are just some of the best and most popular names for seafood in Los Angeles. Lately, new Hongkong-style seafood houses have opened in the Westside and Santa Monica as well, tempting a wider American audience to explore the likes of sautéed shrimp in XO sauce, steamed rock cod, and abalone *shabu shabu*.

Unlike most other types of Chinese restaurants, which are owned by families and individuals, Hongkong-style seafood houses are built with significant amounts of overseas capital. Competition is especially keen these days, as each new restaurant is built bigger and more opulent than the last, and chefs are traded around like free agents in baseball. Whenever a new dish is invented, it is quickly emulated by other competitors. And when a price cut is advertised, it is immediately undercut across town. Hongkong-style seafood houses exemplify Hongkong-style competition – cutthroat and raw at its core. The winners, as always, are food-lovers who get to sample some truly spectacular creations.

X MARKS THE XO SAUCE

Deeply immersed in Hongkong's seafood cuisine is the mysterious XO sauce – a spicy condiment that is golden in color, coarse in texture, and with a taste that is unlike anything else in the league of Guangdong's cooking sauces. Made with dried scallops, shrimp, garlic, and a secret combination of spices, XO sauce

has piqued the curiosity of food lovers for over 40 years. Although its exact origins are unknown, one thing about the XO sauce is certain: it does not contain a single drop of XO, the cognac that gives the sauce its name. "XO" is merely a marketing moniker used to attract people's attention and to command higher prices. XO cognac is a status symbol in Hongkong, and a sauce named XO naturally elevates itself to a higher level of sophistication, perceived or otherwise.

Like many Chinese culinary traditions, no one knows for sure how the XO sauce was first invented. Many people speculate that it originated from Fook Lam Moon, a famous seafood restaurant in Kowloon. In the 1960s, Fook Lam Moon was confronted with a business dilemma – competition from other seafood houses was heated, and customer patronage was sliding. To woo customers and boost its image, Fook Lam Moon came up with this golden sauce. People flocked to the restaurant to try it, shelling out top money to get a taste. A firestorm soon raged around this sauce, and overnight every seafood house in Hongkong touted its own XO sauce.

Forty years later, the craze for the XO sauce has not faded. It is found in nearly every restaurant and home pantry, and it has truly become a classic condiment in both Guangdong cuisine and Hongkong-style seafood cuisine.

Although the XO sauce's fame was propelled by ingenious marketing, its continued popularity is grounded in pure substance. The XO sauce has proven itself to be the perfect condiment for stir-frying seafood such as squid, lobster, scallops, and crab. The play of natural flavors is the quintessence of traditional Guangdong cooking, and the XO sauce is just light and spicy enough to complement the delicate flavors of the sea.

LIVE FISH TANKS

Hongkong-style seafood houses are identifiable by the live fish tanks that line one side of the wall. Some of the larger places have their fish tanks filled with local- and imported seafood. A selection of crab, shrimp, clam, fresh- and saltwater fish make up the general offering. Upscale restaurants will stock exotic creatures for big appetites and bigger bank accounts. When they are in season,

Maine lobsters are as obligatory as Tammy Faye's mascara. Favorite imported seafood include geoduck clams (pronounced "gooey-duck") from the Pacific Northwest, snow crabs from Alaska, and imperial crabs from Australia.

The fun of eating in a Hongkong-style seafood house – besides people watching and yelling over the din of diners – is ordering from these fish tanks. Dishes on the printed menu with "seasonal price" next to them usually use the fish tank seafood. Frequently, these are the chef's specialties that make stopping by a Hongkong-style seafood house an exciting and rewarding experience.

Another way to order from the fish tanks is to specify the ways by which the fresh seafood is prepared. All of this is negotiated with the waiter, and they can be very helpful with suggestions. The general concept is that fresh seafood should be cooked simply – by steaming, boiling, stir-frying or deep-frying. Sauces are light enough so that the natural flavors of the seafood are not overwhelmed. Fresh and good quality seafood does not have offensive odors, so Guangdong's light sauces are perfect complement to even the subtlest qualities of crustaceans and fish.

Specifying the way by which seafood is prepared can be made with a three-step approach. The first is to select the catch – whether it is a fish, crab, shrimp, or whatever else that is in the fish tanks. Then, choose a way to cook it. Depending on what is ordered, seafood can be fried, steamed, boiled, braised, pan-fried, et cetera. Finally, select a sauce. Depending on the cooking method, ideal sauces for seafood include the XO sauce, black bean sauce, "red-cooked" sauce, or simply a garnish of ginger and scallions.

When ordering from the fish tanks, prices are determined by weight. The waiter theatrically nets the seafood out of the fish tank, and then brings it in a plastic bag or tub to the table for inspection. At that time, the weight of the catch and its approximate price are revealed. The seafood is then brought into the kitchen, and the next time it reappears is on a plate beautifully prepared.

However, not all the dishes in the Hongkong-style seafood house will use the fresh seafood from the fish tanks. Generally, seafood that requires a lot of preparation, like shelled shrimp or filleted fish, will not take the live ones out of the tanks. The seafood is assuredly fresh, just not freshly killed. Ask the waiter for any clarification if you are unsure.

A more adventurous way to order seafood is to have a single catch prepared into several different courses. This means that the catch has to be big enough so that it could be reasonably split into several parts.

For example, a five- to six-pound rock cod is large enough for three to five courses. Of course, it could also be eaten whole in a single course. An imperial crab, which can weigh up to 20 pounds and cost $300, is almost always prepared into many different courses. Though not cheap, sharing a large crab like this among five or six people in the party makes the tab easier to digest.

If you ordered a fish, the fish head could be made into a casserole, served in an earthenware hotpot. If you ordered abalone – one of the most expensive items in a seafood house – a *shabu shabu* makes a good appetizer, or perhaps eaten raw as Japanese-style *sashimi*. The rest can be braised with bamboo shoot and mushrooms. Lobsters can also be eaten in several courses. The brain matter can be stir-fried with seasonal vegetables, and the tail sautéed with XO sauce. There are almost endless possibilities with preparing seafood

in the Hongkong style. Just discuss with the waiter how you want them to be prepared.

COOKING METHODS FOR SEAFOOD:

The cooking techniques of southern China are ideal for preparing seafood, because they resort to simplicity and lightness that help maintain the ingredients' natural flavors and textures. Basic cooking techniques such as steaming, boiling, stir-frying, and deep-frying are usually enough treatment that the seafood needs. Any further elaboration or complexity in the cooking often does the seafood more harm than good.

Steaming

For fish, steaming is the most popular way with the Chinese. Whole fish is steamed and served with its head and tail intact, unless you instruct to have the fish head served separately in an earthenware hotpot. Although it sounds simple, a perfectly steamed fish requires precise timing, based on the fish's weight and meat density. It is not easy to do at home. When one orders a steamed fish, it is implied that the accompanying sauce is a light combination of soy sauce and fish stock, and simply garnished with ginger and scallions. Clams, half shell oysters, and shrimp can also be steamed, and they go well either with a fermented black bean-and-chili sauce, or with a similar ginger-and-scallion sauce.

Boiling

Boiled shrimp and prawns are very popular when they are in season.

Seafood houses often offer two-for-one specials to be competitive and keep the foot traffic flowing. On almost every table, Chinese families can be seen peeling shells off piles of giant pinkish shrimp, which they dip in a soy sauce flavored with fresh chili peppers. Chaozhou-style boiled shrimp is served with a tangy orange sauce and slices of cantaloupe and honeydew melons. These boiled shrimp are usually eaten as an appetizer. Although boiled shrimp is popular, lobsters are almost never boiled in the way that Americans are accustomed to. The Chinese prefer to stir-fry or steam lobsters instead.

Stir-frying

If a whole fish were to be eaten in two or more courses, the fillets can be stir-fried with fresh vegetables like asparagus, onions, or green peppers. In ordering stir-fried seafood, you must specify if you want the fresh catch taken from the fish tanks. Typical mainstays on the menu like Kungpao Shrimp need preparation and shellimg beforehand, but if you specify to have it made with live shrimp, they will do it with the shrimp unshelled and the heads intact. Clams, squid, lobsters and abalone can all be stir-fried to great results, using black bean sauce, XO sauce, or oyster sauce, et cetera.

Deep-frying

Any seafood can also be deep-fried, although with the Chinese, deep-frying tends to be greasy and of mixed quality. A deep-fried fish, which is generally battered with flour or starch, can be drizzled with a "red-cooked" sauce on top. Otherwise, a "chili-and-garlic" sauce is also popular, as is a simple seasoning of salt and pepper.

ACCOMPANYING SAUCES FOR SEAFOOD:

The basic sauces that accompany seafood are generally simple and light. However, restaurants often call them by different names, so that mentioning a "Shanghai-style" or Sichuan-style" sauce often elicits different results. It is best to ask the waiter for clarifications, or just describe exactly how you want it made.

"Red-Cooked" Sauce
紅燒

Often called "Shanghai-style" sauce, but sometimes (mistakenly) called "Sichuan-style," this sauce echoes the red-cooking method in Jiangzhe and Shanghai cuisines. Soy sauce, sugar, and star anise are the fundamental ingredients used to create a rich and aromatic sauce, giving the dish a reddish coloration and tangy taste. "Red-cooked" does not suggest the color of red chili peppers, which is why many people mistakenly assume that the red-cooked sauce is spicy.

Sichuan-style
四川式

The Sichuan style of preparing fish is to create a spicy sauce of chili peppers, garlic, and scallions, which are stir-fried in the wok and poured over a steamed or deep-fried fish. Since Hongkongers cannot tolerate hot and spicy foods, they make this sauce sweet, with a hint of hotness instead of the firebrand commonly associated with Sichuan cooking.

Sweet-and-sour (sugar-and-vinegar) Sauce

甜酸

One type of sweet-and-sour sauce is a brown sauce flecked with chopped green scallions. It goes well with steamed fish, or all varieties of deep-fried seafood. The brown color comes from *Zhenjiang* black vinegar, added with sugar for the sweet-and-sour taste. The sweet-and-sour sauce that Americans are familiar with is made from salted plums and red food coloring. In such a case, the sauce almost always accompanies deep-fried foods. Any restaurant is capable of working with both kinds of sauces, but they usually assume that Americans want the red plum sauce without asking. Therefore, be sure to specify the kind sweet-and-sour sauce you want when ordering.

XO Sauce

This is a sauce with sweet and spicy flavors, and which has ridden the fad wave for over forty years since its introduction at a Kowloon seafood house. But the gleam of its popularity has not waned. The XO sauce is still considered trendy among the Chinese, and it is easy to understand why. It is perfect for stir-fried crustaceans, such as clams, octopus, crabs and lobsters.

Black Bean Sauce

豉椒

Made from fermented black beans or bean paste, this sauce has been a longtime favorite for steamed- and stir-fried dishes. Often seen in dim sum/yum cha is a dish of steamed pork spareribs in black bean sauce. A similar style of steaming using black bean sauce can be applied to clams and half-shell oysters. Stir-fried clams, crab, fish, and lobster can also attain great heights when highlighted with a black bean sauce, which has a slightly pungent, earthy fragrance.

Salt-and-Pepper "Sauce"

椒鹽

Not really a sauce but a seasoning, this is a flavoring created by combining salt with ground black pepper and star anise. Salt-and-pepper always goes with deep-fried foods, and it can either be coated into the food by tossing, or served on the side as a dipping salt.

Garlic-and-chili "Sauce"

蒜爆

Also called "bursting garlic" in some places, this is another "sauce" that is more like the salt-and-pepper dipping salt described above. Chopped garlic is sautéed with hot chili, and then tossed into deep-fried foods.

TYPICAL DISHES IN A HONGKONG-STYLE SEAFOOD RESTAURANT

Hongkong-style seafood houses are not places for cheap meals. The ingredients used in the seafood cuisine are, more often than not, top quality items that are fitting for the Hongkonger's spendthrift appetite. Typical exotica begin with all grades of shark's fin, swallow's nest, and abalone – the "Seafood

Trio" of precious ingredients that can cost anywhere from $5 to $100 per serving. The rest of the Hongkong-style seafood house menu is filled with favorite Guangdong-style dishes, all suggestive of the fundamental roots of this emergent cuisine.

Shark's Fin

Shark's fin has no distinctive flavor. Instead, it is treasured for its exquisite, chewy texture. A piece of dried shark's fin, no bigger than a flour tortilla, can cost more than $800 a pound. Shark's fin is popularly served in a soup, but extravagant displays of wealth will feature shark's fin braised or stir-fried with other precious ingredients, or even alone on its own (if cash is no problem). At top seafood restaurants, a section of the menu is devoted entirely to shark's fin dishes.

Swallow's Nest

Although it is considered a seafood item, swallow's nest is actually the dried saliva of several species of swallows that live along the rocky cliffs of southern China and Southeast Asia. It is a primary specialty in traditional Chaozhou cuisine. Skilled men climb up the high, dangerous perches to harvest these nests, which must then be cleaned to remove twigs and undesirable dregs from the saliva collection. The use of swallow's nest in cooking is very similar to shark's fin; they have similar textures (also no flavor), and are considered with equal esteem by the Chinese for their said medicinal values to cure and prevent all sorts of ailments.

Abalone

The Chinese are partially blamable for the dwindling worldwide supply of abalone, especially in California where their numbers are in danger of depletion, and the harvest is now severely regulated. These giant clams have that chewy texture that the Chinese cannot seem to get enough of. Even for the astronomical prices that abalone command, the Chinese continue to consume them with religious fervor. Abalone can be prepared in any way imaginable:

HONGKONG-STYLE SEAFOOD HOUSES IN LOS ANGELES

There are so many seafood houses in the San Gabriel Valley that it takes months to eat at every one of them. By then, more seafood houses will likely have opened. Trends and fads also pass quickly. In order to keep up, seafood houses put up huge advertising banners for the latest promotions, making them regular features (and eyesores) of the local street scene.

The quality of seafood houses in Los Angeles is predictably high, thanks to the abundance of fresh Pacific catch, and also the accessibility of prized seafood from all over the world. Intense competition also keeps restauranteurs grounded; poor performers are quickly dispatched from the food scene like J-Lo changes her beaus. By coupling world-class seafood with Guangdong cuisine's simple cooking techniques, Los Angeles's Hongkong-style seafood cuisine is another wonder of the city that is the envy of the world.

Empress Pavilion

Standing in the location of the former Harbor Village – the spearhead of the Chinese Culinary Revolution in Los Angeles – Empress Pavilion has languished like a spring tulip under the August sun. Blame that to competition, which has whittled this original seafood house down to a shadow of its former self. The food is still good, but not the cutting-edge seafood cuisine that first set it apart from the unflattering domain of "Chinese Food" that once pervaded in Los Angeles.

111 N. Atlantic Blvd., #350, Monterey Park
(626) 300-8833

MPV

Smaller and more modest than the seafood palaces in Monterey Park, MPV serves some of the best seafood without extravagant embellishments. MPV's wintermelon soup is quite popular here. The half-wintermelon is filled with stock, bamboo shoot, ham, and mushroom. The whole thing is then steamed, and upon serving placed in a decorative brass tureen. The wintermelon can be scooped from the inside, and eaten with the rest of the soup. MPV is open until 3 a.m. to countenance any case of midnight hunger attack.

412 S. Garfield Ave., Alhambra
(626) 289-3018

NBC

Generally considered as one of the best seafood restaurants in Los Angeles, the history of NBC goes way back to the middle of the 1980s. It is one of the few seafood houses in town that does not succumb to discounting. None is necessary, so claims NBC, because the diners who come there know the restaurants serves top quality food. NBC's reputation has remained solid through the years, serving ever-creative dishes newly arrived from Hongkong.

404 S. Atlantic Blvd., #A, Monterey Park
(626) 282-2323

Ocean Star

One of the largest seafood houses in Los Angeles, Ocean Star is consistently regarded as one of the two best in town, the other being NBC. The sheer palatial dining hall seats more than 800, with rooms for private parties and large banquets.

145 N. Atlantic Blvd., Monterey Park
(626) 308-2128

More restaurants are listed in Appendix II.

sliced raw as sashimi; served in a soup; braised with sea cucumbers, et cetera. Together with shark's fin and swallow's nest, abalone rounds up the "Seafood Trio," and it is perhaps the most precious among the three.

Lobster and Fruit Salad

龍蝦鮮果沙津

A recent invention, Lobster and Fruit Salad has caught the popular rage. This appetizer dish can be found in almost every seafood restaurant today. Cold pieces of steamed lobster are tossed with seasonal fruit to create a light, refreshing – and unusual – start to a seafood meal or banquet.

Kungpao Shrimp with Macadamia Nuts

夏果宮保蝦球

The latest adaptation of the famous Sichuan dish is to substitute chicken with tender shrimp. Peanuts are also replaced by the alluring crunchiness of roasted macadamia nuts. The combination creates a lively contrast of textures and flavors, and the use of a foreign ingredient such as macadamia nuts – found in abundance in Hawaii – suggests the experiences of Guangdong immigrants working as contract labor in the Hawaiian sugarcane fields during the 1850s.

Steamed Half-shell Oysters

薑蔥生蠔

Oysters, like other expensive seafood, have extremely delicate flavors that are easily overwhelmed by strong sauces or spicy ingredients.

Therefore, basic cooking techniques, such as steaming, are superior for preparing seafood. In this timeless dish, half-shell oysters are simply steamed, then served in a light soy sauce with no more than julienne ginger and scallions as garnish.

Boiled Geoduck Clam

白灼象拔蚌

Geoduck is simply boiled in water, sliced, and served with a chili-and-soy sauce dipping sauce. Guangdong people heap praises for the clam's chewy texture and delicate flavors, which, at around $20 a pound, suggest why such a simple dish is one of the most expensive items on the menu.

Sea Cucumber and Abalone in a Brown Sauce

紅燒海參鮑魚

The combination of sea cucumber and abalone is a classic in Chinese cooking. Sea cucumber has a gelatinous, almost crunchy texture, and good quality abalone is chewy but not rubbery. The brown sauce is a light mixture of soy sauce and oyster sauce – light enough so that it does not compromise the already delicate flavors of sea cucumber and abalone.

DIM SUM/YUM CHA HOUSE

"People know their dim sum from Abilene to Zürich, and in many U.S. cities, dim sum is as popular as sushi and pizza."

On any given weekend, the typical dim sum/yum cha house in Los Angeles roils with a controlled sort of cacophony. Families, friends, and children arrive by the carloads, and the wait in the lobby could be as long as an hour. Inside in the dining room, hundreds are already embattled in a loud feeding frenzy of *shao mai*, *har gow*, and grilled *chong fun*. Hawker women push silvery handcarts around the tables, taunting the diners with dim sum dishes stacked high on their carts. And all around, people are busily engaged in people watching, talking, and whiling away time with good company and good food.

The institution of dim sum/yum cha has now become a worldwide sensation. People know their dim sum from Abilene to Zürich, and in many U.S. cities, dim sum is as popular as sushi and pizza. These days, dim sum can also be found at some ballparks and cafeterias, blurring the boundaries between ethnic and mainstream American foods.

Contrary to popular belief, dim sum/yum cha was not invented in Hongkong. Rather, it evolved from a traditional breakfast eaten in Guangzhou, the provincial capital of Guangdong and the nexus of all southern Chinese cooking styles. Whereas the typical Chinese breakfast consists of some sort of steamed *baozi*, rice cakes, or grilled pancakes eaten with soymilk as the breakfast beverage of choice, people in Guangzhou drink tea instead. Thus, the foundation is laid for dim sum/yum cha's inseparable association with tea drinking.

Traditionally, the neighborhood restaurants of Guangzhou started serving breakfast as early as 4 a.m. The customers were mainly merchants from the nearby vegetable and auction markets, who began their workdays well before the break of dawn. They did not spend much time over their breakfasts, resorting to quickly devouring two steamed dumplings accompanied by a pot of *Pu-er* tea. This breakfast became popularly known as Guangzhou's "One Pot, Two Items" breakfast – the pot of Pu-er tea was absolutely essential, and a plate of food always contained two pieces of some sort of dumplings or pastries.

In Hongkong, creative chefs reformed this traditional Guangzhou breakfast by transforming the hearty dumplings into a sampling of small snacks – called dim sum. Sweet pastries, steamed baozi, and specialties such as rice cakes and steamed chicken feet all found their ways into the dim sum selection. Gradually, dim sum/yum cha moved from neighborhood restaurants into larger establishments – primarily to the opulent seafood houses that began appearing in Hongkong in the 1960s. These restaurants began employing specialty dim sum chefs who created ever artistic snacks that were delicate in texture, and appealing in appearance. The portions of dim sum also became smaller – made intentionally delicate and small so that people could sample more varieties of them without quickly becoming sated.

The terms "dim sum" and "yum cha" are interchangeable in Chinese, as they both refer to the same dining tradition. *Dim sum* means "snacks," and *yum cha* means "drinking tea." In actuality, both terms used together portray the complete experience, which is both the excitement of sampling snacks, and the enjoyment of drinking tea.

Drive-by Congee

In typical L.A. fashion, dim sum is always available for people on the run.

SOUTHERN

The portions of dim sum dishes are small – each piece is no more than a bite or two. A single order of dim sum is no longer constrained by the old "One Pot, Two Items" custom of containing only two dumplings. It can come with as many as three or four pieces per order. Dim sum/yum cha is unique among Chinese dining customs in that it is ideally suited for individuals or small groups, not large families. On weekday mornings, when the pace of action slows down considerably, many businessmen come to make deals over dumplings and tea. Many individuals also stop by to read their morning papers. Few other eating activities are as congenial and productive as dim sum/yum cha.

THE DINING MORES OF DIM SUM/ YUM CHA

For the most part, the quality of dim sum depends on the skills of the dim sum chef. Many large seafood houses employ two sets of chefs: one for making dim sum in the morning, and another for making regular seafood cuisine later on. Making dim sum is no cakewalk, and it gets to be a competitive blood sport of sorts. While basic, traditional dim sum dishes such as *har gow* and *shao mai* can be found in the cavalcades of dim sum offerings anywhere, what sets the best dim sum/yum cha houses apart are the creative dim sum dishes that come out of the chef's imagination. Sampling these innovative creations further adds to the excitement of the dim sum/yum cha experience; it

provides additional impetus for the development of *haute cuisine* dim sum/yum cha.

Unlike the rigid tea ceremony of Japan, the "yum cha" part of dim sum/yum cha is relaxed and informal. However, it does nevertheless follow certain procedures. Drinking tea is obligatory in dim sum/yum cha, so once you are seated at a table, the waiter does not ask if you want tea, but rather the kind of tea you want. The primary tea of choice is Pu-er, the standard black tea of the Guangdong people and the Hongkonger. Jasmine, Oolong, and *Ju-pu* (a blend of Pu-er tea with chrysanthemum flower) are common alternatives. It is said that Pu-er and Ju-pu have especially good grease-cutting abilities that are the appropriate counterbalance for some of the rich, fatty dim sum dishes.

The teapot can be repeatedly refilled with hot water – without changing the tealeaves. Lifting the pot lid and leaving it at the edge of the table gives waiters the cue to refill the pot; they are generally very swift at spotting an open pot lid, and adept to quickly refilling it.

The dim sum/yum cha experience is typically eaten for breakfast, but opening hours generally extends well past lunchtime. Once seated at a table, people can stay as long as they want, with the teapot repeatedly refilled with hot water until closing. Orders are taken by flagging down the hawker women (men are never employed to hawk dim sum) who rove around the dining room, carrying an assortment of dim sum on handcarts or shoulder trays. The handcarts are actually a recent invention, and a modern generation of dim sum/yum cha houses have gone retro – no longer employing hawkers and instead taking orders from menu cards placed on the table. Either way, just point to anything you like or find interesting. At the end, a tallying card is used to calculate the final tab.

Dim sum Spotter's Guide

There can be more than thirty dim sum dishes offered at one time, so the choices could be bewildering even for people familiar with eating dim sum. Orders are stacked on carts four or five baskets high, or in dome-covered plates. What is contained inside is not always obvious, but dim sum dishes are arranged in a more or less systematic manner so that just the appearance of these carts gives a good indication of what they have. Otherwise, the next best thing would be to guard your table like Checkpoint Charlie, and not let any hawker woman go by without a thorough interrogation.

Small Steamer Baskets

Shrimp Dumplings (*har gow*)
蝦餃

These small, bite-sized dumpling are made of whole shrimp and mashed shrimp, all wrapped in a translucent rice flour wrap. Har gow has a pale pink color from the shrimp inside.

Pork Dumplings (*shao mai*)
燒賣

Pork filling is stuffed into a egg noodle wrap and shaped to resemble a small teacup. It is yellow all around, except for the exposed top, where the steamed pork filling shows a slightly pink color.

Shark's Fin Dumplings
魚翅餃

Shark fin adds extra mileage for this otherwise ordinary steamed pork dumpling. Don't expect high quality shark's fins in a dumpling like this.

Fun gor
粉果

Typical Chinese dumplings are made with a flour wrap, but this Chaozhou specialty is made with a rice flour wrap, nearly transparent so that the contents inside are visible. Fillings for fun gor can include shrimp, pork, and basil for a Southeast Asian tint.

Beef Meatballs

牛肉丸

These meatballs are lightly seasoned with soy sauce, and steamed over a bed of spinach leaves. Beef meatballs are not coated with any kind of sauce – they are eaten straight from the steamer basket, with or without dipping into the provided chili sauce and mustard.

Fish Balls and Octopus Balls

魚蛋，墨魚蛋

Fish balls are made of fish fillets pounded into a smooth paste. Octopus balls are like fish balls with pieces of chopped octopus wrapped inside. Some places offer these dishes with distinctively Chaozhou overtones, by steaming them in a sauce using curry and coconut milk.

Dumplings Wrapped in Tofu Skin

腐皮捲

A variation of traditional dumplings, tofu skin is used to wrap these dumplings instead of flour wraps. The fillings are generally vegetarian, since the use of tofu skin has an immediate association with Chinese vegetarian cuisine.

LARGER STEAMER BASKETS

Chicken and Glutinous Rice Wrapped in Lotus Leaf

糯米雞

A meal in itself, a single portion of this is substantial enough for one person. It, of course, can be shared so that there is room for other dim sum dishes. Lotus leaf is used to wrap the contents into a dense, square package. The hawker woman will cut it open to reveal a fragrant mound of glutinous rice with a lightly seasoned piece of chicken stuffed in the center.

Red-cooked Chicken Feet

紅燒鳳爪

Chicken feet are steamed in a savory soy and chili sauce until the meat almost falls off the bones. They virtually melt in the mouth, and can generally be eaten without hands. There is not much meat on the chicken's feet, but that is not the point in eating chicken feet. The Chinese enjoy chicken feet primarily for its gelatinous texture, which is like eating Jell-O with tiny bones in it, only more flavorful.

Spareribs in Black Bean Sauce

豉汁排骨

A dish of pork spareribs is steamed

in a black-bean sauce until the meat is tender. This is a typical home-style dish of Guangdong cuisine, reduced to bite-sized portions for dim sum consumption.

Steamed Tripe
牛百葉

Cooked in similar fashion as steamed spareribs, steamed tripe has a chewy texture that many people love. Fashionable dim sum restaurants make this dish in a spicy XO sauce.

Assorted *baozi*
包子

There are all sorts of steamed baozi, including fillings of red beans (sweet), mashed lotus seeds with duck egg (combination of sweet and salty), and roast pork (salty).

PLATES SHIELDED BY DOME COVERS

Steamed *Chong Fun*
蒸腸粉

Inside the dome covers contains a rice noodle roll called *chong fun*, which literally means "rice noodle sausages." They have an appearance resembling shiny white enchiladas. Chong fun are made by wrapping a broad, flat sheet of rice noodle with an assortment of fillings such as beef,

shrimp, barbecue pork, or even the infamous *youtiao*. A light soy sauce is poured on top prior to serving. This can also be grilled, which is served from a cart with a roving grill (see "Roving Grill" below).

ASSORTMENT OF COLD CUTS

Fried Taro Nuggets
炸芋角

Mashed taro is shaped into palm-sized nuggets, and stuffed with a spicy pork filling. The golden, lacy outer layer of taro nuggets is created by deep-frying, which suggests that it is a hot item. However, fried taro nuggets are actually cold dumplings.

Shredded Jellyfish
海蜇皮

Preserved jellyfish is cut into strips, marinated with salt and vinegar, and served like a cold salad. They look like rubber bands, have a slithery, crunchy texture, and absorb all the flavors of the marinating sauce.

SOUTHERN

Cold Roast Duck
烤鴨

Leftover roast duck from the barbecue shop the day before is served cold the morning after, coated with a thin sprinkling of *au jus*.

Cold Roast Pork
叉燒肉

Just like cold roast duck, leftover roast pork (charsui) is chopped and served as a snack item.

Boiled Chicken Feet
鹽水鳳爪

Unlike steamed chicken feet, the boiled ones are eaten cold, and are cooked not as tender. Thus, these have a slightly more sinewy texture, and require eating with hands.

SWEETS

Egg Custard Tart
蛋撻

Learned from the French, egg custard tarts are so popular with the Chinese that they have become an obligatory item in any dim sum lineup. A creamy egg custard is baked into a flaky piecrust, showing masterful blending of western influences into Guangdong cuisine – using butter, cream, and eggs not typically used in other Chinese cooking styles.

White Sugar Rice Cake
白糖糕

This soft steamed rice cake is leavened with yeast and allowed to ferment slightly. A classic Guangdong tea pastry, it is eaten either for breakfast or throughout the day as an in-between-meals snack.

Coconut Milk Pudding
冰凍椰糕

The coconut milk used in this gelatin dessert gives the dish an unmistakably tropical- and Southeast Asian character, showing some of the outside influences that transformed the humble "One Pot, Two Items" breakfast into snacks with an international flair.

Dɪᴍ sᴜᴍ/Yᴜᴍ cʜᴀ Hᴏᴜsᴇs
ɪɴ Lᴏs Aɴɢᴇʟᴇs

The dim sum/yum cha experience in Los Angeles is leagues above that in other U.S. cities, mainly because the San Gabriel Valley is now home to some of the world's best dim sum chefs. Many travelers to Hongkong have even returned to confirm that the dim sum/yum cha in L.A. are better than the originals back home. The large dim sum/yum cha houses, which moonlight as seafood houses at night, have deep financial backing to hire the best dim sum chefs. Tasting their innovative dim sum dishes is the main attraction at these restaurants, and on weekends, the wait can be well over an hour.

Smaller Guangdong-style restaurants and bakeries make traditional dim sum of the early "One Pot, Two Items" breakfast of Guangzhou. These dim sum items can also be taken away to be enjoyed at home or work. Chinese supermarkets have also jumped into the dim sum fray, operating their service delis as conduits of quick snacks and microwaveable dim sum.

Fong's Dim Sum Food To Go

This traditional Guangdong-style bakery sells many basic types of dim sum, including steamed barbecue pork baozi, shao mai, har gow, and steamed glutinous rice wrapped in lotus leaf. No tables or chairs in this smallish strip mall fixture implies that the goodies are to be enjoyed at home.

311 E. Valley Boulevard #103, San Gabriel
(626) 280-0490

NBC Seafood Restaurant

For over 20 years, NBC has consistently been one of the best places for dim sum/yum cha in the San Gabriel Valley. The waiting crowd that spills out to the parking lot every weekend is confirmation of this assessment. Many of NBC's dim sum dishes are creative innovations by the chef; they cannot be found anywhere else, even back in Hongkong.

404 S. Atlantic Blvd., #A, Monterey Park
(626) 282-2323

SOUTHERN

Ocean Star

Another great place for dim sum/yum cha, Ocean Star's dining room is larger, more opulent, and even more crowded than NBC. Noteworthy dim sum dishes not found elsewhere include: Shark's Fin Soup; Tapioca Tarts; and Bird's Nest *Jiaozi* served in a soup, resembling upscale wontons.

145 N. Atlantic Blvd., #201-203, Monterey Park
(626) 308-2128

Sea Harbour Seafood Restaurant

A new entrant to the competitive dim sum/yum cha scene in the San Gabriel Valley, Sea Harbour is also the current pacesetter of *haute cuisine* dim sum. The entire menu is comprised of delicate, imaginative re-creations of traditional favorites. The green baozi are colored by using spinach juice; the shao mai is flecked with *tobikko* (flying fish roe); and the beef tripe is steamed in XO sauce. There are no hawker ladies pushing carts around at Sea Harbour – orders are taken directly from a menu card placed on the table. The ordinary pot of *Pu-er* tea, like the old tradition, remains unchanged.

3939 N. Rosemead Blvd., Rosemead
(626) 288-3939

More restaurants are listed in Appendix III.

STEAMING POT OF BOILING WATER

Boiled Gai Lan
水煮芥蘭

This cart with a pot of boiling water serves a dim sum/yum cha stalwart – blanched *gai lan*, often called "Chinese broccoli." Oyster sauce is poured on top upon serving.

LARGE RICE COOKERS OR POTS

Congee
皮蛋瘦肉粥

Guangdong-style restaurants serve a large variety of congee flavored with all sorts ingredients. The most popular flavor of congee is ground pork and thousand-year-old eggs. This is generally the only type of congee served in dim sum/yum cha houses.

Ox Stew with White Radish
蘿蔔牛什湯

A fortifying bowl of ox stew contains table scraps: beef tripe, intestines, liver, and sometimes pig blood. All is simmered together with white radish in Chu Hou Sauce.

Hot Soybean Gelatin
豆花

Soy gelatin ("*douhua*") is eaten throughout China for breakfast. It is a flimsy solid made by adding edible plaster to soymilk. Dim sum houses only serve douhua hot and sweet, by pouring a ginger-flavored syrup on top, or otherwise sprinkled with boiled whole peanuts.

ROVING GRILL

White Radish Rice Cake
蘿蔔糕

This steamed rice cake is flavored with white radish and minced Guangdong-style sausage. The rice cake is cut into square pieces, and grilled until brown on both sides.

Water Chestnut Cake
馬蹄糕

This steamed rice cake has a yellow color, and is actually sweet. The unusual combination of flavors and textures makes the water chestnut cake a perennially popular item on the roving grill.

Grilled Chong Fun
煎腸粉

Grilled chong fun can come in a beef, pork, or shrimp filling. There are also plain rolls with no fillings at all. Instead of a topping of soy sauce (as is the case with the steamed ones), grilled chong fun is served with one of two sauces: either a sweet bean sauce or a peanut sauce.

HONGKONG-STYLE COFFEESHOP

"Hongkong-style coffeeshops are places where tea meets coffee, baozi meets toast, and chow mein meets mac-and-cheese."

Americans generally perceive Chinese food with a stereotype as inaccurate as Columbus's new route to India. Things like egg fu-yung, chop suey, and fortune cookies are as foreign to the Chinese as tamales, pizza, and *mille feuille*. But what goes around comes around. The Chinese have an equally distorted stereotype of American food, believing that things like "Spam Macaroni" are as American as Apple Pie. Culture clash often results in comedic misunderstandings, and this is certainly the case between the perceptions of the Americans and the Chinese. When the cooking traditions of America and China are mixed together, funny things are bound to come out of the kitchen.

In Hongkong, the Chinese fascination for American food manifests itself in an interesting breed of coffeeshops that proliferate throughout the city. To Hongkongers, these coffeeshops broaden their perception of American food beyond the sebaceous swamp-land of McDonald's, KFC, and Pizza Hut. But to Americans, Hongkong's coffeeshops do not serve what one will typically find in an American coffeeshop. Rather, they serve a roughshod fusion of American and Chinese foods – practical in style, with flavors tilted to satisfy the Chinese palate.

Hongkong-style coffeeshops are places where tea meets coffee, *baozi* meets toast, and chow mein meets mac-and-cheese. Just as Columbus's errant ways changed world history, the Hongkonger's gross misinterpretation of American cuisine created a new line of dishes that further adds to the city's colorful food scene.

Some coffeeshop dishes are interpretations that bound on the purely farcical, such as a bowl of Top Ramen served with a hotdog on top. Yet, despite the number of rather strange and curious concoctions, there are also versions of American food icons that are quite straightforward. Steaks for example, look like the real thing in Hongkong as they do in Houston. Mostly, the food served in Hongkong-style coffeeshops runs in the spectral range that transcends any cultural borders. Typical dishes such as Ox Tongue Curry Stew, Indonesian-style *Chow Fun*, and Roast Chicken with Spaghetti show a well coordinated fusion of eastern- and western elements, blended together to create a completely new, stylish, and trendy cuisine.

Hongkong-style coffeeshops first surfaced in Los Angeles in the early 1990s, after sensationalizing the food scenes in Hongkong and Taipei. Today, there are scads of Hongkong-style coffeeshops in the San Gabriel Valley, and the competition among them is quite intense. On a two-mile stretch of Valley Boulevard, between Alhambra and San Gabriel, there are more than ten coffeeshops vying for the curious- and food-conscious appetites of the locals.

Hongkong-style coffeeshops are noted for their brasserie décor and extended hours. Some are open 24 hours a day, while others stay open until 3 or 4 a.m., only to open again by 7. Coffeeshops are hosts to a fascinating panoply of characters traversing through their doors every day. Old folks come in the morning, followed by *salarypersons* at lunch, then joined by families in the evening, and capped out by an assortment of insomniacs, miscreants, partygoers, and the simply hungry in the overnight hours. Like American coffeeshops, breakfast-, lunch-, and dinner dishes can be ordered throughout the day.

Coffeeshops are usually outfitted with a busy bar that serves a full range of nonalcoholic beverages, which, like many dishes on the menu, are quite surprising to the uninitiated. While the timid can stay with cola,

SOUTHERN

Rice

The Guangdong people typically eat rice as their main staple, and they assume that the Americans do the same. Generally, the Chinese believe that Americans eat rice by pouring a sauce on top of either plain- or stir-fried rice. The most popular "American-style" sauce is a minced beef soup thickened with scrambled eggs and starch. *Cream of Corn with Chicken* is also a popular sauce, as is Oxtail Stew.

tea, or coffee, there is another world of hot Ovaltine, lychee ice, and boba tea waiting to be discovered. Further into the depths of coffeeshop beverageology is the domain of taro milkshakes, red bean shaved ice, and "*yuanyang*" – a bizarre combination of half coffee and half tea. Although some courage may be required to tackle these drinks, they are – more often than not – surprisingly good and irresistibly refreshing.

DISHES OF HONGKONG-STYLE COFFEESHOPS

Hongkong-style coffeeshops share the distinction with Guangdong-style restaurants in that the dishes on the menu are best described in categories. As with Guangdong cuisine, a wide variety of ingredients are thrown together to create a bewildering combination of dishes, resulting in menus that are typically as thick as a book. Some small coffeeshops break away from this practice by offering only a limited selection of rice- and pizza dishes.

In Hongkong-style coffeeshop menus, there is also a wide variety of stir-fried rice dishes with geographical associations: "Singapore-style" rice is a stir-fried rice seasoned with curry; "Yangzhou-style" rice is fried rice with scrambled eggs and charsui pork; "Fuzhou-style" rice features a sauce of roast duck, chicken, and shrimp. If you are still not sure where is what, ask the waiter for a clarification.

Curries

Curry is popular in Hongkong, although the mild palates of the Hongkonger cannot tolerate such fiery curries of India as the *madras* or the *vindaloo*. Curry served in Hongkong-style coffeeshops closely resemble Japanese-style curries: soupy, heavily starched, and sweet. Beef-, oxtail-, and chicken curries are popular, as is a plain curry poured on top of a breaded pork chop. Curries are typically served over plain- or fried rice, but more adventurous souls can try a curry served over spaghetti.

like seafood, liver, liver-and-kidney, meatballs, chicken, chicken-and-mushroom, and even tofu-and-corn have made their way among the head-spinning choices on the menu.

Congee

Congee is a rice cereal eaten much like oatmeal for breakfast. Rice is boiled with soup stock until it becomes a gooey slop. In Guangdong cuisine, congee is combined with different ingredients for a large variety of flavors. Since congee was just a thrifty way of extending the use of rice, any kind of meats and vegetables can go into it. The classic Guangdong congee is pork with thousand-year-old eggs. In addition, combinations

Eggs

The Chinese perceive egg dishes as typically American food, since the Chinese do not typically eat eggs as eggs themselves. They see eggs as an ingredient used in other dishes,

not as the main element of the dish. In Hongkong-style coffeeshops, any kind of fried- or scrambled egg dish, from sunny-side-up to an omelet, is served "American-style" with toast, pork chops, steaks, or chicken fillets. Some places even serve a fried egg over a bowl of Top Ramen noodles.

Spam

Hongkong-style coffeeshops are perhaps the only places in North America where Spam is prominently featured on the menu without fear of ridicule. The Hormel folks must be proud of them. Spam is wildly popular in Asia, including Hongkong and especially throughout Southeast Asia where Spam is popularly served with plain rice. In the coffeeshops, Spam is a popular substitute for ham, found in dishes such as Eggs and Spam, Spam Macaroni, and Top Ramen with Spam.

Salads

Salads are a touch of exotica for the Chinese, since they rarely eat raw vegetables. Salads served in Hongkong-style coffeeshops tend to stick with the familiar American forms, with very little alteration. Caesar's salad, chef's salad, chicken salad, tuna salad, and the run-of-the-mill garden salad all look like they could be served at any Denny's or Waffle House.

Steaks and Pork Chops

It is rare to see thick slabs of steak or pork chop anywhere in Chinese cuisine, but Hongkong-style coffee-shops are popular places for steaks with the Chinese. Steaks are typically seasoned with just salt and pepper, then meticulously grilled to order. Upon serving, a white wine sauce is doused on top. Sides of garden salad and plain rice usually accompany

Hongkong-style coffeeshops are great places for **steaks**.

HONGKONG-STYLE COFFEESHOPS IN LOS ANGELES

Hongkong-style coffeeshops caught on in the San Gabriel Valley during the early 1990s, after creating quite a stir first in Hongkong, and later in Taipei. Today, their popularity has not waned. Many of them offer a standard menu chock full of hybrid dishes, while others have developed distinctive personalities, offering smaller menus that focus on only one or two specialties.

Sampling beverages is also a primary reason for visiting a Hongkong-style coffeeshop. A quick glance through the beverage menus will undoubtedly reveal that the coffeeshop experience is far from typical. All beverages are non-alcoholic, and icons such as boba tea and *yuanyang* are expertly prepared by bartenders who also twist out all sorts of unusual drinks.

Garden Cafe

Garden Cafe is the grand potpourri of Hongkong-style coffeeshops. A large selection of steak and pasta dishes is its main draw, along with many varieties of rice- and congee dishes. The menu also includes several selections featuring Top Ramen. A busy bar offers a substantial menu of western-style desserts and not-so-western beverages.

18406 E. Colima Rd., #H, Roland Heights
(626) 913-1188

228 W. Valley Blvd., #101, Alhambra
(626) 289-1833

California Stonegrill Cafe

At this unique restaurant, the steaks are served on a slab of hot stone for some added "western" touch. The other dishes are more or less standard Hongkong-style coffeeshop fare: curries, pork chops, rice- and noodle dishes, and a slew of drinks concocted from behind the bar. Another anomaly about this place is the "early" closing time (10 p.m. on weekends), and breakfasts are not offered.

1631 S. Azusa Ave., Hacienda Heights
(626) 581-3222

J.J. Hong Kong Cafe

A comprehensive menu the thickness of an IKEA catalog makes this popular restaurant a very interesting place to visit, not just for people watching, but also for the sampling of many unfamiliar dishes. There is never a dull moment in a restaurant that serves ten kinds of congee and forty variations of noodle dishes – at last count.

447 W. Garvey Ave., Monterey Park
(626) 280-3833

Savoy Kitchen

A charming corner spot on busy Valley Boulevard marks the location of this small café. Menu is limited to a few pasta-, curry-, and pizza dishes. The main attraction, however, is the specialty Hainan Chicken Rice, which comes drizzled with chicken fat and served with the requisite three dipping sauces. Outdoor tables on the pedestrian-less sidewalk are a welcomed exception from the florescent-lit and super-chilled dining rooms that haunt too many Chinese restaurants.

138 E. Valley Blvd., Alhambra
(626) 308-9535

More restaurants are listed in Appendix IV.

SOUTHERN

the steaks. Pork chops are grilled in a similar fashion as steaks. Another popular way to prepare pork chops is to deep-fry them in a breading or batter, resulting in something similar to the Japanese *tonkatsu*.

Spaghetti and Pasta
Hongkong-style coffeeshops serve spaghetti with an ordinary spaghetti sauce on top. Curry, as is mentioned above, is a popular sauce to go with pasta. Other spaghetti sauces include seafood stir-fried in XO sauce, oxtail soup, or a garlicky and spicy variation of the jarred pasta meat sauce found in American supermarkets.

Chow Mein and Stir-fried Noodles
These noodle dishes are similar to the ones found in traditional Guangdong-style restaurants. Chow mein is egg noodles first steamed, then fried to a crisp. A sauce is then poured on top. Stir-fried noodles are more straightforward – all the ingredients are stir-fried in the wok. A curiosity at some coffeeshops is the presence of Top Ramen noodles, often served as a breakfast item with a fried egg on top.

Beverages
There is a whole lot of shaking going on behind the bar of a coffeeshop. All the beverages are non-alcoholic, and many of them defy verbal descriptions. *Yuanyang* is an interesting mixture of half coffee and half tea, and has an acquired taste. Cola can be flavored with lemon, cherry, vanilla, et cetera, just like the soda fountains from the 1950s. Though odd to consider red beans as a sweet treat, putting them over shaved ice is pleasantly edible. Additionally, "taro milkshake" may not sound all too appetizing, yet after a few slurps it is hard to put down.

CHAOZHOU CUISINE

"Chaozhou cuisine is a colorful cooking style of Guangdong foundations influenced by decidedly Thai- and Vietnamese characteristics."

When American troops withdrew from Vietnam in 1973, it was clear that the Vietnam War was imminently over. For the ethnic Chinese living in South Vietnam at the time, this marked the beginning of their tumultuous odyssey, which plunged them into persecution and suffering, culminating in a desperate flight for freedom as Vietnam's Boat People.

The Chinese were among the first targets of the Vietcong, which sought to eliminate the country's merchant class. Like elsewhere in Southeast Asia, especially Indonesia and Malaysia where anti-Chinese sentiment is high, the Chinese controlled most of Vietnam's wealth, but exerted almost no political power. The Vietcong quickly took steps to confiscate Chinese property, and limited their personal freedoms.

In some instances, ethnic violence was delivered to the Chinese with abject brutality.

By 1978, most of the Chinese in Vietnam felt that they had no choice but to flee. Even though Vietnam was the only home they had, the situation was becoming desperate. Most of them chose to take to the seas. The "Vietnamese Boat People," as they were called, became a term synonymous with human cruelty, suffering, and death. At sea, they not only faced plights of sickness, starvation, and thirst, the Chinese also had to worry about Thai pirates that scoured the seas, indiscriminately robbing, raping, and killing anyone who came in their way. Between one-third and one-half of the Vietnamese Boat People perished at sea.

The large ethnic Chinese population living in Vietnam originally emigrated from a region in Guangdong province surrounding the city of Chaozhou (Chiu Chow, or Teochew), near the border of Fujian province. During the 19th century, poverty, overcrowding, and social unrest in China forced many Guangdong people to search for better lives elsewhere. The Chaozhou people, as these people are called, settled throughout Southeast Asia. Other Guangdong people, such as those from the city of Guangzhou, migrated to Hawaii, the U.S., and the Caribbean.

A large part of Vietnam's ethnic Chinese population, or more precisely the Chaozhou people, now lives in the Los Angeles metropolitan area. They are most visible in Los Angeles's Chinatown and Westminster in Orange County. Their presence is an ugly reminder of the recent past, yet, as the Chaozhou people have prospered in America, their survival gives an inspiring lesson to life – that through determination, tenacity, and an unwavering work ethic, people can overcome insurmountable obstacles.

A bottle of **Siracha chili sauce** *instantly reveals the restaurant's Chaozhou connection.*

COOKING CONDIMENTS IN CHAOZHOU CUISINE

The Chaozhou people have also graced Los Angeles with their unique cuisine, which is a colorful cooking style of Guangdong foundations influenced by decidedly Thai- and Vietnamese characteristics. The biggest distinctions of Chaozhou cuisine include the use of fresh herbs like mint, lemongrass, and basil, as well as condiments like fish sauce and siracha chili sauce.

Fish Sauce
魚露

The fish sauce is the lifeline of Chaozhou cuisine. It has a thin consistency like a light soy sauce, and often works as its replacement. The fish sauce is made from fermented fish, giving it an unmistakably rural and coastal flavor. Southeast Asian cooking – in particular Thai and Vietnamese – are inseparable from it. The Chaozhou people use it in everything from steamed fish to flavoring congee.

Siracha Chili Sauce
是拉差辣椒醬

Chaozhou cuisine is also the starting point for the spicy world of Southeast Asian cooking, which becomes progressively hotter and spicier further down the subcontinent. Unlike the Guangdong people, who are afraid to eat spicy foods, Chaozhou people love dishes laden with chili peppers. Included in the Chaozhou pantry are many different types of chili pastes and hot sauces, including the sriracha chili sauce, frequently referred as "Thai ketchup."

TYPICAL CHAOZHOU-STYLE DISHES

Seafood is a notable Chaozhou specialty, prepared in similar ways as Hongkong-style seafood cuisine, but simpler and even lighter. It is worth comparing the flavors of Chaozhou-style seafood with that of Hongkong, both of which are exemplary styles of cooking seafood. In other Chaozhou dishes, Southeast Asian overtones often predominate, with flavors such as curry, mint, lemongrass and chili infused into the delicate dishes.

Steak Salad (Beef Loc Lac)
法式牛柳

An interesting Cambodian dish, it is sometimes called "French-style Beefsteak." This salad features pieces of cubed grilled beefsteak, marinated in a tangy sauce of lime or tamarind water, and punctuated by the mildly sweet, cool sensations of seared mint leaves. The steak is served with whole lettuce leaves, and can be either eaten like a salad or wrapped taco-style.

Hot-and-sour Shrimp Soup, Thai-style
泰式蝦湯

A soup that is very similar to Thailand's *Tom Yum Koong*, this hot-and-sour soup gets its flavors from lemongrass, lime leaves, fish sauce, and lots of chili peppers. Although it is very spicy, the overall dimensions of the soup remain light and refreshing, and it is ideally suited for eating during the summer.

Hot-and-sour Fish Soup, Vietnamese-style
越式魚湯

The Vietnamese version of the hot-and-sour soup, or *canh chua*, calls for a tangy, light fish broth flavored with pineapples, star fruit, tamarind, bean sprouts, and chili peppers. Like the Thai-version, it is preferably eaten very hot and spicy, and ideal for the summer months.

Scallop and Asparagus with Mint
香茉蘆筍帶子

When scallops, asparagus, and mint are stir-fried together, the delicate flavors of the three ingredients come alive. However, none of the flavors overpowers the other, and the dish remains light, with subtle hints of the sea and the earth playfully intermixing within the dish.

Crab in Tamarind Sauce
酸枳螃蟹

Tamarind is used throughout Southeast Asia, but it is nearly unheard of elsewhere in Chinese cuisine. The sour, tangy flavors of tamarind are used for both cooking and confectionery, and at the same time add a distinctly tropical dimension to the dishes. Crab in Tamarind Sauce is a simple dish featuring fried crab drizzled with a lightly seasoned sour sauce derived from tamarind water.

Thai Curry Crab
泰式咖喱焗蟹

A very popular Chaozhou dish, the curry sauce used over the fried crab is quite spicy, although it is much sweeter than the curry commonly associated with Indian cuisine. Some Chaozhou-style restaurants use coconut milk for a richer, more tropical flavor; others stick with ordinary stock and fish sauce.

Boiled Prawns

Boiled prawns are served with fresh slices of honeydew melon and cantaloupe, along with a dipping sauce made from oranges. The tartness

of the orange sauce complements well the lightness of the boiled shrimp and sweetness of the fruits.

Frog Legs with Lemongrass
香茅田雞

Saying that frog legs taste like chicken is not a cliché. Loosely translated, the Chaozhou people euphemistically call frogs "field chickens." A stir-fry of frog legs with a light sauce flavored with lemongrass and sriracha chili sauce reveals unmistakably Southeast Asian characteristics – light yet refreshingly spicy.

NOODLE BASKETS AND BIRD'S NESTS

Stir-fries served in an edible, decorative basket are Chaozhou specialties. The menus generally have two types of baskets to choose from. Noodle baskets are "woven" by deep-frying strands of egg noodles, as the name suggests. Bird's Nests are made from julienne taro. They should not be confused with "Swallow's Nest," which is a special seafood ingredient. (See chapter on Hongkong-style Seafood House).

RICE NOODLE DISHES

Rice noodles are eaten much like any other kinds of flour-based noodles. They are never deep-fried, however, because of their high moisture content. Many of the Chaozhou-style rice noodle dishes resemble the *Chow fun* dishes served in Guangdong-style eateries.

SOUTHERN

Hu tieu
粿條

The most important and instantly recognizable rice noodle in Chaozhou cuisine is the versatile hu tieu, which the Vietnamese call *pho*. Hu tieu can be served either stir-fried or in a soup. Typical hu tieu dishes include Chaozhou-style Duck Hu Tieu, Rice and Egg Hu Tieu, and Stir-fried Satay Beef Hu Tieu.

Bahn Loc
粘米粉

This is a different type of rice noodles. Bahn loc is made from a particular type of rice with an extraordinarily high starch content. The rice flour dough is pressed through a sieve, creating short, slippery slivers of rice noodles that are thick in the center and tapered to pointed ends. The coarse, uneven texture of the bahn loc is its main attraction; it has similar appeal as the knife-cut noodles of northern China.

Fish Balls
魚蛋

A popular way of preserving fresh fish is by pounding fish fillets into a paste, and then shaping it into marble-sized balls. Once cooked, fish balls have a firm, chewy texture, and can be used in place of meats in stir-fries, soups, and noodle dishes. Fish balls are also one of the few truly healthy foods in all of Chinese cuisine. They are low in cholesterol and fat, as well as having high nutritional values inherent in fish.

CHAOZHOU-STYLE RESTAURANTS
IN LOS ANGELES

There are two main types of Chaozhou-style restaurants: small rice noodle shops and seafood restaurants. Rice noodle shops mainly serve simple stir-fries and dishes featuring a type of flat, white rice noodle called *hu tieu*. As suggestive of Chaozhou cuisine's ties with Guangdong cuisine, these rice noodle shops feature dishes that are very similar to those of Guangdong-style restaurants, albeit with unmistakably Southeast Asian overtones.

Seafood restaurants serve more substantial – and expensive – Chaozhou-style dishes, with seafood taking center stage. Although only a few of these seafood restaurants are large enough to challenge the palatial trappings of Hongkong-style seafood houses, the food is arguably better. If not for Chaozhou's lighter- and simpler cooking styles, the fusion of Thai- and Vietnamese cooking elements makes this one of the most unique eating experiences to grace Los Angeles's food scene.

Kim Tar Restaurant

Many people mistakenly assume that Kim Tar is a Vietnamese restaurant because of the Vietnamese translations on the menu. However, with all those dishes similar to a Hongkong-style seafood house, Kim Tar reveals itself as an archetypal Chaozhou-style restaurant. Dishes are thoughtfully arranged into categories such as: shark's fins, sea cucumbers, lobsters, sizzling plates, noodle baskets, and so on, making the choices among unfamiliar dishes easier to spot. Southeast Asian flavors like curry, mint, tamarind, and Vietnamese-styles shrimp soup are very popular. Additionally, Kim Tar also makes its own hu tieu, which is distributed throughout many area supermarkets.

964 E. Garvey Ave., Monterey Park
(626) 307-9139

Mien Nghia Noodle Express

This airy restaurant features a very simple menu of rice- and egg noodle dishes, served with overwhelmingly Vietnamese flavors. An occasional Vietnamese-style sandwich using French bread rolls can also be spotted. Special to this place are the satay beef rice noodle dishes.

304 Ord Street, Los Angeles
(213) 680-2411

7755 E. Garvey Ave., Rosemead
(626) 288-0177

406-408 W. Valley Blvd., San Gabriel
(626) 570-1688

Kim Chuy

A small, warm eatery set in a charming roadside shack, Kim Chuy serves up a variety of rice-, and noodle dishes. The cooking here is more Guangdong-style in substance than Vietnamese, but specialties like Mint Leaf Chicken and Satay Beef Rice Noodles show genuine Southeast Asian influences. Kim Chuy's fish balls are justifiably popular, made fresh in the back and can be taken home for a fragrant touch to soups and stir-fries. Interestingly, Kim Chuy's menu also features a "Chinese Food" section, just in case someone is in need of a Chop Suey or Moo-goo Gai Pan fix.

501 W. Valley Blvd., Alhambra
(626) 282-9080

Newport Seafood

The casual and brightly-lit dining room has all the appearances of a Hongkong-style seafood house, except that the fish tanks are absent. Newport's menu, translated in four languages: Chinese, English, Thai, and Vietnamese, also suggests that the food inside is very different. As typical for Chaozhou-style seafood, dishes are very simple and light, yet hot from an unabashed use of chili peppers. Also typical for Chaozhou-style restaurants are the very reasonably prized set menus, featuring soup and a variety of unpretentious dishes for two to ten people.

18441 E. Colima Rd., Rowland Heights
(626) 839-1239

835 W. Las Tunas Dr., San Gabriel
(626) 289-5998

More restaurants are listed in Appendix V.

RICE DISHES

The number of rice dishes offered in Chaozhou-style restaurants is not as abundant as Guangdong-style restaurants. This is probably because all other rice dishes play second fiddle to the almighty Hainan Chicken, which is as ubiquitous in Southeast Asia as *Yoshinoya* is in Japan.

HAINAN CHICKEN RICE

For a short while, the idyllic name *Hainan* was hijacked by the EP-2 incident of early 2001. What was normally a tranquil island resort became the center of espionage and political intrigue. Now that all the diplomatic rhetoric has faded off the radar screens, Hainan has reclaimed much of the sanity, as well as its association with a famous chicken dish.

Hainan is a tropical island at the southernmost tip of China, once on the direct route of the Chaozhou people's migration to Southeast Asia 150 years ago. From their brief stays in Hainan before continuing south, the Chaozhou people transplanted a simple local dish of boiled chickens to Malaysia, Thailand, Vietnam, and Singapore. There, Hainan Chicken Rice became what it is today – a transformation of ordinary Chinese cooking into a distinctively Southeast Asian dish. Hainan Chicken Rice is so popular in Singapore that it is its de facto national dish.

Hainan Chicken Rice is a plate of boiled- or fried chicken, accompanied by plain rice drizzled with chicken fat. The chicken is cooked until it is very tender, much more so than the Guangdong-style boiled chicken found in the barbecue shops. Fragrant, long-grained Thai rice further adds aromas to the dish, which, when drizzled with the rich chicken fat, soaks up all of the chicken's essential flavors.

There are always three dipping sauces for Hainan Chicken Rice: a sweet soy sauce; a sauce of minced ginger marinated in oil; and a spicy *sambal* of fresh red chilis and lime juice (the Malaysian equivalent of salsa).

In Los Angeles, Hainan Chicken Rice can be found in the usual culprits of Southeast Asian cuisines, including Chaozhou-style restaurants. It is also a regular staple in Hongkong-style coffeeshops.

HUNAN CUISINE

"Little has changed with Hunan cuisine, mainly because the province has had limited contact with outsiders."

Legends have it that Hunan's famous son, Mao Zedong, lived such a simple and frugal life that when he died, among the things he left behind was a pair of old pajamas patched in 73 different places. Sartorial tastes aside, it is awfully difficult to imagine Mr. Mao this way. After all, the same man killed over 40 million of his people in less than thirty years of his rule. However, the pajamas story fitted nicely with the Communist propaganda machine, which shaped Mao as the champion of China's working class, fighting against the dual evils of foreign imperialists and greedy capitalists.

Made more plausible was also the fact that Mao Zedong came from the backwaters of Hunan province – in rural parts of southern China that is long associated with poverty and the peasantry. Indeed, Mao's communist revolution succeeded in part because of his Hunan roots – his humble beginnings convinced Mao's followers that he was truly one among them.

In reality, Mao was far from the frugal peasant as was portrayed to be. A recent memoir by Mao's personal physician, Li Zhisui, suggests that Chairman Mao carried out a much more decadent existence, compulsively indulging in food and sex to the pinnacles rivaling Roman emperors. However, Mao's love for down-home Hunan cooking remained incontrovertible to the end. Being a southerner, he never regarded Beijing and the northern cuisine with much affection.

Inside the government compound at *Zhongnanhai*, Mao preferred to fete fellow despots and communist allies with official banquets consisting entirely of Hunan dishes. Mao's eccentric style of hospitality eventually earned it the moniker

"Chair Mao's Banquet," which was invariably tied to the practical, unsophisticated cooking styles of Hunan.

Over the years, Hunan cuisine has remained the most traditional form of Chinese cooking. Little has changed with Hunan cuisine, mainly because the province has had limited contact with outsiders. In the mid-1800s, when the Western Powers busily carved out parts of China for themselves, Hunan province was completely ignored for more accessible seaports like Guangzhou, Shanghai, Qingdao, and Tianjin. Hunan's capital and largest city, Changsha, remains an economic afterthought to this day. It never compelled much domestic interest for migration, let alone international investments. Without exposure to domestic and foreign influences, changes in Hunan cuisine were muted; it continues to adhere to rural and peasant characteristics: hearty, generous, and practical.

The geography of Hunan provides another distinctive characteristic of its cuisine. The landlocked province is located between Guangdong and Sichuan provinces, occupying an area that is moderate in climate and lush in vegetation. Its cuisine is an interesting blend of Guangdong- and Sichuan cooking styles. It is especially interesting considering that Guangdong and Sichuan cuisines are often at polar opposites in terms of flavor and style. Guangdong cuisine

is light and often sweet, preferring the natural flavors of the ingredients. Sichuan cuisine is hot and spicy, and uses a wide variety of ingredients to construct complex flavors. Hunan cuisine somehow finds a medium between the two, crafting a cuisine that is both reliant on natural flavors like Guangdong, and spicy like Sichuan.

Fresh and local ingredients are emphasized in Hunan cuisine, using a large variety of vegetables. It also employs a lot of stir-frying, like Guangdong cuisine, which give Hunan's dishes a decidedly fresh and natural character. The crunchiness stays crunchy, and the colors remain vibrant. However, and most importantly, Hunan's dishes are more heavily flavored with spices and condiments – a departure from the lightness of Guangdong cooking,

and moving steps into the realm of Sichuan cooking.

Hunan cuisine, like Sichuan cuisine, has a tremendous penchant for chili peppers. However, unlike Sichuan cuisine, Hunan cuisine considers the red chili pepper as a vegetable, preferring to incorporate them in its natural form, and often eating them fresh. This is rarely seen in Sichuan cuisine, where chili peppers are frequently considered as a condiment. Sichuan cuisine uses chili peppers in such forms as pastes, pickles, and powders, in order to create complex flavors that are more than just hot. A spicy dish that contains fresh chili peppers usually gives it away immediately as a Hunan dish; one that uses fermented chili paste, for example, is classically Sichuan.

Also famous in Hunan cuisine is its preserved pork, which looks similar in form to the salted pork of North America. All different cuts of pork can be used – salted and cured until the meat hardens into a blocky shape resembling a solid mound of wax. The Hunan people call this meat preservation technique *la*, meaning "waxification." Accordingly, the preserved pork is called *larou*, or "waxed meat." In addition to pork, all types of meat can be waxified, including chicken, duck, and even fish. These meats can then be used in a variety of dishes, from stir-fries to soups. They contain enough salt through the preservation process that a dish using larou often does not need any further seasonings to enhance the taste.

Another notable characteristic about Hunan cuisine is its use of oversized utensils – big bowls, big spoons, and long chopsticks. The custom of using large utensils is a legacy of Hunan's peasant heritage. Traditionally, several generations of the same family lived and ate under the same roof. The family dining table was large enough for ten or more family members, and the chopsticks had to be long enough so that everyone could be equal participants in the eating action. Similarly, the bowls and spoons are proportionately large for the hefty, practical portions of the Hunan appetite.

TYPICAL HUNAN-STYLE DISHES

Hunan cuisine is best described as a hybrid of Guangdong and Sichuan cuisines, although the extent of their influences varies dish by dish. Two key characteristics of Hunan cuisine are the hotness from chili peppers, and the use of preserved pork (larou). Although most Hunan dishes are very strongly flavored, there are many notable exceptions where the dishes have the lightness and natural flavors similar to Guangdong cuisine.

Pigeon Soup Steamed in Bamboo Cups

竹節鴿盅

This is one of the most unique and famous of Hunan dishes. Minced pigeon is steamed in its broth inside a bamboo cup (which is not edible). The gamy taste of the pigeon is balanced by the delicate and sweet flavors of the bamboo stalk. Each cup makes an individual serving; the portion is small and the soup is generally served as an appetizer. This popular dish is often featured in Hongkong-style seafood houses as well.

Minced Squab Wrapped in Lettuce Leaf

炒明蝦鬆

Minced squab is sautéed, then wrapped inside an iceberg lettuce leaf at tableside to be eaten like a taco. It is frequently served as an appetizer dish in banquets. Some restaurants also offer chicken and shrimp as alternatives to the sautéed squab.

Stinking Tofu

臭豆腐

With a foul-smelling reputation much like the dorian fruit and cordon bleu cheese, this Hunan specialty is a beloved treasure by those who have grown to withstand its noxous odor. Pieces of tofu are allowed to ferment with a certain type of bacteria, which curdles the tofu and covers it with a greenish slime. Many Chinese outside Hunan who are unfamiliar with this dish simply cannot stand it on first contact. However, stinking tofu has a seductive allure to it. Once the tofu is deep-fried, it acquires a much more palatable fragrance, and a crunchy texture that is irresistibly good.

General Tso's Chicken

左宗棠雞

Mao Zedong was not the only Chinese leader in history who despised northern Chinese cooking. There was indeed a General Tso – a Qing Dynasty official (also from Hunan) who served the emperor in Beijing. However, he longed for home cooking so much that he took it on himself to cook this, his favorite dish, every day. Diced chicken is deep-fried until crispy, and then coated with a fiery sauce of red chili peppers, garlic, soy sauce and vinegar. The dish was

SOUTHERN

brought to America by Guangdong immigrants, who altered the recipe by using plum sauce, orange juice, and even pineapples. However, the basic elements of this dish: deep-fried chicken, tangy sauce, and spicy flavors continue to be General Tso's Chicken's distinguishing characteristics.

Steamed Chicken, Hunan-style
富贵鸡

This is one of the most famous Hunan dishes. A whole chicken is marinated with spices and steamed in a lotus leaf wrap. In some restaurants, the steamed chicken is also stuffed with glutinous rice and ham. The unique flavors absorbed from the lotus leaf covering are what give the dish its added attractions.

Larou Stir-fried with Leeks
蒜苗腊肉

The saltiness of larou goes very well with the fresh and pungent flavors of the leeks. Chili peppers enliven the dish with an added dash of spiciness. Sometimes, the leeks are replaced by garlic sprouts, which are not as pungent as the leeks, but have a different intensity in flavor. Another alternative (and a more homey variation) is larou stir-fried with dried white radishes. Generally, larou can be stir-fried with any vegetable for a quick and down-home dish.

Waxified Duck Stir-fried with Chili Peppers
白椒炒腊鸭

Similar to the dish described above, waxified duck – a form of larou – imparts all of the saltiness necessary for this dish. The fresh chili peppers give the dish a enlivened and refreshing dimension. The saltiness of the duck combined with the heat of the peppers creates a curious appeal that draws the tastebuds further into the spicy world of Hunan cuisine.

Baked Larou in Honey Sauce
富贵火腿

Slices of baked larou are coated with a golden, cloying honey sauce, and served between two slices of plain white toast. It is eaten like a finger sandwich, usually as an appetizer. It is also served occasionally at banquets. Larou is considerably drier and saltier than conventional western ham. It is used in small quantities in dishes to provide flavor and texture, and is rarely eaten in such a manner as this, as the main component of the dish.

Tofu Skin Crisps
酥烤素方

Tofu skins are stacked and pressed together to form a thin wafer, then

HUNAN-STYLE RESTAURANTS
IN LOS ANGELES

In the U.S., Hunan cuisine still remains shadowed in obscurity, in due part because there are only a few immigrants native to this province. Also, because Hunan cuisine is a fusion of Guangdong and Sichuan styles, it is routinely left in the footsteps of those two. In Los Angeles, there are only a few true Hunan-style restaurants. There are lots of "Hunan" restaurants, howerver. They are not much different from the "Szechwan" restaurants that all serve Chinese takeout food adapted for Americans. Authentic Hunan cuisine is sorely missed in America, not only because it possesses an interesting fusion of Guangdong- and Sichuan cooking styles, but it is also representative of the last vestiges of traditional Chinese cooking, many of which are otherwise evolving at a breakneck pace.

Hunan-style restaurants often identify themselves as *Xiang* (or *Shiang*) cuisine. Xiang is the historical name of Hunan province, so *Xiang cuisine* and Hunan cuisine are interchangeable terms.

Shiang Garden Restaurant

Some of the Hunan specialties include the house waxified duck, Crispy Clarion Bells, and Steamed Duck Stuffed with Eight-treasure Glutinous Rice. As the nature of Hunan cuisine suggests, many of the dishes on the menu resemble either Guangdong or Sichuan cuisine. Many of them are also very spicy.

111 N. Atlantic Boulevard, #351, Monterey Park
(626) 458-4508

Hunan Restaurant

With a straightforward name, one can only expect down-home Hunan cooking from this place. The hole-in-the-wall is located right next to Shun Fat Supermarket, and its dishes cater to a predominantly mainlander clientele. The menu is full of peasant favorites like Braised Sparerib with Potatoes, Steamed Pork with Taro, and Shredded Beef with Bamboo Shoot. Several dishes on the menu are not translated in English, since they feature parts of the bull's anatomy not typically eaten except by people really down out on the farms.

423 N. Atlantic Boulevard, #101, Monterey Park
(626) 282-2039

fried until crispy. They are often cut into strips, like flat tortilla chips. Tofu skin wafers can be eaten either plain as a vegetarian snack, or served in a hand sandwich along with honey-glazed larou.

Crispy Clarion Bells
酥炸響鈴

The fancy name obfuscates an otherwise mundane dish – fried wontons. Perhaps a redeeming difference for these "bells" is that they are wrapped in thin sheets of tofu skin instead of flour wraps. The meat filling is typically from pork, and is not much different from the ordinary wontons found throughout China. The crunchy sounds from biting into these fried wontons resemble jingling bells, providing the inspiration to the dish's clever name.

Pork Intestines with Bittermelon
苦瓜肥腸

This is a very typical peasant dish, one that uses table scraps with garden vegetables to create an economical and tasty meal. The fiery, red-hot stir-fry uses chili peppers, garlic, and ginger to counter the "coolness" of the bittermelon. The Guangdong people refer to the bittermelon as "cool melon," because it is said that its bitter flavor has a cooling and calming effect in a person. The bitterness of the bittermelon also adds a degree of complexity to this dish, which, albeit simple, contains many of Hunan's best attributes: spicy hot, practical, and full of fresh flavors.

Steamed Fish with Fried Bean Sauce
豆酥鱈魚

Any kind of fish can be used for this dish, which is plainly steamed at first, and then covered with a sauce made from fried soybeans and salt. Although Hunan's fish dishes are not nearly as outstanding as Hongkong- and Chaozhou's seafood dishes, this simple dish demonstrates the best of Hunan's cooking skills. The fried soybean sauce acts as a garnish, adding a slight, crunchy texture to the overall simplicity of a tender, steamed fish.

Shredded Pork Stir-fried with Red Chili Peppers
辣炒牛肉

Nothing can be simpler than this country dish, yet it illustrates the essence of Hunan cooking as the blend of Sichuan and Guangdong elements. Shredded pork and red chili peppers are stir-fried together with a dash of soy sauce. It is a hot dish like Sichuan cuisine, while the use of fresh chili echoes Guangdong cuisine's preference for fresh and natural flavors.

NORTHERN CHINA

If Chinese food had a fly-over country, then northern China must be it. Much maligned by the rest of China, northern Chinese cuisine is a dullard in a land of colorful regional cuisines. Yet, northern Chinese cuisine has successfully maintained a mysterious allure around itself, mainly by harboring some interesting gems that stand out above the daily monotony of Napa cabbage, leeks, and *shaobing* that dominate the average Northern Chinese meal.

The cooking style of Shandong province best represents the cuisine of northern China. Located north of China's Rice-Wheat Line, the main diet of Shandong cuisine is based on wheat, barley, millet, and various types of rough grains. Noodles, pastries, and breads of all sorts are consumed with hardly any rice in the daily staple. Beijing, which in several epochs served as China's imperial capital, does not have much of a cuisine to call its own. Its cooking style is heavily influenced by Shandong cuisine. Beijing does have, however, the world-famous Beijing Duck, as well as a lineup of dessert dishes that are unique in a country nearly devoid of dessert-making traditions.

Northern China is also the home to many of China's Muslim minority. Their Islamic-Chinese cuisine combines Chinese cooking techniques with the dietary laws outlined in the Koran. Another northern specialty is the Mongolian hotpot – a legacy left from the Mongol rule of the Yuan Dynasty (1279-1368).

For the most part, northern Chinese cuisine is practical and simple. Generations of hardship endured by the people of northern China have shaped a cuisine mostly concerned with frugality and survival. Aside from the wheat-based diet, which is wholly different from the rest of China, northern Chinese cuisine is also a testament of the Chinese experience – a compact history of hardship and suffering, as well as glories and riches.

SHANDONG CUISINE

"It is not unusual for the northern Chinese to eat noodles three times a day, and customarily, rice is eaten only a few times a year."

One of the most tragic histories in all of human civilizations resides in Shandong province. The Yellow River, alternately known as the "Sorrow of China," empties to sea in Shandong. For as long as humans have lived in Shandong, this temperamental river has been both a blessing and a curse. Over the last 3,000 years, more than 1,700 major floods were recorded in Shandong province, creating historical bouts of destruction – killing millions and displacing many millions more. A local proverb in Shandong says that if the Yellow River had not flooded in 20 years, it was time to marry off the house pig. The cynicism is not merely pessimism; it bites deeply into the harsh fate that people living along the river must fear each and every day.

The Yellow River gets its name from the extraordinary amounts of sand carried from the deserts of central China. The silt is carried downstream and deposited in low-lying Shandong province, making the land prone to constant flooding. When the river runs wild, which it often does, the Yellow River could shift locations by over 100 miles. Worse, the levees built to control floods have now raised the river level well above the surrounding lowlands. If the levee breaks, the river is liable to create even more damage than it had in the past.

Not all of the Yellow River's destruction was caused by nature. In 1938, during the War with Japan, Generalissimo Chiang Kai Shek deliberately ordered the Yellow River levees blown open in order to slow the advancing Japanese army. The tactic failed to slow the Japanese march toward Nanjing (Nanking), the Chinese capital at the time. Instead, Chiang killed more than 200,000 Chinese in Shandong who were not warned about the approaching flood.

Despite all of its misfortunes, the Shandong people are survivors. They have a hardy, resilient spirit that never ceases to confront the challenges ahead. In good times, Shandong can also make some very good food. Shandong is part of China's northern region, which includes the provinces of Hebei, Shandong, Shanxi, and Shaanxi, plus the self-administered cities of Beijing and Tianjin. Although the province is relatively small in size, Shandong's cooking styles overshadow those of the other northern provinces. It alone represents the cuisine of the entire northern region. Other northern Chinese specialties, such as Beijing's own Beijing Duck, the Muslims' Islamic-Chinese cuisine, and northern-style dumplings and noodles, are profoundly influenced by Shandong's cooking styles.

Relative to the rest of northern China, Shandong has always been a wealthy province. The Yellow River and the sea provide natural avenues for business and commerce, and Shandong's coastal ports have for centuries been some of China's most prosperous cities. Additionally, silt deposited by the river's floods enriched Shandong with fertile farmlands, supporting a variety of crops and produce during the summer growing season. Compared with much of the arid north, which is uncultivatable, Shandong's unique geography provides vital factors for the development of its cuisine, paving way for its influence throughout the region.

TYPICAL INGREDIENTS OF SHANDONG CUISINE

Shandong province lies in the heart of China's wheat belt. Save the short growing season, not much else can grow in northern China except for hardy grains and root vegetables. The climate is similar to the Northern Plains of the U.S., which is well suited for growing grains such as barley, corn, millet, sorghum, and wheat. The areas north of the Rice-Wheat Line are too cold for rice, so the local diet is the only one in China that is wholly dependent on

NORTHERN

breads, dumplings, and noodles. It is not unusual for the northern Chinese to eat noodles three times a day, and customarily, rice is eaten only a few times a year.

Shandong grows only limited varieties of vegetables – usually hearty types such as Napa cabbage, leeks, and white radishes. In the warm but short growing season, a variety of summer vegetables: greens, legumes, white radishes, and squash are harvested. They provide a few months of welcomed deviation, when fresh produce is generally available. During the cold winter months, the whole north basically subsists on Napa cabbage.

The silt-laden waters of the Yellow River are not conducive to large numbers of freshwater fish. However, good quality seafood is plentiful along the seacoast. The most notable seafood caught along the coast of Shandong includes abalone and sea cucumbers. Overall, the variety of fish and seafood in Shandong cuisine lags far behind Jiangzhe and Guangdong cuisines. Similarly, Shandong-style seafood does not generate as much excitement as do the other two.

Shaobing
燒餅

Among the wheat staples, *shaobing* is the most important food item in Shandong cuisine. It is a grilled sesame pancake eaten like bread to accompany all kinds of dishes.

Shaobing can also be eaten plain, or sandwiched with fresh leek slices. In the past, people ate shaobing with leeks because food was short and there was nothing else to eat. Today, people still prefer eating shaobing with leeks for the benign reason that it is also rather tasty. Shaobing defines northern Chinese cuisine like the baguette defines French cooking. Both cuisines would be incomplete without them.

Napa Cabbage
大白菜

Napa cabbage is the most important vegetable of northern China, especially in the winter when it is eaten like a staple. Beginning in the autumn harvest, stacks of Napa cabbage are stockpiled in northern Chinese homes. By the time winter arrives, they are piled up to the roof, and allowed to freeze in the cold. The hardy Napa cabbage can withstand freezing without rotting, so it provides the northern Chinese with a vital source of nutrition during those months when other fresh vegetables are unavailable.

Pickled Napa Cabbage
酸白菜

Northern Chinese cuisine is famed for its varied ways of preserving vegetables – a necessity borne out of the lack of fresh produce during the long winter months. One way of preserving Napa Cabbage is by pickling them with salt and vinegar. The entire head of Napa Cabbage is salted immediately after harvest – without washing – and piled into a large ceramic urn with a vinegary brine. This Shandong specialty food item is similar to the German sauerkraut. It is used in various types of soups and stir-fries.

Leeks
大蔥

Leeks are also important to the northern cuisine. They resemble scallions in appearance, and are commonly called "giant scallions" by the Chinese. Leeks have pungent flavors that are much stronger than scallions. They also grow easily. Even during the toughest times, leeks provided vital nutrition that helped people sustain through famine and hunger.

Caramelized Shallots
糖蒜頭

Entire cloves of shallots are preserved by marinating them in a sugary brine, which turns them translucent and red, while retaining the crunchy texture of the shallots. Caramelized shallots resemble marinated pearl onions, and

are used much like any pickles: eaten as-is; as part of a cold salad; or with shaobing in a sandwich for breakfast.

COOKING STYLES OF SHANDONG CUISINE

Repeated bouts of flood and famine have taught chefs to practice thrift and frugality. Despite Shandong's tradition of wealth, Shandong cuisine's cooking techniques were developed with the economies in mind. Because floods and famine often left fuel and ingredients in short supply, Shandong's cooking techniques evolved to embrace methods that cooked food quickly in order to save firewood and cooking fat.

Flash-frying
爆

A large variety of Shandong dishes are flash-fried, involving very high heat in the wok, and cutting ingredients into thin- or small pieces. Flash-frying is different than ordinary stir-frying in that flash-frying requires a hotter wok, less oil, and a shorter cooking time. When ingredients first enter the wok, they create loud, crackling sounds that give the technique its Chinese name – bao, meaning "to explode."

Pan-frying
鍋塌

The technique is different to pan-frying in the western tradition. Food is first coated with flour and then egg wash – a reverse order in comparison

NORTHERN

105

with typical western-style battering. The food is then fried in a shallow layer of oil. Finally, a seasoned broth is added into the frying pan, allowing the ingredients to cook until all of the liquids are absorbed into the food. Fine examples of pan-frying in Shandong cuisine include Pan-fried Tofu Squares and "Potstickers." This cooking technique is rarely found in dishes from other parts of China.

Fermented Rice Mash
糟溜

Glutinous rice is fermented with yeast and sugar to create a rice wine mash that has a sweet taste, with a savory scent of rice wine. One way of using fermented rice mash is to simmer meats in a stew flavored with this fermented rice. Another way is to use it in a sweet soup typically eaten as a snack. A famous Shandong dish is Fish Fillets Braised in Fermented Rice Sauce.

Candied Flossing
拔絲

Malt sugar is caramelized over heat until it achieves a consistency that produces thin strands when pulled, like dental floss. Fruits such as apple- and pineapple slices are coated with this candy to give off a visually spectacular appearance. Other food items commonly found in candied flossing dishes include lotus seeds and sweet potatoes. Typically, a sweet dish like this is served hot. Diners use chopsticks to pick up the pieces from the plate, allowing the flossing to form. Then, they dip the pieces into a bowl of ice water, which hardens the candy. The appeal of candied flossing is not only in its visual appearance. The contrasting textures of the crunchy candy and soft fruit, as well as the balance between the hot and the cold, are interesting to the tastebuds. Candied dishes can also be served cold, but in such cases, the sugar is hardened and the flossing will not form.

Soups

Shandong cuisine makes use of a lot of soups – generally starting with one of two basic types of soup stock: clear broth and milk broth. A clear broth is made by slowly simmering meat bones until the liquid acquires all of the essential flavors. A milk broth is produced by boiling the same kinds of meat bones over very high heat. No milk is used in the milk broth, even though the appearance and consistency is white and creamy. The duck soup served in a Beijing Duck meal is a typical example of this Shandong-style milk broth.

Noodle-making

Shandong chefs are master noodle makers. In a cuisine based wholly on wheat, inventive ways of using wheat flour have become artistic skills. In Shandong cuisine, the variety of noodles is bewildering. Common types of northern Chinese noodles include Knife-cut Noodles, Yi-fu Mian, and Cat's Ears. (See chapter on Noodles & Dumplings.)

SAUCES IN SHANDONG CUISINE

The use of cooking sauces in Shandong cuisine is not as prevalent as it is in Guangdong cuisine. However, there are several sauces whose use immediately reveals clues to the dish's northern Chinese origin.

Sweet Bean Paste
甜麵醬

This thick, reddish-brown sauce is quintessentially northern Chinese. There is something similar in Guangdong cuisine called "Hoisin Sauce," which is basically the same thing. Made with puréed fermented soybeans, the sweet bean paste often contains enough salt to provide the necessary seasoning in the dishes. The sweet bean paste also gives off a rustic character. In Shandong, it is often used like butter to flavor shaobing – spread thinly on the inside and eaten with leeks sandwiched in between. The sweet bean paste is also the main condiment in the famous Shandong dish called "Shredded Pork Flash-fried in Sweet Bean Paste."

Sesame Paste
芝麻醬

Although sesame paste can be found throughout China, it is closely associated with northern China because of the region's history with the Muslim population. Sesame was brought to China from Africa (through Arabia) over 1,000 years ago, and it is used widely in Shandong cuisine. Whole sesame seeds are spread on top of shaobing. Ground sesame are frequently used for sweet desserts. Sesame can also be pressed into oil. Sesame paste is used for a wide variety of stir-fries, giving the dishes a sweet, nutty flavor. It also forms the basis for the dipping sauce used in northern-style lamb hotpots.

Nira Flower Paste
韭菜花醬

The flower bud of the nira grass is the most desirable part of this vegetable. Nira flower paste gives off a pungent flavor typically associated with the nira plant, and it is commonly used in making the dipping sauce for the northern-style lamb hotpot.

Osmanthus Flower Paste
桂花醬

Osmanthus is a fragrant flower grown from a small, compact bush with broad, green, and leathery leaves. The Chinese preserve the flowers by salting them or marinating them in oil or water. The preserved flowers are then made into a fragrant paste that can be used both as a vital ingredient in traditional medicine, as well as a flavoring agent. Any dish that uses it has an attractive and immediately identifiable fragrance suggestive of the actual flowers.

NORTHERN

TYPICAL SHANDONG DISHES

Shandong cuisine is practical and simple – resorting mainly to economic ways of cooking that saves fuel and cooking fat. Flavorings of Shandong dishes do not venture far from the doldrums, relying primarily on salt, vinegar, and the flavors of preserved vegetables such as the sweet bean paste. There are no spicy dishes to speak of, and foreign influences are largely limited to contact with Arabs and Mongolians centuries ago. Many Shandong dishes are boiled in large pots, with most of them invariably featuring the ubiquitous Napa cabbage.

Braised Napa Cabbage with Dried Shrimp

開洋白菜

Napa cabbage is the most important vegetable in northern Chinese cuisine, and this dish is probably the most famous of them all. Napa cabbage is braised with dried shrimp and mushroom in a light broth, and boiled down to a soft and tender consistency. The cooking liquid, which turns into a rich vegetable bouillon, is fully absorbed into the Napa cabbage.

Napa Cabbage in White Vinegar Sauce

醋溜白菜

A different way of braising Napa cabbage is cooking it in white vinegar and broth. Sometimes, white tree fungus is added to provide a crunchy contrast to the dish. This dish has strong ties to Shanxi province, where nearly all of the local dishes are flavored with white rice vinegar.

Dry-sautéed Green Beans

干扁四季豆

This vegetarian dish is now so famous and pervasive throughout China that many people forget its Shandong origins. Dry sautéing involves flash-frying the vegetables inside a covered wok, using only oil and no liquid. This way, the natural textures and colors of the green beans are not cooked down. After removing the green beans from the pan, the skin of the green beans cool down and contract, creating attractive wrinkles that give the dish its interesting visual appearance.

Shredded Pork Flash-fried in Sweet Bean Paste

京醬肉絲

This is also called Beijing-style pork. Any dish using sweet bean paste as its main flavoring ingredient has an immediate association with northern China. This is a typical home-style dish that, like Flash-fried Lamb with Leeks in Islamic-Chinese cuisine, is an ideal side dish to eat with shaobing or a roughage like millet congee.

NORTHERN

SHANDONG-STYLE RESTAURANTS IN LOS ANGELES

Much maligned northern Chinese cuisine is often perceived as nothing more than a bonanza of leeks and Napa cabbage. However, many exemplary dishes exist in Shandong cuisine to make a visit to a northern-Chinese restaurant worthwhile. Although the number of Shandong cuisine restaurants in the Los Angeles area is not anywhere like the prevalence of Guangdong cuisine or Hongkong-style seafood, there are a few additional choices are available.

In the following chapters are descriptions of Beijing Duck, Islamic-Chinese cuisine, and Dumplings and Noodles. Although these categories of northern-Chinese cuisine have their own distinguishing characteritics, all of them are heavily influenced by Shandong's cooking styles.

NORTHERN

Three Family's Village Restaurant

Noodle dishes play a dominant position in this restaurant's menu, which features *baozi*, *jiaozi*, Cat's Ears, regular noodles, and knife-cut noodles. It also serves the traditional *shaobing* with leeks, recalling the humbler, famine-plagued days in the past. The rest of the menu includes home-style dishes, many featuring the nothern Chinese staple/vegetable: Napa cabbage. Unfortunately, no dessert dishes are served here.

18438 E. Colima Rd., #102, Rowland Heights
(626) 810-4993

More restaurants are listed in Appendix VII.

Stir-fried Pickled Napa Cabbage
炒酸白菜

One way of preserving Napa cabbage for the winter is by pickling it with salt and vinegar. The typical northern Chinese method of pickling calls for salting and air-drying an entire head of cabbage, and then allowing it to age inside a clay urn. Although this pickled Napa cabbage suggests obvious similarities with sauerkraut, it is versatile for use in stir-fries such as this, as well as in soups and Mongolian hotpots.

Pan-fried Tofu Squares
鍋塌豆腐

Square pieces of tofu are pan-fried until golden brown, and then simmered in a clear Shandong-style broth until all of the cooking liquids is absorbed into the tofu. The dish, though simple, skillfully transforms an otherwise bland piece of tofu into a tender, savory piece of nutrition-packed gem.

Dalu Mian
打鲁麵

The most famous noodle dish from Shandong province is Dalu Mian, which is just a bowl of ordinary noodles served in a starchy egg-drop soup. Any variety of ingredients can go into the soup itself, but a typical northern Chinese style of soup includes Napa cabbage, mushrooms, and leeks. This simple but hearty noodle soup says much about Shandong cuisine, which relies on noodles, soups, and Napa cabbage to endure through the long winters.

Chop-suey with a Hat on Top
合菜戴帽

An assortment of flash-fried vegetables (hecai) includes Chinese favorites such as bean sprouts, black tree fungus, yellow nira, bamboo shoot, and carrots. Shreded pork, dried tofu and cellophane noodles are also added to make an opulent chop-suey. The flash-fry is flavored with just ordinary condiments including salt and sugar. A thin sheet of grilled scrambled eggs is layered on top, like a hat, to complete the dish. Frequently, this chop suey is served with shaobing and sweet bean paste.

NORTHERN

Beijing Duck

"The fat marbled in the interstices of the meat tissues is essential for creating the duck's distinctive tenderness and rich flavor."

Beijing Duck is a 600-year old tradition, favored by emperors and subjects in the past and enjoyed worldwide today. It is also a survivor – having endured through countless famines, plagues, and floods, then wars, sieges, and dictators. Today, Beijing Duck is the most famous dish from the Chinese capital, and it is the most popular duck dish in the world. Some of Beijing's largest duck restaurants seat over 2,000 people, and chefs around the world routinely emulate its recipe. Even Wolfgang Puck, an Austrian-born Provençal chef living in Los Angeles, has found a way to put Beijing Duck on his pizzas.

Preparation of the Beijing Duck is a complicated and well-guarded secret, with each step faithfully followed in order to achieve the duck's desired qualities: mahogany color, crispy skin, and tender meat. The drying process alone, a crucial step that creates the crispy skin, could take up to 12 hours. Because of this, making Beijing Duck is practical only when it is mass-produced in large duck restaurants. Otherwise, smaller restaurants require preordering at least a day in advance so that they could make all the necessary preparations.

Photo courtesy of J.Z.Y. Cafe

The ducks for the Beijing Duck are raised in specialty duck farms, where they are force-fed a diet of grains and soybeans through a funnel and tube. Although the ducks do not bask in a similar sort of pastoral luxury enjoyed by the Kobe Beef cows, they nevertheless grow to contain around 40 percent body fat. The fat marbled in the interstices of the meat tissues is essential for creating the duck's distinctive tenderness and rich flavor.

Before roasting the duck, air is pumped into the skin, and the body cavity is filled with hot water. This way, roasting takes place on the outside while simmering takes place from the inside. The result marks one of the most unique and ingenious cooking techniques – producing a roast duck perfectly balanced by the contrast between the mahogany, crispy skin, and the white, succulent meat.

Eating Beijing Duck follows a certain tradition, although it is by no means a rigid custom – like most everything else in Chinese food culture. The duck must be carved and served immediately after roasting, or otherwise the contrast between the crunchiness and tenderness would be lost. Some large duck restaurants add theatrics to the Beijing Duck experience by rolling out the whole duck into the dining room, and carving it directly by the table.

"ONE DUCK EATEN THREE WAYS"

Generally, the skin and meat are served separately in what is commonly called the "One Duck Eaten Three Ways" style. Duck skin is served first as an appetizer, eaten either with steamed lotus leaf-like buns or shaobing (grilled sesame pancakes). They are wrapped together with slices of fresh leeks or scallions, with a daub of sweet bean paste in between. The crispy duck skin, with its slight aroma and fat, is balanced by the cool, pungent flavor of the leeks.

NORTHERN

Wintertime Beijing street scene.

There are two other alternative garnishes for the duck skin. In one, slices of fresh cucumbers and white radish are used instead of leeks. Another way is using granulated sugar instead of sweet bean paste. Both alternatives are popular in Beijing, but they are virtually unheard of elsewhere.

The duck meat – without the skins – is served next as a stir-fry, which comes along with the other dishes making up the main meal. Commonly, this duck meat is stir-fried with bean sprouts and duck fat. Another popular vegetable to stir-fry the duck meat with is yellow nira. Other dishes in the meal – whether they are beef, lamb, or seafood – play deference to the duck meat stir-fry. Although simple, the duck meat stir-fry is the main dish in the "One Duck Eaten Three Ways" style of a Beijing Duck meal, and acts as its focal point.

Finally, a milky soup made from duck bones is served after the meal. This is a traditional Shandong-style soup, which attains the milky consistency by boiling the bones over high heat. Soup is customarily served at the conclusion of a Chinese meal, so a rich but uncomplicated soup like this is ideal for cleansing the palate

for tea and perhaps some desserts afterwards.

OTHER BEIJING DUCK SERVING METHODS

On occasions when one chooses not to indulge in the "One Duck Eaten Three Ways" style, both the duck skin and the duck meat are carved together, and served all at the same time. The duck can thus be eaten either with the buns or the pancakes, or it can come as part of the main meal with the other dishes. The duck soup still comes at the end of the meal.

Beijing Duck is also occasionally featured in Chinese-style banquets, but it is eaten differently than the "One Duck Three Ways" style. In banquets, which consists of ten courses, Beijing Duck is served as a single course, usually the fourth or fifth dish in the procession of increasingly complicated dishes. Waiters bring the duck to the table already carved, and skillfully use a fork and spoon to wrap the duck meat into the steamed buns. Then, they distribute the buns to each person on the table, using the same fork and spoon without touching them with their hands. Once the duck is finished, the banquet moves on to the next course. Duck soup is skipped entirely in banquets.

Although Beijing Duck is popular throughout China and around the world, it retains strong regional ties to northern Chinese cooking. The steamed buns and shaobing used to wrap duck skin reveal northern China's dependence on wheat as its main staple. Also, wrapping leeks or scallions in shaobing was once the peasant's way to beat famine. The milky duck soup is a specialty of Shandong province, whose cuisine is representative of all of northern Chinese cooking, including that of Beijing.

BEIJING DUCK'S "TWIN PANTHEONS"

The stories of Beijing's two largest duck restaurants are as famous and colorful as the Beijing Duck itself. Quanjude and Bianyifang are the twin pantheons of Beijing Duck in Beijing. Each restaurant makes its Beijing Duck differently, and both have their own loyal coterie of followers. In Beijing, bringing up the question about where to find the best Beijing Duck restaurant will likely elicit an answer for either one of these two.

Quanjude
全聚德

Quanjude, or "*Virtue of All Gatherings*," was started in 1864 by Mr. Yang Quanren, a Beijing butcher who opened his shop in the Qianmen (Front Gate) meat market, near the present location of Quanjude's seven-story flagship restaurant. Mr. Yang's innovation was the "open oven" method of roasting, which was done by placing the ducks directly over open flames. Previously, ducks were roasted in closed ovens, in which smoldering, flameless wood provided the necessary heat.

In the first fifty years of the 20th century, Beijing went through the overthrow of the Qing Dynasty, the warlords, the War with Japan, World War II, and the Civil War, in that succession. By 1950, Beijing's economy and social fabric were decimated, and the communist

NORTHERN

government nationalized Quanjude. Today, Quanjude is still state-owned, but it is run like a corporation with over 60 franchises throughout China. There is an additional overseas outlet in the San Gabriel Valley.

"Cheap Restaurant"
便宜坊

Bianyifang, or "Cheap Restaurant," started in 1855 – nine years before Quanjude – in a vendor stall at another Beijing meat market. Originally, it served cafeteria-style box lunches to workers and government officials – a Sino-precursor to the Panda Express juggernaut in America's shopping malls. The difference was that among the choice of dishes, Bianyifang served a succulent Beijing Duck that people raved over. The name "Bianyifang," which originally meant *"Restaurant of Your Choices"* (as in the many dishes to choose from), was changed by local customers to mean "Cheap Restaurant" because everyone loved the cheap prices. Both names are pronounced identically as "Bianyifang," but only written differently in Chinese script.

"Cheap Restaurant" quickly became a citywide sensation, and by 1930 it had nine outlets throughout Beijing. However, by the sunset of the Cultural Revolution in 1976, only one Bianyifang remained, and it did so only by changing its name to "Xinlu Restaurant," and served as a cafeteria-style mess hall for workers. In 1978, the restaurant reverted back to the

Bianyifang name, and rediscovered its old Beijing Duck recipe.

As Bianyifang proudly proclaims, "our ducks see no flame." Its Beijing Duck is distinguished by a closed-oven roasting method. The oven is fired by fruit woods such as cherry and walnut, with millet stalks tossed in to give the flavors some added dimensions. Today, Bianyifang is once again the top Beijing Duck restaurant in Beijing, operating a colossal establishment on Chongwenmenwai Road that rivals Quanjude in size and substance.

TYPICAL DUCK RESTAURANT DISHES

Beijing Duck is essentially a mass-produced fast-food dish in Beijing, and the restaurants that serve them generally specialize in Shandong cuisine as well. These duck restaurants serve Beijing Ducks as its main attraction, and feature a bevy of duck dishes made from every edible part of the duck as well. Because making Beijing Duck is so tedious and painstaking, the most authentic ones are mass-produced in these large, specialty duck restaurants. Many smaller restaurants claim to serve Beijing Duck as well, but their quality may be varied due to the tedious process that they require.

Duck Meat Egg Rolls
鴨絲春卷

Egg rolls are standard fare for the American palate, so these ones made

BEIJING DUCK RESTAURANTS IN LOS ANGELES

In Beijing, the Beijing Duck is actually quite an ordinary dish. Visitors to Beijing who are unfamiliar with the dining mores of the Chinese may find it shocking to see people spitting and tossing duck bones to the floor. Not even upmarket Bianyifang and Quanjude are excepted from this behavior. Thankfully, the Los Angeles Quanjude outlet does not suffer from the same issues of dubious hygiene and social stratification as do the Beijing flagships. There is no spitting and tossing of the bones, and everyone – glitterati or ordinary; rich or pinched – dine in the same, brightly-lit dining room.

Quanjude

The skills required for raising ducks for the Beijing Duck are now practiced at several specialty duck farms in the U.S., so, even though this Quanjude is located almost 8,000 miles from home, the Beijing Duck in Los Angeles is very much like the real thing in Beijing. The menu is small – not surprising considering that people come here for one thing only. However, Quanjude's menu does include some interesting duck dishes for the braveheart: duck egg rolls, marinated duck gizzards, and boiled duck feet.

8450 E. Garvey Ave., #101 Rosemead
(626) 280-2378

J.Z.Y. Cafe

This San Gabriel Valley restaurant is difficult to find inside a nondescript strip mall, but it is worth the effort not only for its decent rendition of the Beijing Duck, but also for a slew of northern Chinese specialties. People come here either for the Beijing Duck or the northern-style hotpot, which features lamb meat and is flavored with pickled Napa cabbage. Also unique about J.Z.Y. Cafe is its dessert tray, which includes many of Beijing's favorite sweets such as Donkey Rolling in Dirt, Black Glutinous Rice Cake, and Empress Dowager Tzu Hsi's favorite: Yellow Pea Cake.

1039 E. Valley Blvd., #102, San Gabriel
(626) 288-8588

NORTHERN

NORTHERN

from duck meat instead of pork are nearly obligatory in a duck restaurant catering to westerners.

Braised Duck Tongue in Basil
三杯鴨舌

This braised meat dish is a variation of a classic Hakka chicken dish. Duck tongues are allowed to simmer slowly in a full-bodied brine of soy sauce and basil, until all of the aromatic flavors are absorbed. The duck tongue, for those who are eager to try, has a tender and chewy texture. The drawback, however, is the small arrowhead-shaped cartilage that one must spit out.

Duck Stir-fried with Yellow Nira
韭黃炒鴨

Yellow nira is an alternative vegetable to the typical stir-fry with bean sprouts. Yellow nira has sweet, less pungent flavors than regular nira, and it gives off a refreshing sensation that also proclaims that summer has arrived.

Braised Napa Cabbage with Dried Shrimp
開洋白菜

Napa cabbage is braised with dried shrimp and mushroom in a light duck broth. Napa cabbage is a very important vegetable in Shandong cuisine, because it is hardy and can be stored easily in the open air for the duration of winter. Napa cabbage dishes appear very frequently in Shandong- and Beijing-style restaurants.

Napa Cabbage in White Vinegar Sauce
醋溜白菜

With Beijing Duck, this light dish is an ideal match. The acidity of the vinegar sauce provides a good counterbalance to the greasiness of the duck meat. The white vinegar in this dish suggests a heavy Shanxi province overtone. The province has a much-maligned cuisine, because nearly all of its dishes are sour from vinegar.

NORTHERN

ISLAMIC-CHINESE CUISINE

The cooking of the Hui minority of China adheres to the halal diet, based on the guidelines expressly stated in the Koran.

A curious aspect of Chinese cuisine is the cooking style that follows strict Islamic dietary laws. China has a small but visible Muslim minority population, with about 10 million people called the "*Hui*" – accounting for just under 1 percent of the total population. Muslim presence in China dates back to about 750 A.D., when Arab and Persian traders first arrived in the ports of southern China.

Today, the Huis live mainly in large northern cities such as Beijing, Tianjin, and Xian. In the countenance of a dominant Han culture, Chinese Muslims have largely assimilated to the Han way of life. Many also adopted Sinicized names, and have become nearly indistinguishable in appearance through intermarriage. However, the Hui's faith in Islam never wavered, and neither did their adherence to the *halal* diet. Their style of cooking, called Islamic-Chinese cuisine, mirrors the social assimilation of the Huis in China. It is, in essence, Chinese cooking based on Shandong cuisine, while adhering to the dietary laws outlined in the Koran.

Although they represent only a small part of China's minority population, Chinese Muslims are not a single, monolithic group. Another large group of Muslims called the *Uigurs* lives in the remote northwestern provinces of Gansu, Ningxia, Qinghai, and particularly in Xinjiang, where their populations far outnumber the Hans. The Uigurs share similar cultures and heritages as neighboring Afghanistan, Tajikistan, and Kazakhstan, and because the Hans never had much influence on them, their cuisine is more related to Central Asia, with no affinity to either the Islamic-Chinese cuisine or any other regional cuisine of China.

DEVELOPMENT OF ISLAMIC-CHINESE CUISINE

Arab Muslims once enjoyed great political- and social prominence in China, especially during the Yuan Dynasty (1279-1368), a period of history when China was conquered by the Mongols. During this time, Arabia had the most educated- and technically advanced civilization in the world, and Arabs were welcomed in Yuan's official bureaucracy in Beijing. The Arabs held a higher social status than the Hans, who were regarded as third-class citizens in their own country. Also during this time, Marco Polo made his visit to China, and trade between China and the West flourished from a borderless frontier stretching from Hangzhou to the gates of Prague.

The fortunes of the Huis in China changed when the Ming Dynasty (1368-1644) reclaimed China under Han rule. Xenophobia was the natural reaction to the suffering of the Chinese under the brutal Mongols. The Ming rulers led the popular mood of detesting and denigrating anything foreign. Muslims, especially those living in large Chinese cities, were forced to adopt Chinese customs. Their wholesale assimilation to Chinese culture during this time – except for their religious beliefs – formed the basis of their Islamic-Chinese cuisine today.

Worse fate awaited the Huis during the Qing Dynasty (1644-1911), which discriminated against the Muslims as a matter of official policy. Although the Qing were essentially foreign rulers (they were of Manchu ethnicity), the "Last Dynasty" was suspicious that Islamic beliefs were irreconcilable with Chinese culture. The fact that

the Muslims had joined with the Hans in an unsuccessful rebellion against the Qing did nothing to win the emperor's sympathy either. The Qing took many steps, often violently, to force Muslims out of prominent positions in government and society. The indignities suffered by the Huis during the Qing Dynasty nevertheless damaged the relationship between the Hans and the Huis forever.

CHARACTERISTICS OF ISLAMIC-CHINESE CUISINE

The Koran gives strict guidance on food and drink, which outlines specific foods deemed to be "lawful" for consumption – or *halal*. Islamic dietary laws also reveal the ways by which Muslims select, prepare, and eat food. For example, the slaughtering of animals requires a ritualistic process that stresses the virtues of cleanliness, humanity, and the *humility* of killing animals for consumption. Blood, a forbidden item for food, is completely drained from the meat, retaining freshness and preventing contamination as well. The skills of Muslims in animal slaughter suggest why they make up a large proportion of the butchering profession in China.

Among the foods expressly forbidden by the Koran – or *haram*, the most important example is pork. Pigs are considered forager animals, and are viewed both as filthy and carriers of disease. Other banned foods in Islam include crustaceans such as clams, crabs, and shrimp. Also, the consumption of alcohol is completely haram; beers, wines, and liquors play no role in the Muslim diet, either as a beverage or a cooking condiment.

Another major difference between Islamic-Chinese cuisine and other regional cuisines is the type of meats used. Instead of pork, Islamic-Chinese dishes frequently feature beef and lamb. The Hans do not typically eat beef, because cattle are generally domesticated for use as a beast of burden. Families often feel a sense of gratitude to their cattle, and their emotional attachment made it uncommon for them to eat beef. Lamb meat is rarely eaten outside northern China. It is thus a distinctly northern Chinese meat, and also one that typifies Islamic-Chinese cuisine.

Similar to Shandong cuisine, the main staple of Islamic-Chinese cuisine is based on wheat. *Dabing*, or "big pancake," is the basic bread in Islamic-Chinese meals. Similar to shaobing – its smaller brethren, dabing is eaten like bread to accompany all sorts of dishes. It is the size of a large pizza – up to sixteen inches in diameter and around two inches thick. Some are covered with roasted white sesame, and others are flavored with chopped leeks. Dabing is grilled in a shallow cast iron pan until it is golden brown – crispy on the outside with a soft, fluffy dough in the center.

Noodles are also popular feature in Islamic-Chinese cuisine, mirroring the noodle-making traditions in Shandong cuisine. Hand-pulled noodles are made by chefs who turn out thin strands of flour noodles from a single ball of dough. It is often performed in front of an incredulous audience. Knife-cut noodles are slivers of flour dough gradually shaved with a sharp knife. They have a coarse and uneven texture, and are served either in a noodle soup or stir-fried with meats and vegetables.

TYPICAL DISHES OF ISLAMIC-CHINESE CUISINE

The entire lineup of Islamic-Chinese dishes is profoundly influenced by Shandong cuisine. This means that flash-frying and the use of soups are important cooking techniques that shape the cuisine's primary characteristics. Lamb dishes are also numerous and varied. Additionally, any Islamic-Chinese meal cannot be complete without a dabing, which is always eaten instead of rice.

Dabing and Shaobing
芝麻大餅, 燒餅

A large, grilled sesame pancake, or dabing, is about the size of a Chicago-style deep-dish pizza, while shaobing is the shape of a business-size envelope. Both are eaten like bread to accompany all meals. A dabing is ample for six to eight people, while the smaller shaobing is an individual serving. Some people prefer eating these pancakes with leeks. In restaurants, it could take about a 20-minute wait for a dabing, since each one is made to order. So, people immediately order one even before reading the menu.

Pancakes in a Lamb Soup
羊肉泡饃

This is the ultimate frugal food of northern China. A piece of dabing is dunked under a bowl of lamb (or beef) soup to sop up all of the juices and flavors. It is not unlike the French, who like to soak pieces of stale baguettes in soup to avoid waste.

Knife-cut Noodles
刀削麵

A northern Chinese specialty is knife-cut noodles, which are broad, flat

ISLAMIC-CHINESE RESTAURANTS IN LOS ANGELES

On the surface, Islamic-Chinese cuisine appears to have only limited appeal in Los Angeles, mainly because it is overshadowed by more flamboyant cuisines from other parts of China. But look around an Islamic-Chinese restaurant, you can usually find all kinds of people: Malaysians, Iranians, Pakistanis, Arabs, and Chinese, dining together with their families and friends. It is almost ritualistic to order a dabing before even looking at the menu, since it is the most important element in an Islamic-Chinese meal.

Unfortunately, some Islamic-Chinese restaurants now also serve familiar takeout dishes like Kungpao Chicken, Broccoli Beef, and Beijing Duck, just so that they could keep their businesses going. However, for the genuine Islamic-Chinese dining experience, stick with the coarse and unsophisticated repertoire of dabing, noodles, lamb dishes, and traditional Shandong-style flash-fries.

Islamic Chinese Restaurant

The décor is Spartan and clean, with white walls and florescent lights. Only a photograph of Mecca breaks the uniform monotony of the restaurant's setting. Islamic Chinese Restaurant recalls the simple *hutong* restaurants of Beijing's Muslim quarter. It is relaxed, straightforward, and filled with locals and Muslim families who know this is some of the best and most authentic stuff in town.

7727 E. Garvey Ave., Rosemead
(626) 288-4246

Tung Lai Shun Restaurant

This restaurant serves good pancakes and lamb dishes, although the menu strays far and wide to include seafood and Beijing Duck. The bright restaurant is located in the San Gabriel Mall, a sprawling, multi-story development featuring a supermarket, department store, and numerous eateries and coffeeshops.

140 W. Valley Blvd., #118-C, San Gabriel
(626) 288-6588

NORTHERN

Beijing Islamic Restaurant

From the outside, the block letters on the restaurant's sign make the place appear quite nondescript and ordinary. The surprise is inside, with a subdued décor that, though understated, provides the right atmosphere for the occasion. Likewise, the food is simple, authentic and faithful to the halal diet. Located at the edge of Palos Verdes, Islamic-Chinese cuisine also makes a pleasant digression from the scads of "Chinese food" restaurants in the area.

3160 Pacific Coast Hwy., Torrance
(310) 784-0846

noodles sliced from a ball of dough. The rough, uneven texture of these noodles suggests the ruggedness of the northern terrain. It also conveys the tough lives the northern Chinese, who endure not only an unforgiving climate, but also repeated bouts of disasters and famine. Knife-cut noodles are best served with a lamb- or beef-soup, or it can also be stir-fried.

Grilled Lamb with Cumin
孜然羊肉

The flavor of cumin is atypical for Chinese cooking. The Chinese generally avoid it like the way vampires scatter to the scent of garlic. Islamic-Chinese restaurants are the few places where a dish like this can be found. Grilled lamb, seasoned with cumin and served in a kabob, gives an unmistakable aura of Central Asia and the Middle East.

Flash-fried Lamb with Leeks
葱爆羊肉

This is perhaps the signature Islamic-Chinese dish. Thin slices of lamb are flash-fried in very hot oil with diced leeks. Flash-frying is a cooking technique from Shandong cuisine, which cooks faster than stir-frying and uses less oil. This dish goes very well as a side dish to a dabing, making a very simple and inexpensive meal. Beef is a common substitute for lamb in this dish.

NORTHERN

DUMPLINGS AND NOODLES

"The entire menu is comprised of foods made from wheat, millet, and soybeans, defying an otherwise solid stereotype of the Chinese as a rice-eating culture."

Wheat is the most important food staple of northern China, and along with millet and soybeans, they comprise the primary diet of the region. Many northerners eat noodles, pancakes and dumplings three times a day, and may go for days without eating rice. Similar to the local diet, northern-style restaurants serve all kinds of wheat-based foods, with nary a rice dish on the menu. This is the primary attraction of the Dumplings and Noodles houses, which serve exactly just that – dumplings and noodles.

Dumplings and Noodles houses are also known for their breakfasts, a rarity among other Chinese restaurants. These restaurants also serve lunch, but they generally close well before dinnertime. Among the breakfast items served in Dumplings and Noodles houses are a wide variety of dumplings and noodles, as well as congee made from millet, oats, and beans – typical roughage for the north. These foods are fortifying enough for the cold, and packed with ample nutrition to get through the day.

For the most part, Chinese breakfasts are an acquired taste. In a culture that loves to eat, it is quite a curiosity that the Chinese pay little attention to breakfast. In all regions except Guangdong province, the traditional Chinese breakfast is unimaginative, bland, and rather unhealthy. If it is not a soggy nira pancake deep-fried in oil, they eat a flavorless bowl of congee accompanied by a square piece of salty fermented tofu. Eating a Chinese breakfast is like watching the rinse cycle of a washing machine – not overly productive and downright boring.

The most notorious Chinese breakfast item is the "*youtiao*," or loosely translated as the "oil stick." It is nothing more than a greasy rod of deep-fried flour dough. Youtiao can be eaten either as-is, or in a manner that many Chinese prefer: flattened between a grilled sesame pancake (shaobing) and eaten like a sandwich. The virtue of youtiao's appeal has always been suspect, but people continue to eat it despite its high fat content, with little nutritional value to speak of.

The customary breakfast beverage is soymilk, consumed hot or cold. It is always flavored in one way or another. Hot soymilk can be either seasoned with soy sauce, chili oil, and pieces of youtiao floating like croutons; or it can be sweetened with sugar. In either case, hot soymilk is always served in a bowl and eaten with a spoon like soup. On the other hand, cold soymilk is always served as a sweet beverage, and drunk from a tall glass.

TYPICAL DUMPLINGS AND NOODLES HOUSE DISHES

It is hard to imagine a Chinese restaurant without any rice dishes, but many Dumplings and Noodles houses do just that – serving just dumplings and noodles, with several sweet pastries rounding out the mix. The entire menu is comprised of foods made from wheat, millet, and soybeans, defying an otherwise solid stereotype of the Chinese as a rice-eating culture.

Soymilk Gelatin (*douhua*)
豆花

Often called *soy brain, soy flower*, or by the Mandarin pronunciation "*douhua*," soymilk gelatin is made by adding edible plaster to soymilk, allowing it to coagulate into a flimsy solid that is much softer than tofu. In all cases, soymilk gelatin is served in a bowl and eaten like a custard. Sweet soymilk gelatin is served by pouring sugar syrup on top, and sometimes garnished with soft-boiled peanuts. Salty soymilk gelatin is served like salty soymilk – seasoned with soy sauce, chili oil, and youtiao croutons.

Hubei Doupi
湖北豆皮

Doupi, or bean wraps, is the only notable dish from Hubei province, which otherwise has a forgettable culinary tradition. The snack resembles a flattened burrito, stuffed with glutinous rice and a compote of pork, mushroom, and bamboo shoots. The ingredients are wrapped with a thin pastry sheet made from mungbean flour, and grilled in a shallow pan until crispy. This popular snack dish originated in the old city of Hankou during the War with Japan (the city is now consolidated into a metropolis named Wuhan).

BAOZI AND JIAOZI

Dumplings come in different shapes and sizes, but basically they are divided between *baozi* (round dumplings) and *jiaozi* (oblong dumplings). Both of them are simply called "dumplings" in many Chinese restaurants, which is unfortunate because these dumplings look and taste differently. To truly enjoy the experiences of eating baozi and jiaozi, it is good to know their characteristics and specify them by their Chinese names when ordering.

Baozi are round dumplings, made with flour wraps of varying thicknesses, surrounding a variety of meat- and vegetable fillings. The flour wraps can either be thick or thin, and leavened or unleavened. Leavened flour wraps benefit from baking soda to become fluffy when steamed. Guangdong-style baozi wraps are usually leavened, and are sweetened with a pinch of sugar. Northern-style baozi also use leavened flour wraps but are generally unsweetened. Shanghai is famous for its Small Soupy Baozi, which uses unleavened flour wraps.

A baozi is shaped by pinching the flour wrap around the stuffing in a circular fashion, creating pillow-like contours with little dimples at the top. Commonly, baozi are steamed. There are also pan-fried baozi cooked in a covered shallow pan. Baozi are never boiled like jiaozi, however.

Jiaozi are oblong dumplings, using only thin and unleavened flour wraps. Fillings for jiaozi can also be of any variety of meats and vegetables. The flour wrap is pinched around the filling in a linear fashion, creating an oblong-shaped dumpling. The most common way of cooking jiaozi is by boiling, but steaming is becoming increasingly popular in the wake of health consciousness in modern society. Jiaozi can also be pan-fried in the Shandong cooking method, in which they are called "potstickers."

Unlike baozi, which can be eaten plain, jiaozi are always eaten with some sort of dipping sauce – either just soy sauce, or a more elaborate mixture of sugar, vinegar, garlic, chili peppers, and sesame oil. The Japanese eat something similar to jiaozi called gyoza, which is actually just the Japanese way of pronouncing the same word.

Small Soupy Baozi
小籠湯包子

Baozi are unusual luxuries for breakfasts that typically consist of soymilk and youtiao, since making baozi is more time intensive. Small soupy baozi are served in steamer baskets, each containing eight or ten bite-sized baozi – enough for an individual meal. They can also be grilled in a pan like potstickers. These baozi are very juicy, and should be eaten with chopsticks in one hand and a spoon in another. Bite into the baozi carefully to release a torrent of hot, savory soup into the spoon, and then eat the baozi with the soup in two or three bites from the spoon. An entire small soupy baozi should not be popped into the mouth like a marshmallow, or the hot soup could scald the mouth. A small dish of shredded ginger is always provided. It should be added with vinegar, soy sauce, and a dash of sugar for a light dipping sauce.

Pork and Napa Cabbage Baozi
菜肉包子

The standard bearer of steamed baozi is made with a filling of pork and Napa cabbage. The size of this baozi is substantially bigger than the small soupy baozi. Each Pork and Napa Cabbage Baozi is about the size of a fist, and one or two will suffice for an entire meal. Pork and Napa cabbage are minced finely, and seasoned simply with salt and pepper. Although these baozi are now found everywhere throughout China, Napa cabbage conveys an unmistakable association with northern Chinese cuisine, and gives away this baozi's true northern roots.

Grilled Pork Jiaozi
鍋貳

Sometimes called "Potstickers," grilled jiaozi start out raw in a shallow pan, where they are pan-fried on the bottom before stock is added to the pan. The jiaozi are then cooked under cover until all the liquid evaporates, cooking the fillings inside. The top part of the jiaozi is chewy while the bottom is crispy.

Vegetarian Baozi and Jiaozi
素菜包子（餃子）

The favorite filling for vegetarian dumplings is nira, a pungent green vegetable with a flavor being the cross between scallions and garlic. Also popular as fillings are mushrooms, Napa cabbage, and cellophane noodles made from mungbean flour. Minced tofu is often added to provide additional protein and meat-like texture to the fillings.

Longevity Peach
壽桃

A specialty *baozi* eaten only on birthdays, longevity peach is a heart-shaped bun that looks like a white-fleshed peach grown in China. Longevity peach is filled with sweet black sesame paste, and the outside flour shell is daubed with red food coloring to simulate the appearance of a peach. Trendy Longevity Peach now comes with fillings such as mashed lotus seeds, date paste, or even pumpkin. Since they are typically purchased in large quantities for birthday parties, longevity peaches are generally unobtainable without preordering.

OTHER BREADS OF NORTHERN CHINA

The standard "breads" of northern China include shaobing, dabing, and the equally ubiquitous *mantou*. A lesser known bread called the "*wowotou*" is a culinary waif much maligned by even the northern Chinese themselves.

Mantou
饅頭

A plain steamed bun, mantou is the sidekick to shaobing as the north's two basic breads. Mantou, or "savage's head," is no more than a lump of leavened flour dough, steamed into a round shape with a bland taste. According to legend, these flour lumps replaced severed human heads in sacrificial rituals way back in the primitive days of Chinese civilization. Mantou is still offered as food at ancestral gravesites and on family shrines inside Chinese homes. Nowadays, mantous also come in designer colors: purple mantou is made with taro starch; brown mantou

is made from whole-wheat flour; yellow mantou from cornmeal, and even green mantou by adding green tea.

Dabing
大餅

A main staple of Chinese Muslims, dabing is large enough to feed the entire family. It is a round bread the size of a Chicago-style pizza, and grilled in a shallow pan. The top is often covered with white sesame seeds. Dabing is eaten like bread to accompany all sorts of stir-fry and soup dishes, and it essentially replaces rice in a northern Chinese meal. Leftover dabing is often used to soak up soup, or stir-fried with an assortment of vegetables in order to avoid waste.

Shaobing
燒餅

Similar to dabing, but much smaller, shaobing has a rectangular shape the size of a business envelope, and can be easily eaten by hand. In northern China, shaobing is an important staple eaten like dabing. Shaobing can also be eaten as a stand-alone food item, by sandwiching it with slices of leek or white radish. Otherwise, shaobing

Unitd Colors of Mantou

Today's mantou come in many designer colors.

is popular for breakfast, typically with a youtiao sandwiched in between.

Wowotou
窝窝头

Another classic northern bread, this one is made from corn meal. It has a distinctive cone shape, which, after steaming, is golden brown in color. The dry, flaky texture is quite different from other types of steamed breads, like mantou. Some detractors opine that wowotou has a consistency of sawdust. Many people also immediately associate wowotou with famine. In the toughest of times, any kind of rough grains and seeds could be gathered to make wowotou, but corn is the customary ingredient. A native crop of 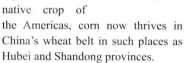 the Americas, corn now thrives in China's wheat belt in such places as Hubei and Shandong provinces.

Grilled Lamb Pancake
羊肉酪饼

A thick, meat-filled pastry the shape of a hockey puck, this pancake is grilled on both sides in a shallow pan. When cooked, the lamb filling becomes quite juicy, similar to small soupy baozi. The pancake is cut into bite-sized pieces before serving, leaving the juices to be soaked up by the flour shell. Beef is often an alternative to lamb in this dish, especially outside northern China where eating lamb meat is less common.

Grilled Nira Pancake
韭菜盒子

Nira pancakes resemble grilled beef pancakes, except that they are often shaped like a crescent or half-moon to distinguish themselves from the meat-filled ones (which are round). Nira is a vegetable that imparts a particularly pungent flavor, and is often used in northern Chinese cooking.

Grilled White Radish Pancake
萝卜丝饼

Another meatless pancake like the nira pancake, the grilled white radish pancake is filled with shredded white radish. The savory flavors of the white radish are suggestive of autumn, when they are harvested in abundance throughout northern China.

Fried Scallion Pancakes
葱油饼

Scallion pancakes are flat and round pastries the size of a tea saucer. High gluten flour is kneaded with hot water into a highly stretchable dough that can be pulled without breaking. It is also leavened with baking soda so that it becomes fluffy when fried. The dough is rolled with scallions, then flattened into a round disk before frying in a shallow pan. Many people prefer adding an egg to their scallion pancake, which makes for a tasty breakfast food item.

NORTHERN

Youtiao

油條

"Oil sticks" are the most popular breakfast item among the Chinese. It uses high gluten flour so that the dough could be stretched without breaking. The dough is leavened with soda so that it immediately swells to ten times its size when deep-fried in oil. This also produces youtiao's distinctive crunchy texture. Although youtiao is similar to doughnuts, there is only one flavor for youtiao – salt. Some people like dipping youtiao into a bowl of hot soymilk – akin to dipping doughnuts in coffee. Others float pieces of it in hot soymilk, like croutons.

RICE DISHES

Interesting about Los Angeles's Dumplings and Noodles houses is that many are owned by the Taiwanese. Before 1949, the Taiwanese were generally unaccustomed to the wheat-based foods of northern China, but over the years, they mastered the noodle-making skills passed down from mainland refugees who fled there. Nevertheless, these restaurants find it worthwhile to offer a limited menu of rice dishes: rice milk, rice cakes, glutinous rice rolls, et cetera.

Glutinous Rice Balls

湯圓

These small marble-shaped dumplings can contain one of a variety of fillings: pork, shrimp, ground peanuts, red bean paste, sesame paste, et cetera.

They are served in the same water in which they are boiled. Salty-flavored glutinous rice balls can be eaten as a main course, and sweet glutinous rice balls are generally eaten as snacks. Glutinous rice balls filled with sweet sesame paste are a traditional holiday food item, eaten on the 15th day of the Lunar New Year.

White Radish Rice Cake

蘿蔔糕

Rice cakes are made from steamed rice milk. The natural starches of the rice help the cake solidify into form when steamed, and it has a softness that nearly melts in the mouth. White radish rice cake is flavored with shredded white radish and Guangdong-style sausages. It is the same type of white radish rice cake (also called turnip rice cake) served in dim sum/yum cha. Another variation of the rice cake, developed in Taiwan, uses taro instead of white radishes. It has a pale purple color.

Glutinous Rice Roll

糯米糰

A Taiwanese breakfast invention, the glutinous rice roll has some resemblance to the breakfast burrito. Steamed glutinous rice is used to

DUMPLINGS AND NOODLES RESTAURANTS IN LOS ANGELES

Dumplings and Noodles houses have flourished in Los Angeles over the past decade, thanks in part to the increasing number of northern Chinese who crave for the rice-less diet like they had back home. Among the most important "dumplings" in the northern diet are baozi, jiaozi, shaobing, and the almighty mantou. Noodle dishes run the gamut from soups to stir-fries; beef to vegetarian. They can also feature all different sizes of noodles, from thin hair-like strands to broad, knife-cut noodles. Many Dumplings and Noodles houses also serve traditional Chinese breakfast, which are an eye-opener for many in more ways than one.

Interestingly, many Dumplings and Noodle houses in Los Angeles are owned by Taiwanese entrepreneurs. Many mainlanders who fled to Taiwan in 1949 found success selling dumplings and noodles in Taipei. Now they have handed down their skills to the next generation, who are venturing out to the U.S., offering truly authentic northern-style wheat-based dishes, as well as a limited selection of rice dishes from Taipei's street snack scene.

NORTHERN

Dumpling 10053

Steamed seafood jiaozi are the specialties at this smallish but busy restaurant. Among the more daring creations is steamed jiaozi filled with Pacific salmon, a cross-border tribute to the fabled North American fish. The restaurant also serves limited varieties of rice- and noodle dishes that recall street-side snacks of Taipei, such as Fried Pork Chop with Rice, and Beef Noodle Soup.

10053 Valley Blvd., #2, El Monte
(626) 350-0188

Yung Ho Tou Chiang Restaurant

A hole in the wall that serves up genuine northern-style gems, Yung Ho is another famous Taipei shop name that transplanted some of its pastry-making skills to America. The restaurant's décor is less than spectacular – grease stained walls and florescent lights complete an old-school atmosphere that nevertheless faithfully portrays northern China's humble realities. Everything else – from soymilk dishes to glutinous rice rolls, are hugely popular, which is why mornings are packed every day of the week.

533 W. Valley Blvd., San Gabriel
(626) 570-0680

NORTHERN

Malan Noodles

This noodle house is an overseas branch of a Beijing-based fast-food franchise, but on the surface it does not look anything like the sort. The specialty here is hand-pulled noodles, made partly by hand, with five different shapes of varying thicknesses. When boiled to *al dente*, the slippery noodles are perfect accompaniments to a standardized assortment of northern-style soups. The house soup is Lanzhou Beef Soup, featuring a clear, mild beef broth garnished with slices of beef brisket and chopped yellow nira. Strictly a noodle house, this restaurant does not serve breakfast or dumplings.

2020 Hacienda Blvd., Hacienda Heights
(626) 369-5602

Ding Tai Fung

A trendy Taipei chain, Ding Tai Fung was started by a Shanxi refugee who originally vended peanut oil on Taipei's streets before saving money to open a baozi shop. Today, Ding Tai Fung's Small Soupy *Baozi* are the talks of the towns in Taipei, Tokyo, and Los Angeles – cities where the chain operates gleaming, postmodern – and crowded – outlets. The restaurant also makes an assortment of northern-style dim sum, including its longevity peach, which requires preordering. A smattering of stir-fried rice dishes round out an otherwise complete lineup of wheat-based foods.

1108 S. Baldwin Ave., Arcadia
(626) 574-7068

More restaurants are listed in Appendix X.

wrap a selection of fillings, ranging from youtiao to salted duck eggs. Everything is pressed tightly into a handy burrito-shaped roll for people to eat on the go.

NOODLES

Not all noodles are created equal. Many of the north's favorites, such as Shandong's hand-pulled noodles, require special skills from the noodle chef. Neighboring Shanxi province is also renowned for several types of noodles, such as knife-cut noodles and "cat's ears."

Hand-pulled Noodles
拉 麵

A Shandong specialty, the makings of hand-pulled noodles require a certain degree of dexterity and acrobatic skill. From a single ball of dough, the chef gradually kneads and pulls the noodles into long, sinewy strands of more than twenty feet in length. Long noodles are a symbol of longevity, so hand-pulled noodles are typically served at birthday banquets for elders over 80 years in age.

Knife-cut Noodles
刀 削 麵

This Shanxi specialty is shaved with a knife by hand from a single ball of dough. Its uneven texture is the primary attraction to this pasta, which is thin around the edges and thick near the center. Once cooked, knife-cut noodles can be used like other noodles – in stir-fries or soups.

"Cat's Ears"
貓 耳 朵

Pieces of flour dough are flattened into a thin disk the size of a penny, and pressed with the thumb to create small, curled pasta shaped like cat's ears. This noodle is very similar to the Italian *orecchiétte*, and has some resemblance to the Swabian *Spätzle* as well. Cat's Ears are cooked by boiling them in water, and then served either in soups, stir-fried, or covered with a sauce of assorted meats and vegetables.

Beef Noodle Soup
牛 肉 麵

This is by far the most popular style of noodle soup. The favorite type of beef soup is the numbing-hot Sichuan-style, which was actually popularized in Taiwan during the 1950s, and has eventually become the icon of Taiwan's legendary snacking culture. A non-spicy "red-cooked" beef soup features a savory beef stock with tender pieces of beef. Though by no means less flavorful, the non-spicy beef soup is generally overshadowed by the popularity of the fiery kind.

THE MONGOLIAN HOTPOT

"Cooking-it-yourself and huddling around the table with everyone bring a sense of warmth, communion, and kindred spirits among family and friends."

The Mongols under Kublai Khan conquered China in 1279, establishing the Yuan Dynasty (1279-1368). It was the first of two epochs in Chinese history when the country was ruled *entirely* by foreigners. The Yuan was a relatively short-lived dynasty; Mongol rule lasted only 70 years before they were driven back across the Gobi Desert. Today, few legacies remain from the Mongols' stay, but the Mongolian hotpot has endured the test of time. In a food-loving culture like the Chinese, it should come as no surprise that among the few remaining reminders of this bitter past is a food of the Mongols – the Mongolian hotpot. Today, the hotpot is so widespread in China that it is as much a part of the national identity as pandas, the Great Wall, and portraits of Chairman Mao.

During the Yuan Dynasty, the Mongols ruled China from Beijing. Consequently, much of their influences were left in northern China. The hotpot is considered a northern Chinese dish for this reason, even though every region in China has some claim to its own style of hotpot nowadays. In Beijing, the local hotpot features lamb meat cooked in a sour broth flavored with pickled Napa cabbage. In Sichuan, the hotpot resembles a roiling cauldron of chili oil, dotted with floating Sichuan peppercorns. In Taiwan, the people rage over the *yuanyangguo* – a combination hotpot with a slotted pot filled with a bland broth on one side and a numbing-hot Sichuan-style broth on the other. Even the Japanese have picked up the hotpot custom. Their hotpot, called *shabu shabu*, uses a light broth flavored with *kombu* kelp.

Hotpots are cook-it-yourself meals: meats, vegetables, and a large variety of ingredients are cooked in the hotpot's boiling broth. The pieces are plucked out of the hotpot with chopsticks, and dipped into an individually prepared sauce before eating. The hotpot can be enjoyed in restaurants as well as at home. It is often eaten for special family gatherings such as holidays and birthdays, but can also be eaten as an ordinary meal any day.

The allure of the hotpot is the fun and experience of it. Cooking-it-yourself and huddling around the table with everyone bring a sense of warmth, communion, and kindred spirits among family and friends. They also recall the hotpot's primitive origins – cooking communally around an open fire. Some people may be set back by sharing the same hotpot with others, but this is the main attraction of the hotpot meal. Otherwise, separate utensils can be provided for communal use, so that people would not need to use their own chopsticks in the hotpot.

The claims of the hotpot as a unifier of families and friends are genuine. Around Christmastime, New Year's, and Chinese New Year, Chinese supermarkets are filled with shoppers stocking up on meats, fish cakes, and hosts of hotpot supplies for what has become the traditional holiday meal for the Chinese. Not to be outdone, hotpot restaurants do brisk business during this time of the year, capturing the spirit of the season with bubbling broth, fogged glasses, and sounds of people's cheer.

The physical hotpot is itself a unique cooking vessel. Traditionally, it is a donut-shaped bowl set on a coal-burning chamber. A chimney in the center sets rising smoke above the faces of the diners, while the coals heat up the hotpot from below. However, people are less inclined to mess with the cumbersome coal-burning hotpot these days. More likely, today's hotpots use gas- or electric tabletop stoves with just an ordinary cooking pot set on top.

There is nothing complicated about a hotpot meal. Everything is cook-it-yourself, and the selection of ingredients is dependent entirely on the individual. Meats are sliced

NORTHERN

thinly, to around an eighth of an inch thickness. Just about any kind of meat can be used: lamb, beef, pork, chicken, and fish. Others such as tripe, liver, and kidney, as well as all kinds of seafood, offer additional possibilities. Vegetables include the hotpot requisite: chrysanthemum leaves, as well as Napa cabbage and an assortment of mushroom, white radish, taro, and wintermelon. Other things cover the gamut from cellophane noodles to fishcakes and meatballs.

When everything is put to the table, everyone gathers around to help themselves to the food and all the cooking. All the food should not be placed into the hotpot at the same time. Otherwise, the food would be boiled down to a sloppy mess by the end. The small, thinly sliced meats need only a few seconds of swishing in the hotpot before they are ready. Napa cabbage may need a few minutes. Everyone should time the cooking by dropping the food into the hotpot just before eating.

MONGOLIAN HOTPOT RESTAURANTS IN LOS ANGELES

Although the Chinese prefer eating hotpots in the warmth and intimacy of their own homes, they often find themselves intrigued by hotpots with a regional twist. As a result, eating hotpots in Los Angeles is never a dull experience, with restaurants offering regional-style hotpots featuring unusual flavors and flair that attracts constant crowds and entices them back for more.

The current "hot" hotpot is the *yuanyangguo,* a combination hotpot that the Taiwanese have popularized. Smaller restaurants serving regional cuisines also offer local-style hotpots in addition to the ordinary dishes prepared from their kitchens. Assuredly, these hotpots have strong regional flavors, commensurate with the types of dishes that they serve.

Kingswood Teppan Steak House

On one side of Kingswood is the kind of *teppanyaki* service that made Benihana a household name in America. On the other side, the tables are outfitted for the Taiwan-style yuanyangguo hotpot. Hotpot customers choose a variety of meats and vegetables from a menu card. Among the selections are customary cuts of beef, lamb, chicken and pork, as well as unusual hotpot ingredients such as pig's blood rice cakes, tempura fishcakes, goose intestines, and the ubiquitous youtiao. Kingswood is very popular with families, especially on weekends.

18900 E. Gale Ave., #B, Rowland Heights
(626) 912-1382

J.Z.Y. Cafe

This restaurant not only serves a good Beijing Duck, it also offers northern-style lamb hotpot. Northern-style hotpots are invariably flavored with pickled Napa cabbage, which gives the white broth a slight, vinegary flavor. Lamb is the customary meat for this type of hotpot, but beef can also be used as a substitute. Other items for this hotpot range widely, but the Chinese almost always order chrysanthemum leaves, pig's blood rice cakes, and tofu. J.Z.Y. Cafe is decorated in the style of a traditional Chinese inn, with small, lacquered tables and chairs – an ideal setting for two to four people to enjoy the intimacy of the hotpot experience.

1039 E. Valley Blvd., #102, San Gabriel
(626) 288-8588

NORTHERN

Cocary Bar B. Q. Restaurant

The attraction of this popular hotpot restaurant is its strange-looking hotpot vessel, which is a hybrid of a hotpot fused with a grilling hotplate. In the center is a deep cast iron pot in which a broth is used to boil foods. The flanged sides are flat panels on which food can be grilled, allowing people to cook their personal Mongolian barbecue. Everything is self-service; a well-stocked refrigerator is stacked with plates of meats, vegetables, eggs, and tempura fishcakes. The empty plates are tallied at the end to calculate the bill.

112 N. Garfield Ave., Monterey Park
(626) 573-0691

B.B.Q. King Buffet

The *Las Vegasification* of the Mongolian hotpot craze has turned what is normally a fun and intimate eating experience into a grotesque feeding frenzy. For $10, you get a boiling pot of broth, and unlimited dibs to the buffet bar laden with sliced meats, vegetables, and all the essential hotpot ingredients. What is missing in this all-you-can-eat madness is any semblance of regional characteristics that set one style of hotpot from another. But you can't beat the price, and it is a good introduction to the Chinese love for the hotpot.

140 W. Valley Blvd., #212, San Gabriel
(626) 289-2889

More restaurants are listed in Appendix XI.

A dipping sauce is essential to good hotpotting, and there are as many ways to make a dipping sauce as there are jambalaya recipes in New Orleans. Generally, the Chinese like their dipping sauce thick and strongly flavored. In the north, the vinegary Beijing-style hotpot calls for a sesame paste, flavored with nira flower paste, soy sauce and a piece of salty, fermented bean curd. The Sichuan hotpot is spicy enough already, so that it needs no additional sauce. Many people still like a light sesame paste-based sauce to tame down some of the numbing-hotness. In Taiwan, a barbecue-style sauce made from bonito fish flakes is popular.

Mongolian hotpots should not be confused with Mongolian barbecues. The latter is a buffet style free-for-all, in which people pile a maddening array of ingredients onto a plate: meat, vegetables, and seasonings altogether. Then they bring it to a communal flat grill for a quick stir-fry. Hotpots, on the other hand, are cooking by boiling food at the table, using the distinctive hotpot that gives the dish its name.

NORTHERN

Western China

China's most creative cuisine comes from the "Heavenly Kingdom" – as Sichuan (Szechwan) province is popularly known. Sichuan is an isolated province located in the blessed western part of China, surrounded by tall, misty mountains and swift-flowing rivers. Free from many of the warfare and famines that plagued the rest of China, Sichuan developed a mind of its own with just about everything it does. Its cuisine, supported by a fertile land that produces three rice crops a year, stands alone for a single characteristic – the *numbing-hot* flavor – a strange and strangely mystifying sensation that is unmatched by anything else in this world.

Sichuan cuisine is the dominant force in the cooking of western China, but a few distinctive dishes exist from Sichuan's neighbors. Yunnan province, located to the southwest of Sichuan, is known for a dish called *Across the Bridge Rice Noodles*, and a curious cooking vessel called the *airpot*. Guizhou, a backwards- and poor province to the southeast, is credited for gracing the world with Gongbao (Kungpao) Chicken, the codified mainstay of Chinese takeout restaurants. The rest of Guizhou's cuisine, unfortunately, is awash with mediocrity.

For a long time, restauranteurs and chefs in Los Angeles were afraid to offer authentic Sichuan cuisine, because they assumed Americans could not tolerate its spicy and strongly flavored dishes. However, the blazing popularity of Sichuan cuisine today has emboldened many new restaurants to insist on serving the real thing – fiery red and deeply aromatic dishes that recall both the snacking culture of Chengdu and the urban refinements of Chongqing.

SICHUAN CUISINE

"Chefs were inspired to invent imaginative dishes that are far more complex and flavorful than any other regional cuisine of China."

If a friend ever invites you to a dinner of "Strange-flavor Chicken," "Fish-flavor Eggplant," and "Ants Up a Tree," perhaps the immediate reaction is to find new friends. But relax, these are some of the best dishes in Sichuan cuisine, which, aside from the weird names, are some of the most unique in the world.

Fiery, flamboyant, and fragrant, the dishes of Sichuan are not for the timid palates. They exude an addictive mystique about them that, once hooked, lures people back for more. Making ingenious use of ingredients, coupled with creative cooking skills, Sichuan cuisine is easily the most imaginative and flavorful cuisine in China. Deservedly, it is China's most popular cuisine, and it enjoys good recognition around the world as well. Dishes like Gongbao (Kungpao) Chicken, Twice-cooked Pork, and Hot-and-Sour Soup are now household names in America, and chefs throughout the world have copied their recipes over and over again.

Sichuan, which means "Four Rivers," is a province surrounded by mountains on all sides. Most of the 110 million inhabitants live in the large and fertile Chengdu Plains, fed by rivers and streams that flow down from the Tibetan Plateau from west to east. The namesake four rivers that cross the Chengdu Plains empty into the Yangtze, which passes through the southern part of the province, and zigzags through impassable gorges swept constantly by dangerous whitewater currents.

Such a rugged geography has kept Sichuan isolated from the rest of China, and which has repeatedly worked to Sichuan's favor. Invading armies were kept away to pursue easier targets elsewhere, sparing Sichuan from warfare that ravaged other parts of China. Even in times of turmoil, Sichuan was always the last place to fall. During the War with Japan (1931-45), the Chinese capital retreated several times before finally settling in Chongqing. Then, despite repeated and savage bombings by the Japanese, Chongqing never submitted. A few years later, during the Chinese Civil War, Chengdu remained the last bastion of Kuomintang resistance before Mao Zedong's Communists finally completed the "Liberation."

Sichuan is also graced with many natural wonders within its borders. Aside from being the only natural habitat of pandas, Sichuan is well known for its congenial climate. In good years, it can produce three rice crops. Sichuan is commonly called "Heavenly Kingdom," because its blessed environments have earned the envy from the rest of China. The province's two major cities: Chengdu ("Successful Metropolis") and Chongqing ("Re-Celebration") are names that give further testament to the province's legend of wealth and prosperity.

Shielded from the turmoil that constantly dogged the rest of China, the Sichuan people found their

security translated into a perpetual love for food. Chefs were inspired to invent imaginative dishes that are far more complex and flavorful than any other regional cuisine of China. Although the food is mainly peasant fare, the cuisine evolved from a lifestyle that only prolonged periods of peace and prosperity could afford.

The full range of Sichuan condiments and spices are bewildering to contemplate. The most well known among them include: star anise, fermented chili-bean paste, preserved mustard greens, chili powder, pickled chili, lily buds, black tree fungus, black vinegar, and Sichuan peppercorns. From them, Sichuan chefs created an array of unique flavors unheard of elsewhere: "Strange-flavor Chicken" uses five different spices, a "lychee-flavor" dish uses no lychees at all, and "Fish-flavor Eggplant" is purely vegetarian.

Comparing Sichuan cuisine with other regional styles of China, Guangdong cuisine is its polar opposite. Sichuan, a landlocked province, has access to limited quantities of seafood, so its cuisine is completely devoid of it. Meanwhile, Guangdong sits on some of the most fertile fishing waters in the world, so its cuisine makes full use of all kinds of seafood. Also, Sichuan cooking loves to construct complex flavors from the ingredients, while Guangdong cooking is very simple, and dominated by natural flavors.

WESTERN

Although it is unimportant to debate whether one cuisine is better than the other, the comparison between Sichuan and Guangdong cuisines reveals interesting contrasts between these two distinct and great cooking traditions.

With such a wide variety of spicy dishes, Sichuan chefs turned the use of chili peppers into an artistic skill. Chili peppers are used dried, whole, ground, crushed, fried, pickled, fermented, and even roasted. Curiously however, they are rarely used fresh. This is the main difference between Sichuan- and Hunan cuisine, which also has a reputation of being hot and spicy. Hunan cuisine uses fresh chili peppers like vegetables, and exhibits similarities with Guangdong cuisine in that the natural characters of the chili are preferred. On the other hand, in Sichuan cuisine the chili pepper is considered a condiment, so its role is to provide added dimensions in the construction of complex flavors.

The flavors constructed from chili peppers can be so varied that the Sichuan people have different ways of describing their hotness. A "dry-hot" dish is made by stir-frying dried chili or chili powder, while a "wet-hot" dish uses fermented chili paste. "Sour-hot" is a classic flavor popular throughout the world, and in Sichuan, it comes from blending rice vinegar with ground white pepper. Finally, a "numbing-hot" dish combines chili

peppers with the legendary Sichuan peppercorns, which meld to achieve an almost indescribable sensation in the mouth.

PEPPERCORNS ÜBER ALLES

The Sichuan peppercorn is, in essence, central to Sichuan cuisine's uniqueness. If there is one ingredient that separates Sichuan cuisine from all of the rest, it is not the chili pepper but the Sichuan peppercorn. Sichuan peppercorns resemble ordinary black peppercorns in size and appearance, but taste nothing like them. Sichuan peppercorns are not peppercorns actually, but are the fruit berries of a prickly ash tree (*pimpinella anisum*), which grows in the temperate mountain climates of China, Japan and North America. While the Chinese and Japanese varieties are edible, only the Sichuan ones impart a peculiarly numbing sensation akin to receiving a minor electric shock in the mouth.

When Sichuan peppercorns are combined with chili peppers, the chili pepper's hotness not only tastes hotter, it leaps with a dry, numbing sensation that lingers in the mouth. The Chinese call this flavor "numbing-hot," and go crazy for it. Numbing-hot flavor is distinctive to Sichuan cuisine – not easy to duplicate outside Sichuan because Sichuan peppercorns cannot grow anywhere else. This strange and alluring flavor is a sole Sichuan propriety, and whoever that wants to accurately emulate the numbing-hot flavor must import these peppercorns from Sichuan.

Unfortunately, the FDA bans fresh Sichuan peppercorns from being imported to the U.S., because they are believed to carry a tree blight that attacks citrus trees (but not harmful to humans). Only pre-roasted Sichuan peppercorns are allowed, but they often lose their full numbing punch soon after roasting. This has not stopped the Chinese from giving up on their love for the numbing-hot dishes, however. Somehow, stashes of genuine Sichuan peppercorns always find their way into the kitchens of authentic Sichuan restaurants in Los Angeles.

DIVISIONS OF SICHUAN CUISINE

There are two primary divisions of Sichuan cuisine. They revolve around Sichuan's two major cities – Chengdu and Chongqing.

Chengdu, the provincial capital, is known for its teahouses and street-snack culture. The teahouses are one of the most colorful institutions dedicated to tea drinking, but they actually have no contribution to the development of Chengdu's culinary heritage. Snacks, on the other hand, dominate the city's food culture. Throughout the city, snack vendors line the streets and alleys, serving bite-sized snacks on the go. Many vendors invented their own snack

dishes – noodles, pastries, and small meat dishes – of which many became quite famous and are now served in restaurants.

Chongqing, a major industrial city on the Yangtze, has for centuries attracted migrants from the surrounding countryside. Chongqing's cuisine reflects the peasant heritage of those migrants, with some added big-city refinements. Some also say that Chongqing's flavors are hotter than Chengdu's dishes.

TYPICAL SICHUAN DISHES

Many dishes in Sichuan cuisine have strange-sounding names, equaling the unique flavors of the region. Some dishes are also fabled legends – their stories preserved in the annals of Chinese culinary history. Moreover, Sichuan cuisine's flavors are challenging more Americans to venture into the hot and spicy world of its cooking. All it takes to begin the adventure are a little curiosity, some courage, and lots of ice water.

Gongbao (Kungpao) Chicken
宫保鸡丁
Some people dispute that this fiery dish actually originated in neighboring Guizhou province, but claimants of Gongbao Chicken under Sichuan jurisdiction maintain that it has all of the essential characteristics as a Sichuan dish. This lychee-flavored dish relies upon *Zhenjiang* black vinegar as the pivotal ingredient, a

WESTERN

dash of which creates a tart, fruity dimension that reminds one of eating a fresh lychee fruit. Gongbao Chicken consists only of diced chicken, peanuts, and slivers of dried chili. Green peppers are sometimes added, but the crunchiness of the roasted peanuts is absolutely essential for the authenticity of this dish. Gongbao Chicken's recipe is copied all over the world, and in America, Guangdong immigrants have altered it into "Kungpao Chicken," using anything from plum sauce to pineapples.

Pockmark-face Lady's Tofu
麻婆豆腐

The story of the pockmark-face lady is now a culinary legend. During the War with Japan, a tofu-making lady in Chengdu, with her face marred with acne scars, sold this tofu dish from a ramshackle street stand. Chengduers were immediately drawn to its aromas and flavors, enhanced in part by the fried ground beef simmering in the wet-hot chili sauce. People talked about this dish all over town, referring to it by recalling the image of the poor-complexioned lady. The original tofu stand still exists in Chengdu – it

is now modernized, state-owned, and converted into a full-size restaurant. The pockmark-face lady's recipe is also copied all over world. This dish can be found in homes as well as in restaurants, with variations that even follow the Islamic and vegetarian dietary rules.

Husband-and-Wife Beef Slices
夫妻肺片

This is another snack invention that emerged from Chengdu's streets, and has now attained world fame. A young Chengdu couple originally made this dish out of table scraps: intestines, kidneys, and beef tongues – cooked in a brine, allowed to cool, and then sliced and served with crushed peanuts and a fiery, numbing-hot chili sauce. The couple called this dish "*fuqi feipian*." *Fuqi* means husband-and-wife, while *feipian* originally meant "table scraps." However, the idea of "table scraps" turned off many people, so *feipian* was euphemistically altered to mean "liver slices," which has an identical pronunciation. Today's "*feipian*" contains neither table scraps nor liver slices. Restaurants now make it with beef brisket and tripe, which fortuitously provide an interesting contrast in colors and textures. The red beef brisket matches with the white color of tripe, and the brisket's tenderness is balanced by the tripe's chewiness – symbolizing the yin-and-yang of opposites, and complementing the name of "husband-and-wife" with the meaning of a perfect union.

Wonton in Red Oil
紅油抄手

Wonton is a popular snack throughout China, but only in Sichuan are they daring enough to drape wontons in a red-hot chili sauce. Unlike the custom of serving wontons in a soup, Sichuan-style wontons are eaten like meat dumplings, dipped in a distinctively wet-hot chili sauce without soup. The sauce itself is flavored with chili oil, soy sauce and peanut powder.

Water-boiled Beef
水煮牛肉

A most understated dish on the Sichuan menu, the name "water-boiled" suggests nothing of the fiery cauldron that it actually is. Slices of beef are simmered in a red broth, seasoned with chili peppers, fermented chili-bean paste, soy sauce, and Sichuan peppercorns. The taste is numbing-hot, which not only clears sinuses but probably kills some bacteria as well. Upon serving, the rich beef stew is ladled over fresh lettuce or blanched Napa cabbage. The water-boiling technique is also flexible for use on other meats, such as liver, tripe, and fish. Water-boiled Beef is a good representative dish of Sichuan cuisine, displaying many of its unique and distinguishing attributes: numbing-hot, complex flavors, and the opulence of wholesome peasant cooking.

Dan-Dan Noodles
擔擔麵

This is the quintessential street vendor snack from Chengdu. It is a hot, meatless cold noodle dish, sold by vendors who walk around the city carrying an over-the-shoulder balance called the "*dan.*" If you want a bowl of noodles, just flag a vendor down, who proceeds to fill a bowl heaping with cold noodles, then pour a sesame sauce on top of it. The noodles are garnished with chopped preserved mustard green hearts, chili oil, and peanut powder. "Dan-Dan" is an affectionate term simply meaning, "noodles served from the dan."

Ants Up a Tree
螞蟻上樹

Although the curious name suggests something exotic, this dish is no more than heaps of cellophane bean noodles stir-fried with ground pork. Ants Up a Tree is also rather bland – a slim minority in an otherwise fiery lineup of Sichuan specialties. Some people claim that this is actually a Hunan dish, although there is no concrete evidence suggesting that this is true.

Fish-flavor Eggplant
魚香茄子

Although the name suggests that this dish has something to do with fish, there is no fish in Fish-flavor Eggplant. This is actually a vegetarian dish, one of the most creative and flavorful ways to prepare vegetables. The so-called fish-flavor is suggestive of the way Sichuan people prepare fish dishes – by making a reddish sauce simmered in garlic, scallions and chili, and flavored with sugar and vinegar.

Strange-flavor Chicken
怪味雞

The "strange" flavor comes from a seemingly haphazard combination of five conflicting flavors: sweet, hot, sour, numbing, and saltiness. The result is another hallmark of Sichuan culinary skills. Flavors are complex and unique, yet the dish is simple and understated. Cold pieces of boiled chicken are topped with this sauce, allowing the flavors to soak through. It is excellent as an appetizer, or as an in-between-meals snack that goes especially well with beer.

Bang Bang Chicken
棒棒雞

Commonly known as "Bon Bon Chicken" in the U.S., this cold cuts dish is prepared in the same manner as Strange-flavor Chicken above. The difference is in the sauce, which in this case is a slightly numbing-hot mixture based on sesame paste and rice vinegar. A pile of julienne fresh cucumbers make the usual garnish, giving the dish a semblance of a refreshing cucumber salad.

Hot-and-sour Soup
酸辣湯

Like Gongbao Chicken, Hot-and sour Soup is a household name that has now many variations found in America's Chinese takeout restaurants. The hotness comes from ground white pepper, not chili peppers, and the sour comes from black rice vinegar as dark as soy sauce. Ingredients in Hot-and-sour soup vary, and can include bamboo shoots, black tree fungus, mushrooms, lily buds, steamed pig's blood, and tofu.

Twice-cooked Pork
回鍋肉

This is an interesting Sichuan dish in that it uses sweet bean paste – a northern Chinese condiment. Slices of pork belly meat are first boiled in water, and then fried. The frying part is crucial, because it creates a slight crispness in the fat, while keeping the rest of the meat tender. Fermented chili-bean paste provides a wet-hot flavor to the dish, and the sweet bean

SICHUAN-STYLE RESTAURANTS
IN LOS ANGELES

Authentic Sichuan restaurants were rare in Los Angeles until the mid-1990s. Before that, the only one was Fu-Shin Restaurant. There were, however, many "Szechwan" restaurants in town, but they were merely takeout restaurants opened by Guangdong immigrants. The food they served was not necessarily bad, they were just not the kind of food adventure that Sichuan cooking actually is.

A large influx of Chinese immigrants settling in Los Angeles during the 1990s persuaded many chefs to begin serving authentic Sichuan cuisine. Previously, chefs were afraid that Americans could not tolerate Sichuan's legendarily hot dishes, but people's palates proved to be more resilient than they assumed. Dishes like "*Fuqi feipian*" (or just "feipian"), "Water-boiled Beef," "Pockmark-face Lady's Tofu," and "Won Ton in Red Oil" have taken the trailblazing path to stardom, shattering the "Szechwan" restaurant stereotypes of yesteryear.

Oriental Pearl Restaurant

A recent entrant to the competitive Sichuan cuisine food scene in the San Gabriel Valley, Oriental Pearl has already made its mark. For starters, it serves some exemplary examples of authentic Sichuan cooking. Mr. Chen, a Chongqing-trained chef, offers a wide variety of Chongqing-style dishes, including Water-boiled Fish and Chongqing-style hotpots. The modest menu also features many of Chengdu's street-snack dishes, such as Fuqi feipian and Won Ton in Red Oil. A buffet table of cold cuts and appetizers is very popular with the patrons.

621 W. Main St., Alhambra
(626) 281-1898

Szechwan Express

A hole-in-the-wall in a strip mall, this restaurant first started in 1994 by an immigrant family from Chongqing. The ambience here is Spartan – just a few formica tables under florescent lights – but it is the right surroundings for hearty, wholesome country cuisine that defines the true character of Sichuan cooking. In the winter, the steam from the Sichuan-style hotpots fogs up the shop window from ground to ceiling. Pitchers of ice water always stand at the ready nearby, just in case.

732 S. Atlantic Blvd., Monterey Park
(626) 282-8108

WESTERN

Chung King Restaurant

Although it appears to be another hole-in-the-wall, this modest restaurant is owned by a Sichuan chef whose career started Chongqing's 4-star Traffic Hotel. The chef painstakingly designed his dishes by categorizing them into various categories: water-boiled dishes, pickled-chili dishes, et cetera. House specials include Water-boiled fish, which uses the traditional water-boiling method for a Southern Californian ingredient like Pacific snapper. Pickled pepper dishes are especially interesting, stir-fried with anything from frog legs, to eels and squid.

206 S. Garfield Ave., Monterey Park
(626) 280-7430

Fu-Shin Restaurant

By now a San Gabriel Valley institution, Fu-Shin has been around since 1980, when it started in a former IHOP in Alhambra. Refusing to give in to squeamish palates, Fu-Shin was the lone inferno in a flatscape of Guangdong cuisine and Chinese takeouts. More than 20 years later, Fu-Shin has gone upscale – having moved to Pasadena and now offering a menu of more new creations. It triumphs in adapting traditional Sichuan cooking styles to Pacific Ocean seafood, which works surprising wonders on things like rock cod, sea cucumbers, and geoduck clams. Fu-shin also refined many Sichuan favorites, such as *fuqi feipian*, with a slightly sweeter and milder flavors. The food here is as close to *haute cuisine* as Sichuan cuisine ever gets, which also means that Fu-Shin has strayed irreversibly away from the authentic Sichuan dining experience.

2960 E. Colorado Blvd., Pasadena
(626) 792-8898

More restaurants are listed in Appendix XII.

paste adds an unusual – and sweet – dimension to this spicy dish.

Camphor-Tea Smoked Duck
樟茶鴨

The Sichuan answer to the Beijing Duck is not quite as spectacular as its northern cousin. Camphor-Tea Smoked Duck obtains its rich flavors from the marinade made by combining star anise, black tea, and orange peels. All of the flavors are fused into the duck through the smoking process – using more black tealeaves and camphor wood as the smoking base. The finished duck has the crispy skin and tender meat contrast similar to Beijing Duck. In Sichuan banquets, Camphor-Tea Smoked Duck is almost universally served. True to the nature of Chinese-style banquet dishes, this duck is not spicy at all.

Sichuan Hotpot
麻辣鍋

Sichuan has its own style of the Mongolian hotpot, which the people call *malaguo*, or "numbing-hot hotpot." The main attraction of this hotpot is the soup stock, which is covered with a layer of red chili oil. Beneath the oil is a broth containing star anise, chili peppers, and Sichuan peppercorns. When it starts boiling, the hotpot resembles a cauldron that makes Harry Potter proud. The meats and vegetables used in the Sichuan hotpot are very much the same types of meats and vegetables used in other hotpots. Everything seems to go well with this hot and spicy style of cooking broth.

WESTERN

YUNNAN CUISINE

"The cooking styles of Yunnan cuisine are dominated by Sichuan province, Yunnan's next-door neighbor."

Yunnan cuisine comes from a very humble pedigree. The distant province is located in China's southern fringe, long dismissed as a scenic but impoverished backwater. Its food is unpretentious and uncomplicated, with rice being the main staple. The diet of ordinary Yunnan people rarely features meat, since poverty makes eating meat an impractical luxury. Meat is enjoyed only a few times a year, and when they do eat meat, Yunnan people generally eat chicken or pork. Cattle, a vital beast of burden, are rarely slaughtered for meat.

The cooking styles of Yunnan cuisine are dominated by Sichuan province – Yunnan's next-door neighbor. Typical Yunnan dishes are mostly local versions of Sichuan favorites such as Pockmark-face Lady's Tofu, Water-Boiled Beef, and Twice-cooked Pork. However, the flavors of Yunnan's dishes lack the pizzazz that makes Sichuan cuisine so famous, mainly because of the absence of Sichuan peppercorns. The spiciness of Yunnan dishes is more straightforward, relying primarily on chili peppers. They also tend to be very salty, which allow people to eat more rice with sparing amounts of meats and vegetables. In times of famine, people were known to eat only plain rice daubed with salt for flavor.

Despite Yunnan cuisine's lackluster appeal, there are two redeeming dishes that are justifiably famous to make a visit to a Yunnan-style restaurant worthwhile. One is "Across the Bridge Rice Noodles," which is a noodle soup dish similar to the Vietnamese *Pho*. The other is "Chicken in a Clay Airpot," which features a unique cooking vessel that is specific to Yunnan province. These two dishes together constitute Yunnan's contribution to the kaleidoscope of famous regional dishes, and many people instantly identify them with Yunnan. Ironically, both are neither spicy nor salty, which may explain why they have a wider appeal than do other Yunnan dishes.

"Across the Bridge Rice Noodles"
過橋麵線

The Yunnan people eat a type of thin rice noodles similar in appearance to the Vietnamese *Pho*, and they are served in a similar manner. "Across the Bridge Rice Noodles" consists of separate platters of meats and rice noodles, along with a bowl of plain chicken broth all brought to the table for assembly. The waitress deftly slides the meats – thin slices of raw chicken and pork – into the hot broth. Then, the rice noodles are added to the soup, and completed with cilantro, bean sprouts, and pea sprouts on top. The scalding broth quickly cooks the thinly sliced meats, and the fresh scents of the vegetables round out a balanced, refreshing meal.

Legend has it that "Across the Bridge Rice Noodles" was invented by the wife of a Qing Dynasty official. As a student studying for the civil service examinations, the Yunnan native retreated into the forests outside Kunming, the provincial capital, where he could get away from the city's distractions. There, his wife brought him lunch every day, walking a distance that included crossing a bridge that spanned over a river. The food was always cold by the time she got there, but one day the wife found

that the rice noodles and chicken soup she brought surprisingly stayed hot. A layer of chicken fat on top of the soup had kept the soup hot. Thus, this noodle soup became the meal she brought him every day, until he passed his examinations. As gratitude to his wife, the official named the dish after the bridge she crossed every day, which stood as an everlasting symbol of her dedication and love.

Chicken in a Clay Airpot
氣鍋雞

The airpot is a cooking vessel that people often associate with Yunnan cuisine. It looks like a Mongolian hotpot, except that the airpot is made of clay, and has a short chimney that distributes steam inside the pot. When the airpot is immersed in boiling water, steam rising from the chimney is trapped under the lid, cooking the food inside. The airpot can be either small – serving personal-sized portions, or larger serving four to six people. It is ideal for casserole types of dishes where foods are slowly simmered for hours. It is also used frequently to prepare traditional Chinese medicine.

WESTERN

As for the "Chicken in a Clay Airpot" dish, a whole chicken or Cornish hen is simmered in the airport with a broth of herbs, mushrooms, bamboo shoots, and even Chinese medicine. Depending on the types of herbs used, this specialty chicken soup can be eaten to treat a variety of illnesses. Otherwise, "Chicken in a Clay Airpot" is simply a hearty, satisfying dish, warming the soul on wintry days when Pacific storms scour southern California with a moist chill in the air.

WESTERN

YUNNAN-STYLE RESTAURANTS IN LOS ANGELES

Despite Yunnan cuisine's lackluster reputation, Los Angeles's two Yunnan-style restaurants are popular for their "Across the Bridge Rice Noodles" and "Chicken in a Clay Airpot." The rest of the menus show just how dominating Sichuan cuisine is in Yunnan cuisine. Also popular in Yunnan-style restaurants is the buffet-style appetizer table – a typical fixture in western Chinese restaurants – that includes a variety of spicy snack dishes such as fuqi feipian, cold marinated cellophane noodles, and red hot beef jerky. Just point to each item that you want, and the server will heap a plateful of them for you to take back to the table. These heavily spiced dishes are good simply with plain rice.

Hua's Garden

This restaurant's straightforward menu of Sichuan dishes has attracted a large and mainly mainlander following. The star dishes at Hua's Garden are, predictably, "Across the Bridge Noodles" and "Chicken in the Clay Airpot." Besides the Sichuan dishes, there are several obscure Yunnan favorites such as a hot beef jerky (called "Yunnan-style Dried Beef") and spicy squares of salted freshwater fish.

301 N. Garfield Ave., #D, Monterey Park
(626) 571-8387

Hua's Chinese Delicacies

Although the name is similar to Hua's Garden above, these two Yunnan restaurants do not share the same owner. Hua's Chinese Delicacies is a smaller shop, set in upscale Arcadia that serves down-home Yunnan and Sichuan cooking to the local western Chinese appetite. The menu is similar to Hua's Garden: "Across the Bridge Rice Noodles" and "Chicken in the Clay Airpot" receive top billing; the customary buffet-style appetizer table always draws a crowd as well.

921 S. Baldwin Ave., Arcadia
(626) 445-2755

WESTERN

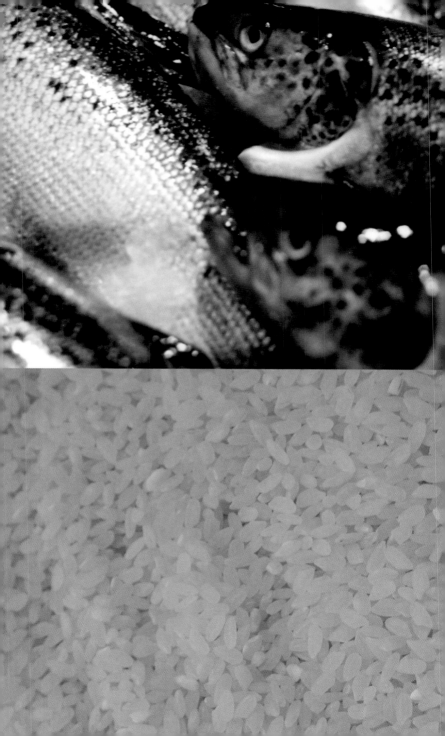

EASTERN CHINA

Eastern – or *"Jiangzhe"* cuisine was for centuries the most sophisticated cuisine in China, but it stagnated under communism over the past 50 years, like all other cultural traditions on mainland China. However, the region's economy is now making a tremendous comeback, bringing renewed vitality to the Lower Yangtze area of eastern China. Likewise, Jiangzhe cuisine is steadily regaining popularity both in China and abroad, eagerly reinventing itself in a bid to become once again the *haute cuisine* of China.

Throughout history, many of China's most famous dishes are from Jiangzhe cuisine. Centuries of prosperity helped make eastern China the most sophisticated region in China. A variation of Jiangzhe cuisine is the cooking style of Shanghai – the most cosmopolitan city on the mainland. Using foreign influences and exotic ingredients, Shanghai cuisine evolved into something that is distinctively its own.

Jiangzhe cuisine also extends to include the cookings of Anhui and Hubei provinces, although both are largely nondescript and unimportant to the primary characteristics of the region's cuisine.

In the last decade, Jiangzhe- and Shanghai-style restaurants have grown profusely in Los Angeles. Although their numbers are still nowhere near the omnipresence of Guangdong-style restaurants, eastern Chinese cuisine can now be found throughout the San Gabriel Valley. The flavors of eastern China are gradually changing the American stereotype for Chinese food. What is once considered the domain of Sweet-and-sour Pork and Kungpao Chicken, the image of Chinese food will soon likely include the likes of *Dongbo* Pork, "Lion's Head," and Wuxi Spareribs.

JIANGZHE CUISINE

" ... the Jiangzhe region was highly educated and literate in comparison with the rest of China, imbuing everything it does with a touch of arrogance and swagger."

The junction where the Yangtze River and the Grand Canal meet has been for centuries the cultural and economic center of China. This crossing of China's east-west and north-south axes linked farmlands with markets, and the government with the people. Historically, this area in eastern China has also been the most prosperous and sophisticated region in China, inspiring a mixture of artists, merchants, peasants and poets to migrate to its environs. The region is dominated by the provinces of Jiangsu and Zhejiang, as well as Shanghai, a self-administered city. Also included are Anhui and Hubei – landlocked and less-prosperous provinces further up the Yangtze.

The Chinese refer to eastern China as "*Jiangzhe*," derived from the contraction of the <u>Jiang</u>su and <u>Zhe</u>jiang names. Many of China's greatest and most historic cities are located in these two provinces:

Hangzhou, Nanjing, Shanghai, Suzhou, Wuxi, and Yangzhou. Some 185 million people live in the region – approximately 16 percent of China's total population while occupying less than 5 percent of the total land area, making it one of the most densely populated regions in the world.

"LAND OF FISH AND RICE"

The waters of Jiangzhe supply the region with ample ingredients for its spectacular cuisine. The Yangtze, the longest river in China and third in the world, run its 3,915-mile (6,300 kilometers) course from Qinghai to just north of Shanghai. Before emptying into the East China Sea, the Yangtze's rapid whitewaters in the upper stretches are slowed to a sweeping, meandering crawl. Fertile soils are deposited along Jiangzhe's banks, covering the lowlands with verdant farmlands that produce an abundance of rice and vegetables.

Mottled and striped in Jiangzhe's landscape are also countless numbers of lakes, streams and canals. They give support to large varieties of fish. More freshwater fish are featured in Jiangzhe cuisine than in any other regional cuisine of China, and the abundance of seafood along the seacoast adds to the diversity of Jiangzhe's dishes. Through the ages, the bounties of Jiangzhe are the envy of the rest of China, and its nickname as the "Land of Fish and Rice" is aptly attributed.

Jiangzhe cuisine was, for centuries, the most refined and sophisticated in China. The wealth of the region's urban centers allowed Jiangzhe cuisine access to a host of fine- and exotic ingredients. Moreover, the Jiangzhe region was highly educated and literate in comparison with the rest of China, imbuing everything it does with a touch of arrogance and swagger. Up until the middle of the 20th century, Jiangzhe cuisine was considered China's *haute cuisine*, and even today, Jiangzhe's lavish banquet cuisine is still the standard for China's banqueting culture.

A striking reputation of traditional Jiangzhe cuisine is its tendency to be sweet and oily. Sweetness is not a common characteristic in Chinese cuisines, because the use of sugar was unaffordable for most people mired in poverty. But more importantly, it is the oiliness that really sets Jiangzhe cuisine apart. Fats and oils were considered as precious commodities, and oily dishes were symbols of opulence. The more fat one ate was indicative of their wealth and success, so Jiangzhe cooking took full advantage of the region's prosperity by using more of the best- and fattiest cuts, such as pork bellies and rumps.

In today's more health-conscious world, oiliness is a major turnoff for many. Unfortunately for Jiangzhe cuisine, which only recently began its long-awaited renaissance, it has yet to pick up on this trend toward lighter dishes.

Prosperity in the Jiangzhe region entered terminal decline in the latter part of the Qing Dynasty (1644-1911), and social order was plunged into complete chaos when Japan

EASTERN

occupied Nanjing (Nanking) in 1938. Doctrinaire communist rule after 1949 did not improve things in China, and Jiangzhe cuisine suffered equally as did the rest of the region. The communists branded dining out as a *bourgeois* excess, and restaurant owners were demonized as "running dogs of capitalist roaders." Jiangzhe cuisine's reputation as the leading cuisine of China was soon eclipsed by a newly emerging cuisine from Hongkong, which, as a free city, thrived with its newfound wealth and an abundance of seafood.

Interestingly, while Jiangzhe cuisine decayed on the mainland under communist rule, its traditions were preserved in Taiwan, where the cooking style still flourishes with tremendous popularity today. Along with the estimated 2 million refugees that fled to Taiwan, many chefs set up a surrogate homeland for Jiangzhe cuisine in Taipei. It proved to be the cuisine's saving grace. Using Taiwanese ingredients, but keeping traditionalist attitudes, Jiangzhe cuisine developed new, considerably fresher and healthier characteristics – using less oil and sugar in cooking. In Taipei today, Jiangzhe cuisine is the de facto cuisine for banquets, and the style is far more popular than Guangdong- and Hongkong-style seafood cuisines.

SPECIALTIES FROM INDIVIDUAL JIANGZHE CITIES

The densely populated areas surrounding the Yangtze River and the Grand Canal are home to many of China's greatest cities. Many of these cities claim to have their own cuisines, but it is probably more accurate to describe them as distinctive local specialties that adhere to most of Jiangzhe's fundamental characteristics. Only Shanghai has a cuisine that is so varied from the traditional Jiangzhe style that it can be considered as a separate cuisine.

Hangzhou

Marco Polo proclaimed Hangzhou as the greatest city in the world when he visited in 1300, and the city enjoyed this prominence – at least as China's greatest city – until the early 19th century. Although it is now overshadowed by nearby Shanghai, Hangzhou is still an important cultural center today; it is also considered as one of China's most beautiful cities. Hangzhou's cuisine still represents the entire Jiangzhe region, and is most famous for two dishes: "Dongbo Pork" and "Westlake Fish in Vinegar."

Suzhou

Suzhou is considered along with Hangzhou as the most beautiful city in China. It is otherwise famous for its silk industry, embroidery-making, and a splendid literary history. Suzhou also has a well-known cuisine that defines China's banqueting culture. The banquet dishes are notable for their showmanship and extravagance. Knife work is especially intricate, introducing a level of artistry into food preparation and presentation rarely seen in other parts of China.

Wuxi

The city is renowned for its "Boat Cuisine," which originated from the nearby Lake Taihu. In the old

days, families hired boats to visit their ancestral graves located on some of the 90 islands dotting Lake Taihu. Boat cuisine recalls the lavish banquets that were prepared for the families on these boats, and today they resemble a dinner cruise featuring Jiangzhe's favorite dishes, enjoyed while contemplating Lake Taihu's beautiful scenery at sunset. Additionally, both Wuxi and Suzhou, which is also located on Lake Taihu, share a similar culinary heritage.

Ningbo

A port city on the East China Sea, Ningbo's cuisine has a local flavor that is still rural in character. Its dishes are mostly plain and unembellished, relying on salt as the main flavoring ingredient. The characterization is largely unflattering, and the Chinese do not spare with their heaping criticisms on Ningbo cooking; it is often derided as grossly egalitarian – equally bad for both the rich and poor.

Yangzhou

A historic trade center on the Grand Canal – and near the border with Anhui province – Yangzhou is a laid-back city with a cuisine most famous for its fried rice. This fried rice is claimed by local boosters to be *the* fried-rice of all of China. Yangzhou is also known for another specialty, a giant meatball called "Lion's Head," which is usually served in a slowly simmered stew.

EASTERN

Nanjing

"South Capital" is most notable for its sizeable *Hui* population dating back to the Arab Muslim traders that first arrived around 750 A.D. Nanjing's most famous dish, *banya*, is a wind-dried duck preserved in salt. This is a dish with Islamic origins, borne out of a dietary tradition that forbids the consumption of pork.

Shanghai

China's brashest city was just a small fishing village at the turn of the 19th century, but its fate was forever changed when the Western Powers forced China to open its doors for trade. Within a century, Shanghai was teeming with foreigners and Chinese migrants, and its cuisine reflected the cosmopolitan atmosphere that existed in Shanghai up to 1949. Eventually, Shanghai cuisine evolved to encompass enough outside influences that it came to be considered a separate cuisine. (See chapter on Shanghai Cuisine.)

COMMON INGREDIENTS IN JIANGZHE CUISINE

The "Land of Fish and Rice" produces a large variety of regional ingredients that contribute to the fascinating kaleidoscope of Jiangzhe's colors and flavors. Unfortunately, much of them are still unknown in America, separated by gaps in culture and geography. However, judging by a renewed spirit to bring Jiangzhe cuisine in step with the 21st century, Americans will soon be discovering this spectacular cooking tradition in exciting and surprising ways.

Hairy Crab
毛蟹

A renowned Jiangzhe ingredient is a river-dwelling crab with hairy claws, found only along the shores of the Yangtze and its tributaries. Although these crabs are harvested between October and May, the best crabs are eaten only during the October and November mating season. During this time, the female crabs have golden roes that are sublimely flavorful, and the male crabs are prized for their unusually sweet meat, which is so soft and delicate that it veritably melts in the mouth.

Jinhua Ham
金华火腿

Ham-making skills for this "*prociutto* of China" carry a 900-year history, with the origins dating back to the Southern Song Dynasty (1126-1279). Jinhua ham is often too salty to be eaten plain. Instead, it is used in a variety of dishes such as: honey glazed ham, which is sliced and eaten like a finger sandwich between two pieces of toast; or red-cooked ham in a honey and lotus seed sauce.

Sea Cucumbers
海参

Jiangzhe's entire array of seafood dishes is justifiably famous, and the sea cucumber is often considered a regional specialty. Having a similar texture as beef tendons, sea cucumbers have been praised as a luxurious delicacy. However, they are much maligned in America for their unseemly appearance. A well-known Jiangzhe sea cucumber dish is red-cooked in a sweet bean sauce with shrimp roe. Another perennial favorite is sea cucumber braised with the classic combination of black mushroom and bamboo shoots.

Eels
鱔鱺

Jiangzhe cuisine also features a large number of eel dishes. Eels grow in abundance in the tranquil lakes and streams along the Yangtze. Eels can be stir-fried, put into a noodle soup, smoked as an appetizer, red-cooked with Jinhua ham, or fried into crispy fritters, et cetera.

APPETIZERS IN JIANGZHE CUISINE

A typical Jiangzhe meal always starts with an appetizer – another symbol of luxury skimped in other regions. There are many appetizer dishes in Jiangzhe cuisine; the most notable ones are often featured as the opening dish in Chinese-style banquets as well.

Drunken Chicken
醉雞

Boiled chicken is chilled, then soaked in a briny sauce made from rice wine and salt. Some restaurants use a special yellow rice wine called Shaoxing, brewed in the city in Zhejiang province of the same name.

Mock Duck
素鷄

Or sometimes called Vegetarian Duck, it is a dish with its origins traceable back to Buddhist monasteries. Dried sheets of tofu skin are pressed tightly together to create a texture similar to duck meat. Spices and seasonings are added to make it taste like the real thing, and many of the well-made ones are quite convincing.

Five-spice Smoked Fish
五香燻魚

Freshwater carp is actually fried to a crisp, not smoked. Then it is allowed to dry, chilled, and marinated with a combination of fruit juices, vinegar, spices, and rock candy to give the fish a smoked flavor.

Crystal Xiaorou
水晶肴肉

Chopped pork is marinated in its own flavorful consomme, then reconstituted into a cool jelly, much like a terrine. Pork skin is layered on the bottom, recreating the appearance of a pork rump. Upon serving, crystal xiaorou is cut into oblong rectangular blocks, and served with a dipping sauce of ginger and Zhenjiang black vinegar. Traditionally, this dish uses saltpeter (potassium nitrate, or "*xiao*" in Mandarin). It is a salt compound with a variety of uses, from making explosives to curing meats. Meats cured with

EASTERN

saltpeter turn bright red, but nowadyas most Chinese prefer making xiaorou with little or no saltpeter (it is a known carcinogen when consumed in large amounts). At most, modern xiaorou is made to be lightly pink or otherwise "crystal clear."

Eight Treasures Meat Sauce
八寶辣醬

The combination of eight ingredients in this appetizer reveals the opulence of the Jiangzhe region. Dried tofu, bamboo shoots, mushroom, lima beans, shrimp, peanuts, *Jinhua* ham, and chicken are stir fried in sweet bean paste to create a savory meat sauce that goes well over plain rice or with just about anything else.

Drunken Crab
熗醉蟹

Not for the faint of heart, raw crab is marinated in a briny mixture of rice wine and salt, which enhances the sweetness of the crabmeat. Raw crab has a gelatinous texture that appeal to many Chinese.

TYPICAL DISHES OF JIANGZHE CUISINE

Jiangzhe dishes are generally opulent, and complicated in their preparation. Unlike Guangdong cuisine, which uses stir-frying to achieve simple, natural textures, Jiangzhe cuisine resorts to techniques such as braising and "red-cooking" to achieve softer textures and full-bodied flavors. Jiangzhe cuisine also consumes a lot of pork – usually the

better cuts such as pork bellies and rumps – which also give its reputation for being exceedingly oily.

Dongbo Pork
東坡肉

The dish's name appears comical, but Dongbo Pork is by far the most famous dish in Jiangzhe cuisine, and ranks up there with Beijing Duck as the most famous dish in all of China. Named after Su Dongbo, a famous Song Dynasty poet who was also an accomplished cook, Dongbo Pork demonstrates the cuisine's main characteristics: sweet, highly sophisticated, but rather oily.

Mr. Su wrote about his own red-cooking technique:

> *"Slow the fire,*
> *Hold the brine.*
> *When it's ready,*
> *Self divine."*

That is exactly how Dongbo pork should be cooked: pork belly is cut into square pieces, tied with string into compact packages, and then slowly simmered in a brine flavored with soy sauce, rock candy, star anise, and cinnamon bark. When completed, it glows red in color, and the meat remains tender to the easy pickings of the chopsticks. This is among the most difficult dishes to prepare in Chinese cuisine, and in the U.S., Dongbo Pork is still as elusive as the Abominable Snowman.

"Reduced-fat" Pork Belly
走油扣肉

In the past, pork belly (bacon) is frequently the meat of choice in Jiangzhe cuisine, prized for its tenderness and high fat content. However, it is not the fat juices but its texture that the Chinese favor. In this complicated and difficult dish, an entire cut of pork belly is first boiled, then marinated in soy sauce, followed by deep-frying and immediate immersion into an ice bath. Then, in its most crucial steps, the meat is sliced and steamed to allow all of the fats to drip away. Expertly prepared, the pork belly has an alluring texture of both crunchiness and tenderness. However, any claim of "reduced fat" is spurious; the fat drippings are returned to the dish by combining with starch to create a rich sauce.

Shrimp stir-fried with Longjing Tealeaves
龍井蝦仁

This is a classic Jiangzhe dish, which uses freshwater shrimp of the Yangtze with *longjing* tealeaves from Zhejiang province. The sweetness of the shrimp is a good complement to the slightly nutty fragrance of the green tealeaves.

Lion's Head
獅子頭

A Yangzhou specialty, Lion's Head is not dish of endangered animals, but an oversized pork meatball. First deep-fried and then simmered separately with clear broth – often in an earthenware hotpot – the meatball resembles the mane of a lion floating in a bubbling stew of Napa cabbage, tofu, and cellophane noodles. Lion's Head can also be red-cooked in a sweet sauce with green vegetables for a strikingly visual appeal.

Braised Crab in Flour
麵拖蟹

Braising ingredients in flour is a cooking method originating from Ningbo, and is similar to the Guangdong cooking style of "baking." Crab is cut up into pieces and lightly breaded with flour, deep-fried, and then braised in a broth. The starch in the flour naturally thickens the cooking broth into a savory sauce.

Yangzhou-style Fried Rice
揚州炒飯

To Americans, fried rice resembles off-brown mounds of flaky rice, dotted with frozen peas, carrots and bits of roast pork. Fried rice to the Chinese is Yangzhou-style, which has a pale color because no soy sauce is used. Rice is stir-fried with eggs, chicken, ham, shrimp, mushroom, bamboo shoot, and peas, retaining a white-and-yellow complexion. Then, a starchy egg-drop soup is poured over the rice like a sauce. Yangzhou-

EASTERN

style fried rice is a lavish substitute for plain rice, and is eaten like a staple to accompany other meat- and vegetable dishes.

Wuxi Spareribs

無錫排骨

It is a signature dish from Wuxi's popular boat cuisine. Red-cooked pork spareribs are slowly simmered in a dark, sweet sauce of ginger, soy sauce, star anise, and rock candy, until the meat is tender and about to fall off the bones.

Sugar-and-vinegar Pork

糖醋排骨

The dish, also called "Sweet-and-sour Pork," has became a takeout superstar in the U.S. It has its origins in Jiangzhe, where the local sweet-and-sour sauce uses sugar and Zhenjiang black vinegar. The pork, cut into small bite-size pieces, is battered and fried until crispy, and then coated with this vinegar sauce. The dish took the slow boat to America with the Guangdong immigrants during the 19th century, and the sugar-and-vinegar sauce was replaced by a tangy plum sauce, often colored with red food coloring.

Shredded Fish with Pine Nuts

松子魚米

Freshwater fish fillet is chopped to the fine texture of rice grains, then quickly stir-fried with roasted pine nuts in a light broth. The fish is tender and the pine nuts are crunchy, and their contrasting colors and textures are the dish's main appeal.

Red-cooked Fish Tail

紅燒划水

The back half of the fish is its most tender part, and Jiangzhe cuisine makes good use of it by red-cooking it in a typical Jiangzhe style of preparing fish: using soy sauce, rice wine, Zhenjiang black vinegar, sugar, and star anise to create sweet and tangy sauce. This popular method has found its way throughout China, and it can be found in other regional restaurants. In Hongkong-style seafood houses, for example, this sauce is often called the "Shanghai-style" sauce.

Westlake Egg-drop Soup with Minced Beef

西湖牛肉湯

This starchy clear soup features minced beef and tofu cut into small

JIANGZHE-STYLE RESTAURANTS IN LOS ANGELES

In recent years, Jiangzhe cuisine has become very popular in Los Angeles, especially in the San Gabriel Valley where a wave of mainland immigrants have turned the focus of the local food scene away from Guangdong cuisine. This is appropriate, perhaps, given the historical fact that Jiangzhe cuisine was for centuries the archetype for the entire array of Chinese cooking. Rich-flavored and sophisticated, Jiangzhe cuisine has already made significant headway in redefining the popular image of Chinese food, at least in Los Angeles.

Several large banquet-sized restaurants now serve innovative and creative dishes of Jiangzhe cuisine. In addition, many small eateries provide heartier, home-style cooking that makes the homesick proud. Although it still has that unshakable reputation for being heavy and oily, Jiangzhe cuisine is showing signs of profound change. This is most apparent in Jiangzhe restaurants transplanted from Taiwan, which preserved the tradition of Jiangzhe cuisine at a time when Chinese traditions were being attacked and destroyed on the mainland. These restaurants serve dishes that are modern and remarkably lighter, but by no means less flavorful.

Green Village Chinese Restaurant

Both locations of this small, cramped eatery are always packed with *easterners* who come here for the authentic home cooking that echo their Lower Yangtze roots. The smallish menu includes many of Jiangzhe cuisine's representative dishes, including Yangzhou's Lion's Head served in an earthenware hotpot, Wuxi's famous spareribs, and Ningbo's Braised Crab in Flour.

18922 Gale Ave., #A, Rowland Heights
(626) 810-0600

833 W. Las Tunas Dr., San Gabriel
(626) 810-0600

Happy Panda Bistro

A very casual neighborhood restaurant in a large strip mall, Happy Panda features mostly everyday rice and noodle dishes, with a limited selection of signature Jiangzhe dishes – particularly those featuring eels and freshwater fish. In the rest of menu are straightforward dishes that do not adhere any regional cooking style, and are not extravagant under any stretch of the imagination.

18406 Colima Rd., #D, Rowland Heights
(626) 839-3822

EASTERN

Gourmet Delight 501

This casual restaurant with an updated décor serves many authentic Jiangzhe dishes, with a small selection of rice- and noodle dishes.

501 S. Atlantic Blvd., Monterey Park
(626) 284-3227

King's Palace

One of the most popular Chinese restaurants in Los Angeles, King's Palace is also a leader in the newfound appreciation for Jiangzhe cuisine. Opened by a Taiwanese proprietor, the restaurant serves dishes that drastically transcend above the heavy and oily reputation of Jiangzhe cuisine. Among the favorites at King's Palace are Braised Sea Cucumber with Shrimp Roe, Vegetarian Yellow Sparrows, and Beggar's Chicken – all of which are richly flavored but not heavy. Jiangzhe-style banquet, the de facto banquet cuisine of China rarely found in North America, also makes its grand appearance here. Unfortunately for Los Angelenos, the elusive Dongbo Pork remains absent from the menu.

18900 E. Gale Ave., #A, Rowland Heights
(626) 854-6686

250 W. Valley Blvd., Suite M, San Gabriel
(626) 282-9566

More restaurants are listed in Appendix XIV.

EASTERN

cubes. Egg-drop is added to thicken the soup, although in some versions, the eggs are dropped completely and the soup is thickened with potato starch only. In the Chinese dining custom, soup is always served as the last dish in the meal.

Braised Shanghai Cabbage in Crab Roe Sauce

蟹黃菜心

Shreds of crabmeat and golden clumps of crab roe are at the center of attention in this opulent vegetable dish. The blanched pieces of whole Shanghai cabbage – often arranged artistically on a large platter – sop up all of the delicate flavors of the creamy crab roe sauce.

Vegetarian Yellow Sparrows

素黃雀

Another vegetarian dish from the tradition of Buddhist monastery cooking, the "yellow sparrows" are actually dumplings wrapped with flat sheets of tofu skin. The fillings consist of a chop suey of sorts, featuring julienne bamboo shoots, salted greens, lima beans, et cetera. The dumplings are braised to a golden brown color, and cooked in a thick, savory vegetable broth.

SWEET DISHES

Despite Jiangzhe's impressive array of dishes, it can only account for a few sweet dishes that are customarily eaten as snacks, and only sometimes eaten as desserts. Nevertheless, these sweet dishes are distinctive to the region.

Eight Treasures Sweet Rice

八寶飯

"Eight treasures" is a popular theme in Jiangzhe cooking, such as the aforementioned appetizer called Eight Treasures Meat Sauce. Similarly, a sweet rice pudding is made from eight "treasures," including: glutinous rice, lotus seeds, red bean paste, plums, raisins, pineapple, mandarin oranges, candied wintermelon, et cetera. All are steamed together with lard to create a hot snack especially popular in the wintertime.

Glutinous Rice Balls in Fermented Glutinous Rice

酒釀湯圓

Fermented glutinous rice is a sweet rice wine mash with a slight alcohol content. It is used as the basis in which glutinous rice balls are simmered. The sweet soup is flavored with mandarin oranges and osmanthus flower petals.

SHANGHAI CUISINE

"Shanghai cuisine is a myriad potpourri of ingredients, flavors, and styles from all over China. Influences from the West can also be spotted."

Shanghai was no more than a fishing village with a population of 10,000 in 1800, but by 1900, it had turned into a roiling metropolis of international standing, surpassing Hangzhou as China's greatest city. The city's tremendous growth was owed to foreign trade, which was forced upon the Qing Dynasty after China's defeat in the First Opium War (1842). The British were granted trading concessions in five Chinese cities, including Shanghai. Because of Shanghai's proximity to major trade routes, it grew quickly to become the most prominent port in China. The British, French, and Japanese set up special quarters in Shanghai, and the architecture constructed along the riverfront *Bund* made Shanghai's skyline resemble a European city.

In the 1920s, Shanghai was called both the "Pearl of the Orient" and the "Whore of China." The city whirled chaotically with all sorts of vices and diversions. On the same stretch of the famous Nanking Road – Shanghai's major thoroughfare – one could find an entire representation of the Chinese society: posh department stores, popular restaurants, calligraphy artists, women wearing fur coats, beggars, orphans, pawn shops, opium dens, brothels, et cetera. Shanghai was also a city brimming with foreigners and Chinese migrants who flocked there in search of fortunes and opportunities. All of these outside influences contributed to Shanghai's local cuisine, which boasts many western characteristics as well as elements from sixteen regions of China.

Shanghai cuisine fell into decline after the Communist takeover, and like other regional cuisines on the mainland, it remained stagnant until China's economic policies were liberalized in the 1980s. The people of Shanghai have always been proud of their city, and as the city rediscovers its culinary heritage, Shanghaiers are once again swaggering and sniffing in the prosperous air currently hovering over the city. A new breed of chefs is determined to bring Shanghai cuisine back into the spotlight of world cuisines, returning Shanghai to the distinguished esteem as a cosmopolitan, world-class city.

The relationship between Shanghai and Jiangzhe cuisines is similar to that between Hongkong and Guangdong cuisines. Both Shanghai and Hongkong were still rural hamlets 200 years ago, so they were not bound by rigid traditions that imbue older, more conservative-minded cities. As they grew into modern cities, Shanghai and Hongkong chefs were free to borrow and experiment with more new ideas than tradition would allow. Consequently, their local cuisines eagerly absorbed all kinds of influences from the outside.

TYPICAL DISHES OF SHANGHAI CUISINE

Shanghai cuisine is a myriad potpourri of ingredients, flavors, and styles from all over China. Influences from the West can also be spotted. Shanghai cuisine's main dishes remain basically Jiangzhe in character, but tucked within the myriad of cooking styles are northern-style meat dumplings, Islamic-inspired lamb dishes, and Hunan-style *larou*.

Chicken and Corn Soup
雞蓉玉米湯

By now, Chicken and Corn Soup is a household name in China, known practically in every Chinese household. The soup started out as *haute cuisine* dish during Shanghai's heyday, as it features corn – a crop native to the Americas. It has since been filtered throughout China as an ordinary soup featuring cream of corn soup flavored with pieces of diced chicken.

Sweet-and-sour Fish, Squirrel-style
松鼠糖醋魚

"Squirrel-style" was the rage of Shanghai during the 1930s at Meiweizhai Restaurant, a local institution that unfortunately did not survive the communists. However, the dish lives on, and it is as famous as ever. Preparation for this dish is difficult because it requires intricate

knifework; the distinctive filleting process creates a piece of fish that resembles the stripes of a squirrel. In typical Shanghai style, the whole fish is red-cooked with sugar and vinegar in the traditional Jiangzhe manner, and combined with "foreign" ingredients such as yellow onions, tomatoes, and ketchup to further enhance the complexity of the sauce.

Braised Fish Head
干燒魚頭

Jiangzhe cuisine is heavier and fattier than Guangdong cuisine, and with seafood there is no difference in that assessment. Likewise, seafood in Shanghai cuisine tends to be heavily flavored. This braised fish head uses a sauce of sweet bean paste, soy sauce, Zhenjiang black vinegar, ketchup, and garlic. Though complex in flavor, it is often the simpler that is the better for seafood. The exemplary examples set by Chaozhou-style and Hongkong's seafood cuisine are marked contrasts to the seafood dishes of eastern China.

Eel Stir-fried with Yellow Nira
韭黃鱔糊

This is a simple stir-fry of eels with yellow nira, both of which are typical ingredients of Jiangzhe cuisine. The flavorings are quite simple – just salt and a dash of soy sauce. Stir-frying is ideal for yellow nira, in order to maintain a certain degree of crunchiness and its sweet, slightly pungent flavor.

Braised Sea Cucumbers with Shrimp Roe
蝦子烏參

This is one of the most famous Shanghai dishes, having first appeared in the 1930s at Dexingguan, one of the most popular restaurants in Shanghai of the time. Slices of tender sea cucumbers are expertly red-cooked in a sauce of sweet bean paste, and speckled with tiny red-orange dried shrimp roe. This opulent dish is both tasty and visually pleasing, and goes far to demonstrate the level of sophistication already achieved by Shanghai cuisine during the first half of the twentieth century.

Shrimp with Walnuts
核桃蝦

This dish is another throwback to the

SHANGHAI-STYLE RESTAURANTS IN LOS ANGELES

Although Jiangzhe- and Shanghai cuisines are widely accepted to be separate cuisines, the distinctions between the two may not be glaringly apparent in Los Angeles. The main reason is that both cuisines are still emerging in popularity here in America, and truly exemplary restaurants of either type are rare. Thus, Jiangzhe- and Shanghai-style restaurants are very similar – except that Jiangzhe-style restaurants are more home-cooking-oriented, and Shanghai-style restaurants feature more seafood and adaptations of other regional dishes.

Although Shanghai-style restaurants in Los Angeles are still overwhelmingly Jiangzhe in character, they will likely begin to absorb the vibrancy of Shanghai in the near future. As Shanghai continues to prosper at an unabated pace, its cuisine will only take off from its already cosmopolitan nature, becoming even more innovative and exciting in substance. Thanks to the steady arrival of Chinese immigrants from Shanghai, it will only be a matter of time before all of the latest in Shanghai cuisine is transplanted right into Los Angeles's backyard.

Wok and Noodle

A typical neighborhood eatery serving a mixture of Jiangzhe-style home-cooking, and Shanghai's cosmopolitan, pan-China cuisine. The menu features many snack- and noodle dishes that show a decidedly northern Chinese influence. Other parts of the menu show authentic Jiangzhe dishes, including Shredded Fish with Pine Nuts, Sweet-and-Sour Fish, Squirrel-style, and Lion's Head casserole.

828 West Valley Blvd., Alhambra
(626) 588-2284

Shanghai Kitchen

This is a modest restaurant that serves a mixture of straightforward Jiangzhe cuisine and interesting Shanghai dishes, with a preponderance of the menu dedicated to home-style dishes.

140 W. Valley Blvd., #211, San Gabriel
(626) 280-4676

EASTERN

Mandarin Shanghai Restaurant

This is one of the oldest Shanghai-style restaurants in Los Angeles, with over 30 years of history at its original Chinatown location. With a revival of interest for Shanghai cuisine currently underway, Mandarin Shanghai is more popular than ever. A lot of the food action is now taking place in the new branch in Arcadia, where the diners are much closer to the local Chinese food scene. The house specialty is a tender braised pork rump served over a bed of blanched spinach. Other dishes exhibit Shanghai cuisine's cosmopolitan nature, including its own Beijing Duck, Yunnan's Chicken in the Clay Airpot, and Japanese-style Lobster Sashimi.

558 Las Tunas Dr., Arcadia
(626) 445-4555

970 N. Broadway, #114, Los Angeles
(213) 625-1195

Lake Spring Shanghai Restaurant

This Monterey Park eatery had first appeared in the 1990s, before the Shanghai cuisine craze. It has since solidified the presence of Shanghai cuisine in the Chinese food scene in the San Gabriel Valley. Lake Spring's modest dishes feature both Shanghai- and Jiangzhe specialties, and among the most interesting are its braised pork rump, the Lion Head casserole, and Eels Stir-fried with Yellow Nira.

219 E. Garvey Ave., Monterey Park
(626) 280-3511

More restaurants are listed in Appendix XV.

"Pearl of the Orient"/"Whore of Asia" days, when Shanghai cuisine was China's *haute cuisine*. Tender whole shrimp is sautéed, then braised in a clear, starcheyd broth with crunchy, honey-glazed walnuts sprinkled on the side. This dish later inspired Hongkong's Walnut Shrimp in Mayonnaise Sauce, which is a more recent creation using mayonnaise as the basis of the braising sauce.

Fish-flavor Scallops
魚香干貝

Sichuan-style fish-flavor sauce is used on seafood in this classic example of Shanghai's adaptation of outside influences. The fish-flavor sauce, generally used for cooking fish, is proven to be versatile for a variety of ingredients ranging from eggplants to scallops.

Red-cooked Bamboo Shoot and Mushroom
紅燒雙冬

The combination of bamboo shoots and mushroom is what the Chinese call *shuangdong*, or "double winter." The connotation of these two ingredients with winter may have something to do with the perception that the best bamboo shoots and mushrooms are harvested during the winter. These days, the shuangdong theme can be found in all Chinese regional dishes, cooked with delicate ingredients such as abalone (Hongkong-style seafood), or alone on its own, such as this one. Sliced bamboo shoot and mushrooms are braised in a sweet, red-cooked sauce, and accompanied by seasonal greens.

Fried Gluten Puff Stir-fried with Shuangdong
雙冬麵筋

Fried gluten puff is stir-fried with the classic combination of sliced bamboo shoots and mushrooms (shuangdong). Flour gluten is an important ingredient in Chinese vegetarian cuisine, because not only is it high in protein and vital nutrients, it provides a meat-like texture that humans naturally crave. When deep-fried, the flour gluten puffs up to resemble a sponge. Then, after it is cooled, the fried gluten collapses and takes on an appearance resembling beef or mutton.

EASTERN

179

Red-cooked Pork Rump using Rock Candy
冰糖元蹄

One of Shanghai's most famous dishes is also one of the heaviest. An entire side of pork rump is slowly red-cooked in a brine of soy sauce, ginger, and rock candy. The rump skin is the most prized part of the dish; it is first deep-fried so that it could absorb all of the cooking liquid's savory flavors. When completed, this pork rump gives off a red color, and has a tenderness that melts in the mouth. Typically, this dish is served over a bed of blanched spinach or Shanghai cabbage.

Stir-fried Rice Cake
上海炒年糕

A peculiar dish that is instantly identifiable as a Shanghai dish. Rice cake, normally grilled or steamed, is cut into small bite-size pieces and stir-fried with different kinds of ingredients. When stir-fried, the rice cake turns sticky, amorphous, and chewy. It is quite an unusual texture, which takes some getting used to. Popular ingredients to go with a stir-fry like this include yellow nira, fried gluten puffs, and pork.

Small Soupy Baozi
小籠湯包子

The northern Chinese skills for making dumplings and noodles were transplanted in Shanghai, and now the city claims Small Soupy Baozi as its own (see chapter on Dumplings and Noodles). The small baozi are served in steamer baskets, each of which contains eight to ten bite-sized dumplings. They can also be pan-fried like potstickers. The baozi should be eaten using both chopsticks and a spoon. First, bite into the baozi to release the scalding soup into the spoon. Then, both the baozi and the soup should be eaten in two or three bites. A dipping sauce of ginger, vinegar, and sugar can be added to provide a more savory flavor.

APPENDICES

GUANGDONG-STYLE RESTAURANTS

AAA B.B.Q. Dim Sum Chinese Restaurant
永發燒臘點心城
711½ New High St., Los Angeles
Phone: 213.687.7333
Hours: 07.00 - 19.00
Cash only

Canton Restaurant
廣州粥粉麵家
8550 Westminster Ave., Westminster
Phone: 714.892.2022
Hours: 09.30 - 21.30 closed Tuesday
Cash only

China Chef Restaurant
富貴樓麵家
8924 Bolsa Ave., Westminster
Phone: 714.891.8775
Hours: 09.00 - 20.00 closed Tuesday
Cash only

Fortune B.B.Q. And Dim Sum
福臨門燒臘點心
18406 Colima Rd., #A, Rowland Heights
Phone: 626.839.0626
Hours: 07.00 - 23.00
Cash only

Guang Zhou Palace
廣州酒家
1463 S. Nogales St., #A, Rowland Heights
Phone: 626.913.2338
Hours: 10.00 - 00.00
opens 09.00 on weekends
Mastercard, Visa

Hong Kong Café
香港茶餐廳
162 W. Garvey Ave., Monterey Park
Phone: 626.288.3282
Hours: 11.00 - 23.00
Cash only

Hop Louie Restaurant
玉宮酒家
950 Mei Ling Way, Los Angeles
Phone: 213.628.4244
Hours: 11.00 - 21.00
All major credit cards

Hop Woo Seafood & B.B.Q. Restaurant
合和海鮮燒臘麵家
721 N. Broadway, Los Angeles
Phone: 213.617.3038
Hours: 10.00 - 01.00
08.00 - 02.00 on weekends
Cash only

Jade Seafood and B.B.Q. Restaurant
翠園海鮮燒腊小館
7808 Garvey Ave., Rosemead
Phone: 626.573.3602
Hours: 11.00 - 01.00
Mastercard, Visa

Lien Hoa Deli
聯合燒腊店
9299 Bolsa Ave., Westminster
Phone: 714.894.1085
Hours: 08.30 - 20.00
Cash only

GUANGDONG-STYLE RESTAURANTS (CONT.)

Lien-Hoa B.B.Q. Restaurant
聯合燒臘海鮮店
721 N. Broadway, Los Angeles
Phone: 213.625.5001
Hours: 07.00 - 19.00
Cash only

Luk Yue
陸羽
123 N. Garfield Ave., Monterey Park
Phone: 626.280.2888
Hours:07.00 - 03.00
Cash only

MPV Express
洛城人家
429 W. Garvey Ave., Monterey Park
Phone: 626.307.7338
Hours: 11.00 - 01.00
Cash only

MPV Garden Restaurant
弘城鮮先仙食府
415 W. Garvey Ave., Monterey Park
Phone: 626.307.7338
Hours: 11.00 - 01.00
Mastercard, Visa

Phoenix Inn
鳳城菜館
208 E. Valley Blvd., Alhambra
Phone: 626.299.1238
Hours: 11.30 - 01.00
Mastercard, Visa

Phoenix Inn
鳳城菜館
1430 W. Valley Blvd., Alhambra
Phone: 626.299.0990
Hours: 11.00 - 22.00
Mastercard, Visa

Phoenix Inn
鳳城菜館
1108 S. Baldwin Ave., Arcadia
Phone: 626.446.7668
Hours: 11.00 - 01.00
Mastercard, Visa

Phoenix Inn
鳳城菜館
301 Ord St., Los Angeles
Phone: 213.629.2812
Hours: 17.00 - 01.00
Cash only

Sam Woo B.B.Q. Restaurant
三和燒臘麵家
514 W. Valley Blvd., Alhambra
Phone: 626.281.0038
Hours: 09.00 - 23.30
Cash only

Sam Woo B.B.Q. Restaurant
三和燒臘麵家
19008 Pioneer Blvd., Cerritos
Phone: 562.865.7278
Hours: 10.00 - 00.00
All major credit cards

Sam Woo B.B.Q. Restaurant
三 和 燒 臘 麵 家
901 South Coast Dr., Ste. C,
Metro Pointe Centre, Costa Mesa
Phone: 714.668.0800
Hours: 11.00 - 22.00
All major credit cards

Sam Woo B.B.Q. Restaurant
三 和 燒 臘 麵 家
15333 Culver Dr., Ste. 722, Irvine
Phone: 949.262.0888
Hours: 10.00 - 22.00
Cash only

Sam Woo B.B.Q. Restaurant
三 和 燒 臘 麵 家
803 N. Broadway, Los Angeles
Phone: 213.687.7238
Hours: 09.00 - 01.00
Cash only

Sam Woo B.B.Q. Restaurant
三 和 燒 臘 麵 家
727 N. Broadway #111, Los Angeles
Phone: 213.687.3763
Hours: 09.00 - 18.00
Cash only

Sam Woo B.B.Q. Restaurant
三 和 燒 臘 麵 家
634 W. Garvey Ave., Monterey Park
Phone: 626.289.4858
Hours: 09.00 - 01.00
Cash only

Sam Woo B.B.Q. Restaurant
三 和 燒 臘 麵 家
18908 E. Gale Ave., Rowland Heights
Phone: 626.913.0213
Hours: 09.00 - 00.00
Cash only

Sam Woo B.B.Q. Restaurant
三 和 燒 臘 麵 家
140 W. Valley Blvd., # 107, San
Gabriel
Phone: 626.572.8418
Hours: 08.30 - 00.00
Cash only

Sam Woo B.B.Q. Restaurant
三 和 燒 臘 麵 家
6450 Sepulveda Blvd., #G, Van Nuys
Phone: 818.988.6813
Hours: 11.00 - 22.00
Cash only

Shun Shing B.B.Q.
順 成 燒 腊 美 食 館
288 W. Valley Blvd., #110-112,
Alhambra
Phone: 626.284.7881
Hours: 11.00 - 01.00
All major credit cards

Tong Sing Seafood
東 昇 燒 臘 麵 家
960 N. Broadway, Los Angeles
Phone: 213.680.3689
Hours: 11.00 - 23.00
Cash only

Won Tin B.B.Q. Restaurant
雲天燒臘
1124 W.Valley Blvd., Alhambra
Phone: 626.289.3616
Hours: 10.00 - 23.00
Cash only

Won Tin Gourmet
雲天
645 E. Main St., Alhambra
Phone: 626.458.8388
Hours: 10.00 - 22.00
Cash only

HONGKONG-STYLE SEAFOOD HOUSES

828 Hong Kong Seafood Restaurant
828 香港海鮮酒家
755 W. Garvey Ave., Monterey Park
Phone: 626.289.9299
Hours: 10.00 - 22.00
Mastercard, Visa

AAA Seafood Restaurant
海珍海鮮酒家
220 W. Garvey Ave., Monterey Park
Phone: 626.571.8898
Hours: 11.00 - 22.00
Mastercard, Visa

ABC Seafood Restaurant
海運海鮮酒家
205 Ord St., Los Angeles
Phone: 213.680.2887
Hours: 10.00 - 22.00
All major credit cards

CBS Seafood Restaurant
海城酒家
700 N.Spring St., Los Angeles
Phone: 213.617.2323
Hours: 08.00 - 22.00
American Express, Mastercard, Visa

China Tea House Chinese Seafood Restaurant
鵬運漁村海鮮酒家
3314 Sepulveda Blvd., Torrance
Phone: 310.325.6716
Hours: 11.00 - 22.00
American Express, Mastercard, Visa

Dragon Phoenix Palace
龍鳳樓海鮮大酒家
9211 Bolsa Ave., #106, Westminster
Phone: 714.893.3682
Hours: 09.30 - 21.30
American Express, Mastercard, Visa

Dragon Regency Seafood Restaurant
龍苑海鮮酒家
120 S. Atlantic Blvd., Monterey Park
Phone: 626.282.1089
Hours: 11.00 - 22.00
Mastercard, Visa

Empress Harbor Seafood Restaurant
海皇翠亨沌大酒樓
111 N. Atlantic Blvd., #350,
Monterey Park
Phone: 626.300.8833
Hours: 17.00 - 22.00
American Express, Mastercard, Visa

Empress Pavilion Restaurant
漢宮大酒樓
988 N. Hill St., #201, Los Angeles
Phone: 213.617.9898
Hours: 09.00 - 22.00
opens 08.00 on weekends
American Express, Mastercard, Visa

HONGKONG-STYLE SEAFOOD HOUSE (CONT.)

Full House Seafood Restaurant
漁 沌 海 鮮 酒 家
1220 S. Golden West Ave., Arcadia
Phone: 626.446.8222
Hours: 11.00 - 22.00
Discover, Mastercard, Visa

Full House Seafood Restaurant
漁 沌 海 鮮 酒 家
963 N. Hill St., Los Angeles
Phone: 213.617.8382
Hours: 11.30 - 03.00
Mastercard, Visa

**Furiwa Chinese Seafood
Restaurant**
富 麗 華 海 鮮 大 酒 樓
13826-13828 Brookhurst St., Garden
Grove
Phone: 714.534.3996
Hours: 10.00 - 22.00
opens 09.00 on weekends
All major credit cards

G.L. Restaurant
東 海 魚 翅 海 鮮 酒 家
1 W. Main St., Alhambra
Phone: 626.289.5072
Hours: 11.00 - 00.00
Mastercard, Visa

Golden City Seafood Restaurant
人 人 海 鮮 酒 家
960 N. Hill St., Los Angeles
Phone: 213.253.2660
Hours: 11.00 - 22.00
Mastercard, Visa

Golden City Seafood Restaurant
人 人 海 鮮 酒 家
108 N. Garfield Ave., Monterey Park
Phone: 626.288.3128
Hours: 10.00 - 00.00
Mastercard, Visa

Harbor Seafood Restaurant
海 霸 魚 沌 海 鮮 酒 家
545 W. Valley Blvd., San Gabriel
Phone: 626.282.3032
Hours: 11.00 - 01.00
Mastercard, Visa

**Hong Kong Palace Seafood
Restaurant**
泮 溪
19101 E. Colima Rd., Rowland
Heights
Phone: 626.854.9829
Hours: 10.00 - 00.00
Mastercard, Visa

Hop Li Seafood Restaurant
合 利 海 鮮 酒 家
526 Alpine St., Los Angeles
Phone: 213.680.3939
Hours: 11.00 - 22.00
All major credit cards

Jade Ocean Seafood Restaurant
新 翡 翠 海 鮮 酒 家
25 W. Valley Blvd., Alhambra
Phone: 626.281.1818
Hours: 11.00 - 00.00
Mastercard, Visa

Main City Seafood Restaurant
明城漁村海鮮酒家
9669 Las Tunas Dr., Temple City
Phone: 626.287.3683
Hours: 11.00 - 22.00
Mastercard, Visa

Mon Kee's Seafood Restaurant
文記海鮮酒家
679 N. Spring St., Los Angeles
Phone: 213.628.6717
Hours: 11.00 - 22.00
American Express, Mastercard, Visa

MPV Seafood Restaurant
弘城魚翅海鮮酒家
1412 S. Garfield Ave., Alhambra
Phone: 626.289.3018
Hours: 11.00 - 01.00
Mastercard, Visa

MPV Seafood Restaurant
弘城魚翅海鮮酒家
18425 Jeffrey Rd., Irvine
Phone: 949.653.9988
Hours: 11.00 - 00.00
Mastercard, Visa

NBC Seafood Restaurant
海運海鮮酒家
404 S. Atlantic Blvd., #A, Monterey Park
Phone: 626.282.2323
Hours: 08.00 - 22.00
Mastercard, Visa

New Capital Seafood Restaurant
半島海鮮酒家
855 S. Baldwin Ave., Arcadia
Phone: 626.445.9998
Hours: 11.00 - 01.00
Mastercard, Visa

New Capital Seafood Restaurant
半島海鮮酒家
7540 E. Garvey Ave., Rosemead
Phone: 626.288.1899
Hours: 09.00 - 01.00
Mastercard, Visa

New Hope City Seafood Restaurant
新合城海鮮酒家
500 W. Garvey Ave., Monterey Park
Phone: 626.289.8329
Hours: 11.00 - 00.00
Mastercard, Visa

NYC Jumbo Seafood Restaurant
新寶城海鮮酒家
203 W. Valley Blvd., Alhambra
Phone: 626.289.4828
Hours: 11.00 - 01.00
Mastercard, Visa

NYC Seafood Restaurant
新港城海鮮酒家
715 W. Garvey Ave., Monterey Park
Phone: 626.289.9898
Hours: 11.15 - 03.00
Mastercard, Visa

HONGKONG-STYLE SEAFOOD HOUSE (CONT.)

Ocean Seafood Restaurant Group, Inc.
富 臨 海 鮮 酒 家
750 N. Hill St., Los Angeles
Phone: 213.687.3088
Hours: 09.00 - 15.00
All major credit cards

Ocean Star Seafood Restaurant
北 海 漁 村 酒 家
145 N. Atlantic Blvd., #201-203,
Monterey Park
Phone: 626.308.2128
Hours: 10.00 - 22.00
opens 09.00 on weekends
Mastercard, Visa

Prince Seafood Restaurant
樂 宮 海 鮮 酒 樓
11828 South St., Cerritos
Phone: 562.809.1812
Hours: 14.30 - 21.30
Mastercard, Visa

Regent Seafood Restaurant
麗 晶 海 鮮 酒 家
739-747 N. Main St., Los Angeles
Phone: 213.680.3333
Hours: 11.00 - 22.00
American Express, Mastercard, Visa

Ruby Palace Restaurant
紅 寶 石 大 酒 樓
1330 Fullerton Rd., #207, Industry
Phone: 626.912.6828
Hours: 10.00 - 22.00
Mastercard, Visa

Sam Woo Dim Sum & Seafood Restaurant
三 和 魚 翅 海 鮮 酒 家
15333 Culver Dr., Ste. 720, Irvine
Phone: 949.262.0688
Hours: 11.00 - 22.00
All major credit cards

Sam Woo Seafood Restaurant
三 和 海 鮮 酒 家
724 N. Hill St., #215, Los Angeles
Phone: 213.680.7836
Hours: 11.00 - 21.00
Mastercard, Visa

Sam Woo Dim Sum & Seafood Restaurant
三 和 魚 翅 海 鮮 酒 家
18922 E. Gale Ave., Rowland Heights
Phone: 626.913.9933
Hours: 10.00 - 22.00
All major credit cards

Sam Woo Seafood Restaurant
三 和 海 鮮 酒 家
140 W. Valley Blvd., #D, 4th Floor,
San Gabriel
Phone: 626.571.8686
Hours: 10.00 - 22.00
Mastercard, Visa

Sea Empress Seafood Restaurant
海 皇 海 鮮 酒 家
1636 W. Redondo Beach Blvd.,
Gardena
Phone: 310.538.6868
Hours: 11.00 - 22.00
American Express, Mastercard, Visa

Sea Food Cove Chinese Restaurant
海景閣
8547 Westminster Blvd., Garden Grove
Phone: 714.895.7964
Hours: 11.00 - 21.30
Mastercard, Visa

Sea Food Paradise
海鮮閣
8602 Westminster Ave., Westminster
Phone: 714.893.6066
Hours: 10.00 - 21.30
Mastercard, Visa

Sea Harbour Seafood Restaurant
海港大酒樓
3939 N. Rosemead Blvd., Rosemead
Phone: 626.288.3939
Hours: 11.00 - 22.30
opens 10.30 on weekends
Mastercard, Visa

Sea Shore Seafood & BBQ Restaurant
海濱海鮮酒家
5137 Calle Mayor, Torrance
Phone: 310.373.0751
Hours: 11.00 - 21.30 closed Monday
All major credit cards

Seafood City Restaurant
海都海鮮酒家
9253 Bolsa Ave., Westminster
Phone: 714.894.1986
Hours: 11.00 - 02.00
Cash only

Seafood Place Chinese Restaurant
海鮮帝
12201 Brookhurst St., Garden Grove
Phone: 714.638.7020
Hours: 11.00 - 21.30
Mastercard, Visa

Seafood Port Restaurant
海鮮港
21180 Hawthorne Blvd., Torrance
Phone: 310.370.8478
Hours: 11.00 - 21.30
Mastercard, Visa

Seafood Town Restaurant
海鮮樓
22922 Hawthorne Blvd., Torrance
Phone: 310.378.0785
Hours: 11.00 - 21.30
Discover, Mastercard, Visa

Seafood City Restaurant & B.B.Q.
金海岸酒家
11612-11616½ South St., Artesia
Phone: 562.860.8383
Hours: 11.00 - 22.00
Mastercard, Visa

Seaworld Seafood Restaurant
海洋海鮮酒家
8118 E. Garvey Ave., Rosemead
Phone: 626.288.2898
Hours: 11.00 - 22.00
Mastercard, Visa

HONGKONG-STYLE SEAFOOD HOUSE (CONT.)

**Ten Ten Seafood Chinese
Restaurant
天天漁港**
18868 Norwalk Blvd., Artesia
Phone: 562.402.2428
Hours: 11.00 - 21.30
Discover, Mastercard, Visa

**V.I.P. Harbor Seafood Restaurant
海景漁村海鮮酒家**
11701 Wilshire Blvd., Los Angeles
Phone: 310.979.3377
Hours: 11.00 - 22.00
American Express, Mastercard, Visa

888 Seafood Restaurant
海珍大酒樓
8450 Valley Blvd., #121, Rosemead
Phone: 626.573.1888
Hours: 09.00 - 15.00
Mastercard, Visa

AAA B.B.Q. Dim Sum Chinese Restaurant
永發燒臘點心城
711½ New High St., Los Angeles
Phone: 213.687.7333
Hours: 07.00 - 19.00
Cash only

ABC Seafood Restaurant
海運海鮮酒家
205 Ord St., Los Angeles
Phone: 213.680.2887
Hours: 08.00 - 15.00
All major credit cards

CBS Seafood Restaurant
海城酒家
700 N.Spring St., Los Angeles
Phone: 213.617.2323
Hours: 08.00 - 15.00
American Express, Mastercard, Visa

Dim Sum Express
326 N. Garfield Ave., Monterey Park
Phone: 626.307.5800
Hours: 07.30 - 19.00
Cash only

Dragon Phoenix Palace
龍鳳樓海鮮大酒家
9211 Bolsa Ave., #106, Westminster
Phone: 714.893.3682
Hours: 09.30 - 15.00
American Express, Mastercard, Visa

Empress Harbor Seafood Restaurant
海皇翠亨邨大酒樓
111 N. Atlantic Blvd., #350, Monterey Park
Phone: 626.300.8833
Hours: 09.00 - 14.00
American Express, Mastercard, Visa

Empress Pavilion Restaurant
漢宮大酒樓
988 N. Hill St., #201, Los Angeles
Phone: 213.617.9898
Hours: 09.00 - 15.00
opens 08.00 on weekends
American Express, Mastercard, Visa

Fong's Dim Sum Food To Go
阿芳點心外賣店
311 E. Valley Blvd., #103, San Gabriel
Phone: 626.280.0490
Hours: 07.00 - 19.00
Cash only

Full House Seafood Restaurant
漁沌海鮮酒家
1220 S. Golden West Ave., Arcadia
Phone: 626.446.8222
Hours: 09.30 - 15.00
Discover, Mastercard, Visa

DIM SUM/YUM CHA HOUSES (CONT.)

**Furiwa Chinese Seafood
Restaurant**
富麗華海鮮大酒樓
13826-13828 Brookhurst St., Garden
Grove
Phone: 714.534.3996
Hours: 10.00 - 15.00
opens 09.00 on weekends
All major credit cards

**Hong Kong Palace Seafood
Restaurant**
泮溪
19101 E. Colima Rd., Rowland
Heights
Phone: 626.854.9829
Hours: 10.00 - 15.00
Mastercard, Visa

MPV Seafood Restaurant
弘城魚翅海鮮酒家
1412 S. Garfield Ave., Alhambra
Phone: 626.289.3018
Hours: 08.00 - 15.00
Mastercard, Visa

18425 Jeffrey Rd., Irvine
Phone: 949.653.9988
Hours: 11.00 - 15.00
Mastercard, Visa

NBC Seafood Restaurant
海運海鮮酒家
404 S. Atlantic Blvd., #A, Monterey
Park
Phone: 626.282.2323
Hours: 08.00 - 15.00
Mastercard, Visa

New Capital Seafood Restaurant
半島海鮮酒家
855 S. Baldwin Ave., Arcadia
Phone: 626.445.9998
Hours: 09.30 - 15.00
Mastercard, Visa

7540 E. Garvey Ave., Rosemead
Phone: 626.288.1899
Hours: 07.00 - 15.00
Mastercard, Visa

Ocean Star Seafood Restaurant
北海漁村酒家
145 N. Atlantic Blvd., #201-203,
Monterey Park
Phone: 626.308.2128
Hours: 10.00 - 15.00
opens 09.00 on weekends
Mastercard, Visa

Prince Seafood Restaurant
樂宮海鮮酒樓
11828 South St., Cerritos
Phone: 562.809.1812
Hours: 11.00 - 14.30
Mastercard, Visa

Ruby Palace Restaurant
紅寶石大酒樓
1330 Fullerton Rd., #207, Industry
Phone: 626.912.6828
Hours: 10.00 - 22.00
Mastercard, Visa

Sam Woo Dim Sum & Seafood Restaurant
三和魚翅海鮮酒家
15333 Culver Dr., Ste. 720, Irvine
Phone: 949.262.0688
Hours: 11.00 - 15.00
All major credit cards

Sam Woo Dim Sum & Seafood Restaurant
三和魚翅海鮮酒家
18922 E. Gale Ave., Rowland Heights
Phone: 626.913.9933
Hours: 10.00 - 15.00
All major credit cards

Sam Woo Seafood Restaurant
三和海鮮酒家
140 W. Valley Blvd., #D 4th Floor,
San Gabriel
Phone: 626.571.8686
Hours: 10.00 - 15.00
Mastercard, Visa

Sea Harbour Seafood Restaurant
海港大酒樓
3939 N. Rosemead Blvd., Rosemead
Phone: 626.288.3939
Hours: 11.00 - 14.30
opens 10.30 on weekends
Mastercard, Visa

Seaworld Seafood Restaurant
海洋海鮮酒家
8118 E. Garvey Ave., Rosemead
Phone: 626.288.2898
Hours: 09.00 - 15.00
Mastercard, Visa

Ten Ten Seafood Chinese Restaurant
天天漁港
18868 Norwalk Blvd., Artesia
Phone: 562.402.2428
Hours: 11.00 - 15.00
Discover, Mastercard, Visa

V.I.P. Harbor Seafood Restaurant
海景漁村海鮮酒家
11701 Wilshire Blvd., Los Angeles
Phone: 310.979.3377
Hours: 11.00 - 15.00
American Express, Mastercard, Visa

California Stonegrill Cafe
石器時代岩燒
1631 S. Azusa Ave., Hacienda
Heights
Phone: 626.581.3222
Hours: 11.30 - 21.30
until 22.00 on weekends
Mastercard, Visa

Garden Cafe
嘉頓港式西餐廳
228 W. Valley Blvd., #101, Alhambra
Phone: 626.289.1833
Hours: 07.00 - 04.00
Mastercard, Visa

Garden Cafe
嘉頓港式西餐廳
18406 E. Colima Rd., #H, Rowland
Heights
Phone: 626.913.1188
Hours: 08.00 - 01.00
until 04.00 on weekends
Mastercard, Visa

Holiday Cafe
又一村港式西餐廳
111 N. Atlantic Blvd., #349,
Monterey Park
Phone: 626.282.1306
Hours: 10.00 - 02.00
Mastercard, Visa

J.J. Cafe
J.J. 港式西餐
447 W. Garvey Ave., Monterey Park
Phone: 626.280.3833
Hours: 07.00 - 04.00
Mastercard, Visa

J.R. Cafe
翠河港式西餐
512 W. Valley Blvd., San Gabriel
Phone: 626.457.8898
Hours: 07.00 - 04.00
Mastercard, Visa

O.K. Cafe
301 E. Valley Blvd., Alhambra
Phone: 626.282.8899
Hours: 07.00 - 04.00
Mastercard, Visa

Oshine Cafe
歐香中式西餐
14805 Jeffrey Rd., #H, Irvine
Phone: 949.654.8899
Hours: 11.30 - 22.00
Mastercard, Visa

Regent Cafe
麗晶港式西餐
1411 S. Garfield Ave., Alhambra
Phone: 626.289.9398
Hours: 10.00 - 01.00
until 03.00 on weekends
Mastercard, Visa

HONGKONG-STYLE COFFEESHOPS (CONT.)

Savoy Kitchen
夏蕙西餐
138 E. Valley Blvd., Alhambra
Phone: 626.308.9535
Hours: 11.00 - 21.00
until 22.00 on Friday and Saturday
closed Sunday
Cash only

U2 Cafe
U2 港式西餐
1200 E. Valley Blvd., Alhambra
Phone: 626.282.1800
Hours: 07.00 - 02.00
Mastercard, Visa

CHAOZHOU-STYLE RESTAURANTS

888 Seafood Restaurant
海珍大酒樓
8450 Valley Blvd., #121, Rosemead
Phone: 626.573.1888
Hours: 09.00 - 22.00
Mastercard, Visa

Battambang Seafood Restaurant
馬德望海鮮酒家
648 New High St., Los Angeles
Phone: 213.620.9015
Hours: 07.30 - 18.30
Cash only

Battambang Seafood Restaurant
馬德望海鮮酒家
1806 S. San Gabriel Blvd., San
Gabriel
Phone: 626.307.3938
Hours: 09.00 - 22.00
Mastercard, Visa

**Capital Seafood Chinese
Restaurant**
金都海鮮酒家
8851 Westminster Blvd., Garden
Grove
Phone: 714.892.4182
Hours: 10.00 - 22.00
Mastercard, Visa

**Capital Seafood Chinese
Restaurant**
金都海鮮酒家
1015 S. Nogales St., #132, Rowland
Heights
Phone: 626.839.7738
Hours: 10.00 - 22.00
Mastercard, Visa

Dong Nguyen Restaurant
東源飯店
1433 E. Valley Blvd., Alhambra
Phone: 626.300.8618
Hours: 11.00 - 21.00
Cash only

Duong Son B.B.Q. Restaurant
唐山燒臘飯店
9081 Bolsa Ave., #105, Westminster
Phone: 714.897.1269
Hours: 09.00 - 21.00
Cash only

Golden Chinese Seafood Restuarnt
金海海鮮酒家
9455 Bolsa Ave., #B, Westminster
Phone: 714.531.4661
Hours: 08.00 - 21.00
Cash only

Hao Vi B.B.Q.
巧味燒臘家
10481 Bolsa Ave., Westminster
Phone: 714.531.2157
Hours: 09.00 - 20.00
Cash only

CHAOZHOU-STYLE RESTAURANTS (CONT.)

Kim Chuy
金水潮州粿條
501 W. Valley Blvd., Alhambra
Phone: 626.282.9080
Hours: 08.00 - 21.00
Cash only

Kim Chuy
金水潮州粿條
727 N. Broadway #103, Los Angeles
Phone: 213.687.7215
Hours: 07.30 - 20.00
Cash only

Kim Fung Restaurant
金鳳潮州粿條餐廳
128 N. Garfield Ave., Monterey Park
Phone: 626.280.8276
Hours: 08.00 - 23.00
Cash only

Kim Tar Restaurant
金塔條飯燒腊飯店
18309 Pioneer Blvd., Artesia
Phone: 562.402.0969
Hours: 10.30 - 00.00
Cash only

Kim Tar Restaurant
金塔條飯燒腊飯店
15475 E. Valley Blvd., Industry
Phone: 626.333.0070
Hours: 10.30 - 21.00
Cash only

Kim Tar Restaurant
金塔粿條海鮮飯店
964 E. Garvey Ave., Monterey Park
Phone: 626.307.9139
Hours: 07.00 - 02.00
Cash only

Mien Nghia Noodle Express
綿義餐室
304 Ord St., Los Angeles
Phone: 213.680.2411
Hours: 07.00 - 16.00
Cash only

Mien Nghia Noodle Express
綿義餐室
7755 E. Garvey Ave., Rosemead
Phone: 626.288.0177
Hours: 07.00 - 16.00
Cash only

Mien Nghia Noodle Express
綿義餐室
406-408 W. Valley Blvd., San Gabriel
Phone: 626.570.1668
Hours: 07.30 - 21.00
Cash only

My Nguyen Restaurant
美源酒家
14282 Brookhurst St., #9-10, Garden
Grove
Phone: 714.839.5541
Hours: 09.00 - 22.00
until 00.00 weekends
Cash only

New Trieu Chau Restaurant
新潮州粿條餐館
9902 Westminster Ave., Garden
Grove
Phone: 714.537.2433
Hours: 08.00 - 19.00
Cash only

Newport Seafood
新港海鮮
18441 E. Colima Rd., Rowland
Heights
Phone: 626.839.1239
Hours: 11.30 - 21.30
Mastercard, Visa

Newport Seafood
新港海鮮
835 W. Las Tunas Dr., San Gabriel
Phone: 626.289.5998
Hours: 11.30 - 21.30
Cash only

Tai Seafood Place Restaurant
漢城潮州海鮮酒家
14541 Brookhurst St., #A-3,
Westminster
Phone: 714.839.1195
Hours: 11.00 - 22.00
Mastercard, Visa

Appendix VI

Hunan-style Restaurants

Hunan Restaurant
湖南小館
423 N. Atlantic Blvd., #101,
Monterey Park
Phone: 626.282.2038
Hours: 09.00 - 21.00
Cash only

Shiang Garden Restaurant
湘園
111 N. Atlantic Blvd., #351,
Monterey Park
Phone: 626.458.4508
Hours: 11.30 - 22.00
Mastercard, Visa

SHANDONG-STYLE RESTAURANTS

Dragon Mark Restaurant
一條龍北平麵點
301 W. Valley Blvd., #110-111, San Gabriel
Phone: 626.282.5953
Hours: 11.00 - 03.00
Cash only

San Tong Restaurant
山東餃子館
18157 S. Pioneer Blvd., Artesia
Phone: 562.865.3003
Hours: 11.00 - 22.00
closed Wednesday
Cash only

Three Family's Village Restaurant
三家村
18438 E. Colima Rd., #102, Rowland Heights
Phone: 626.810.4993
Hours: 11.00 - 22.00
Mastercard, Visa

BEIJING DUCK RESTAURANTS

J.Z.Y. Cafe
京 兆 尹
1039 E. Valley Blvd., #102, San
Gabriel
Phone: 626.288.8588
Hours: 11.00 - 22.00
Cash only

Quanjude Beijing Duck
Restaurant, Inc.
全 聚 德
8450 E. Garvey Ave., #101,
Rosemead
Phone: 626.280.2378
Hours:
American Express, Mastercard, Visa

ISLAMIC-CHINESE RESTAURANTS

Beijing Islamic Restaurant
清眞又一順餐館
3160 Pacific Coast Hwy., Torrance
Phone: 310.784.0846
Hours: 11.00 - 22.00
All major credit cards

China Islamic Restaurant
清眞馬家館
7727 E. Garvey Ave., Rosemead
Phone: 626.288.4246
Hours: 11.00 - 21.30
closed Wednesday
Cash only

Islamic Tung Lai Shun Restaurant
北京清眞東來順餐廳
140 W. Valley Blvd., #118-C, San Gabriel
Phone: 626.288.6588
Hours: 11.00 - 22.00
Mastercard, Visa

V.I.P. Chinese Restaurant
清眞館
18331 E. Colima Rd., Rowland Heights
Phone: 626.810.2499
Hours: 11.00 - 21.30
All major credit cards

DUMPLINGS AND NOODLES RESTAURANTS

Chang's Noodle House
紫琳餃子館
1220 S. Golden West Ave., #F,
Arcadia
Phone: 626.821.9980
Hours: 10.00 - 22.30
Cash only

Din Tai Fung Dumpling House
鼎泰豐
1108 S. Baldwin Ave., Arcadia
Phone: 626.574.7068
Hours: 11.00 - 21.30
opens 10.30 on weekends
Mastercard, Visa

Dumpling 10053
元寶小館
10053 Valley Blvd., #2, El Monte
Phone: 626.350.0188
Hours: 11.30 - 21.30
closed Tuesday
Cash only

Dumpling House Restaurant
老鄉餃子館
5612 Rosemead Blvd., Temple City
Phone: 626.309.9918
Hours: 11.00 - 21.00
closed Tuesday
Mastercard, Visa

Dumpling Master Restaurant
老夫子餃子館
2124 S. Hacienda Blvd., Hacienda
Heights
Phone: 626.369.3788
Hours: 11.00 - 21.30
Cash only

Golden City Chinese Restaurant
金城餃子館
15827 E. Gale Ave., Hacienda
Heights
Phone: 626.333.8739
Hours: 11.00 - 21.30
closed Monday
Mastercard, Visa

Luscious Dumplings
潤豐元餃子店
704 W. Las Tunas Dr., #E4, San
Gabriel
Phone: 626.282.8695
Hours: 11.00 - 21.00
Cash only

Malan Noodles
馬蘭拉麵
2020 Hacienda Blvd., #B, Hacienda
Heights
Phone: 626.369.5602
Hours: 11.00 - 21.30
Cash only

Mandarin Deli
玉堂餃子館
356 E. 2nd St., Los Angeles
Phone: 213.617.0231
Hours: 11.00 - 21.30
Discover, Mastercard, Visa

Mandarin Deli
玉堂餃子館
727 N. Broadway, #109, Los Angeles
Phone: 213.623.6054
Hours: 11.00 - 20.00
Cash only

Mandarin Deli
玉堂餃子館
701 W. Garvey Ave., Monterey Park
Phone: 626.570.9795
Hours: 11.00 - 22.00
Cash only

Mei Lim Restaurant
美林豆漿餐飲店
1257 E. Valley Blvd., Alhambra
Phone: 626.284.1868
Hours: 07.00 - 20.00
Cash only

Ming-Wa Noodle House
明華麵館
1227 W. Valley Blvd., #105,
Alhambra
Phone: 626.458.8338
Hours: 11.00 - 21.00
Cash only

Q Noodle House
陽春麵之家
18930 E. Gale Ave., Rowland Heights
Phone: 626.288.1948
Hours: 11.00 - 22.00
Cash only

Q Noodle House
陽春麵之家
140 W. Valley Blvd., #203, San
Gabriel
Phone: 626.810.5108
Hours: 11.00 - 22.00
Cash only

Supreme Dragon Restaurant
一條龍北平麵點
18406 Colima Rd., #E,F, Rowland
Heights
Phone: 626.810.0356
Hours: 11.00 - 00.00
Cash only

Yi-Mei Restaurant
義美豆漿點心世界
730 S. Atlantic Blvd., Monterey Park
Phone: 626.284.9306
Hours: 07.00 - 20.00
Cash only

Yi-Mei Restaurant
義美豆漿點心世界
18406 Colima Rd., Rowland Heights
Phone: 626.854.9246
Hours: 07.00 - 21.00
Cash only

Yi-Mei Restaurant
義 美 豆 漿 點 心 世 界
1635 S. San Gabriel Blvd., San
Gabriel
Phone: 626.280.8568
Hours:
Cash only

Yung Ho Tou Chiang Restaurant
永 和 豆 漿
533 W. Valley Blvd., San Gabriel
Phone: 626.570.0860
Hours: 06.00 - 18.00
Cash only

Yung Ho Tou Chiang Restaurant
永 和 豆 漿 餐 飲
1045 E. Valley Blvd., #A105, San
Gabriel
Phone: 626.280.9317
Hours: 07.00 - 18.00
Cash only

MONGOLIAN HOTPOT RESTAURANTS

B.B.Q. King Buffet
敦煌火鍋烤肉自助餐館
140 W. Valley Blvd., #212, San
Gabriel
Phone: 626.289.2899
Hours: 11.00 - 01.00
Mastercard, Visa

Cocary Bar B.Q. Restaurant
可加麗餐廳
112 N. Garfield Ave., Monterey Park
Phone: 626.573.0691
Hours: 11.30 - 00.00
Mastercard, Visa

Full-Linetin Restaurant
辣妹啤酒屋，火鍋城
15301 Gale Ave., Industry
Phone: 626.369.0393
Hours: 11.00 - 00.00
Mastercard, Visa

J.Z.Y. Cafe
京兆尹
1039 E. Valley Blvd., #102, San
Gabriel
Phone: 626.288.8588
Hours: 11.00 - 22.00
Cash only

Kingswood Teppan Steak House
上林鐵板燒餐廳
18900 E. Gale Ave., #B, Rowland
Heights
Phone: 626.912.1382
Hours: 11.00 - 23.00
Mastercard, Visa

Kingswood Teppan Steak House
上林鐵板燒餐廳
250 W. Valley Blvd., #L, San Gabriel
Phone: 626.282.9600
Hours: 11.00 - 23.00
Mastercard, Visa

Lu Gi Restaurant
盧記麻辣鴛鴦火鍋
18406 E. Colima Rd., #C, Rowland
Heights
Phone: 626.965.9881
Hours: 11.30 - 22.00
Mastercard, Visa

539 W. Valley Blvd., San Gabriel
Phone: 626.457.5111
Hours: 12.00 - 00.00
Mastercard, Visa

Shabu Express
辣坊麻辣鴛鴦鍋
306 N. Garfield Ave., #A12,
Monterey Park
Phone: 626.573.3421
Hours: 11.30 - 23.00
Discover, Mastercard, Visa

Wu Gee Chinese Restaurant
台 北 吳 記 麻 辣 火 鍋
1330 S. Fullerton Rd., #108, Industry
Phone: 626.854.2668
Hours: 11.30 - 00.00
Mastercard, Visa

SICHUAN-STYLE RESTAURANTS

Best Szechwan
佳味川菜
534 E. Valley Blvd., San Gabriel
Phone: 626.927.9618
Hours: 11.00 - 21.30
closed Monday
Cash only

Chung King Restaurant
重慶川菜
206 S. Garfield Ave., Monterey Park
Phone: 626.280.7430
Hours: 11.00 - 22.00
Cash only

Fu Shin Restaurant
福星川菜
2960 E. Colorado Blvd., Pasadena
Phone: 626.792.8898
Hours: 11.30 - 21.00
All major credit cards

Golden China Restaurant
永華川菜
1015 S. Nogales St., #129, Rowland
Heights
Phone: 626.964.8800
Hours: 10.30 - 22.00
Cash only

Lucky Dragon Chinese Restaurant
3107 S. Colima Rd., Hacienda
Heights
Phone: 626.968.1765
Hours: 11.00 - 21.30
Mastercard, Visa

Lucky Restaurant
欣欣川菜
167 S. Hacienda Blvd., Industry
Phone: 626.369.6819
Hours: 10.30 - 21.30
American Express, Mastercard, Visa

Mandarin Taste Restaurant
川湘園
23391 E. Golden Springs Dr.,
Diamond Bar
Phone: 909.861.1819
Hours: 11.00 - 22.00
American Express, Mastercard, Visa

Manie's Restaurant
龍抄手
18348 E. Colima Rd., #106, Rowland
Heights
Phone: 626.810.7818
Hours: 11.00 - 21.30
Mastercard, Visa

Oriental Pearl Restaurant
重慶川味坊
621 W. Main St., Alhambra
Phone: 626.281.1898
Hours: 11.00 - 22.00
Mastercard, Visa

Red Corner Restaurant
芙蓉鎮
708 E. Las Tunas Dr., #A,
San Gabriel
Phone: 626.286.3223
Hours: 11.00 - 22.00
Mastercard, Visa

SICHUAN-STYLE RESTAURANTS (CONT.)

Shufeng Garden
屬風園
18459 Colima Rd., Rowland Heights
Phone: 626.839.7589
Hours: 11.00 - 21.30
Cash only

Sichuan Palace
川菜王國
19035 E. Colima Rd., Rowland
Heights
Phone: 626.854.1700
Hours: 11.00 - 22.00
Mastercard, Visa

Szechwan Express
小四川
732 S. Atlantic Blvd., Monterey Park
Phone: 626.282.8108
Hours: 10.00 - 21.00
Cash only

YUNNAN-STYLE RESTAURANTS

Hua's Chinese Delicacies
雲 南 過 橋 園
921 S. Baldwin Ave., Arcadia
Phone: 626.445.2755
Hours: 11.30 - 21.30
Cash only

Hua's Garden
雲 南 過 橋 園
301 N. Garfield Ave., #D, Monterey
Park
Phone: 626.571.8387
Hours: 11.00 - 21.30
Cash only

JIANGZHE-STYLE RESTAURANTS

Gourmet Delight
采味樓
501 S. Atlantic Blvd., Monterey Park
Phone: 626.284.3227
Hours: 11.30 - 21.00
Mastercard, Visa

Green Village Chinese Restaurant
綠楊村
18922 Gale Ave., #A, Rowland
Heights
Phone: 626.810.0600
Hours: 11.30 - 21.30
closed Tuesday
Mastercard, Visa

833 W. Las Tunas Dr., San Gabriel
Phone: 626.289.6228
Hours: 11.00 - 22.00
Cash only

Happy Panda Bistro
江浙小吃
18406 E. Colima Rd., #D, Rowland
Heights
Phone: 626.839.3822
Hours: 11.00 - 22.00
Cash only

King's Palace
江浙敍香園
18900 E. Gale Ave., #A, Rowland
Heights
Phone: 626.854.6687
Hours: 11.30 - 22.00
Mastercard, Visa

King's Palace
江浙敍香園
250 W. Valley Blvd., #M, San Gabriel
Phone: 626.282.9566
Hours: 11.30 - 22.00
Mastercard, Visa

Mei Long Village
梅龍鎮
301 W. Valley Blvd., #112, San
Gabriel
Phone: 626.284.4769
Hours: 11.30 - 21.30
Mastercard, Visa

New Shanghai Restaurant
萍聚閣
5408 Walnut Ave., #B, Irvine
Phone: 949.733.3836
Hours: 10.00 - 21.30
Discover, Mastercard, Visa

New Shanghai Restaurant
萍聚閣
8450 E. Valley Blvd., Rosemead
Phone: 626.288.9299
Hours: 10.00 - 21.30
Cash only

Jiangzhe-style Restaurants (cont.)

New Shanghai Restaurant
萍聚閣
1015 S. Nogales St., #131, Rowland
Heights
Phone: 626.964.8458
Hours: 10.00 - 23.30
Mastercard, Visa

SHANGHAI-STYLE RESTAURANTS

Food World Restaurant
新世界上海飯店
640 W. Valley Blvd., Alhambra
Phone: 626.458.1918
Hours: 11.00 - 22.00
Mastercard, Visa

Jin Jiang Restaurant
錦江江南名點
301 W. Valley Blvd., #109, San
Gabriel
Phone: 626.308.9238
Hours: 11.00 - 00.00
Cash only

Lake Spring Shanghai Restaurant
上海錢塘春
219 E. Garvey Ave., Monterey Park
Phone: 626.280.3571
Hours: 11.00 - 22.00
Mastercard, Visa

Mandarin Chateau
上海美味齋
970 N. Broadway, #114, Los Angeles
Phone: 213.625.1195
Hours: 11.30 - 21.30
All major credit cards

Mandarin Shanghai Restaurant
上海美味齋
558 Las Tunas Dr., Arcadia
Phone: 626.445.4555
Hours: 11.00 - 21.30
until 22.00 on weekends
American Express, Mastercard, Visa

Shanghai Kitchen
上海喬家柵
140 W. Valley Blvd., #211, San
Gabriel
Phone: 626.280.4676
Hours: 07.00 - 21.30
Mastercard, Visa

Shanghai Yau Fat Restaurant
上海有發飯店
1721 W. Valley Blvd., Alhambra
Phone: 626.282.8634
Hours: 10.30 - 21.30
Mastercard, Visa

Wok and Noodle
上海小吃
828 W. Valley Blvd., Alhambra
Phone: 626.588.2284
Hours: 11.00 - 22.00
closed Wednesday
Mastercard, Visa

INDEX

M

madras 79

Manchus 1, 121
See also Qing Dynasty

Mandarin (dialect) 2, 37, 129, 167, iii

mandarin oranges 8, 173

mantou
See bread

Mao, Zedong 3, 92, 95, 147

maotai
See beverage, alcoholic,
kaoliang

Marco Polo 20, 121, 164

mayonnaise 179

meatball 48, 70, 79, 140

medicine
See Chinese medicine

Meiweizhai 175

milk broth
See Shandong, cuisine

millet 19, 21, 101, 103, 108, 116,
128, 129

mille feuille 76

Minced Squab Wrapped in Lettuce
See Hunan, cuisine

Ming Dynasty 18, 121

mint 42, 85, 86, 89

Mock Duck
See Jiangzhe, cuisine

Mongolia 5

Mongolian barbecue 142, 143

Mongolian hotpot 25, 101, 138, 155,
157
northern style 107
Sichuan style 153, 155
yuanyangguo 138, 141

Mongols 18, 101, 138
See also Yuan Dynasty

Monterey Park v, vi

mooncake
See dessert

mungbean 19, 20, 129, 131

Muslims 20, 103, 120, 121, 122, 132
See also Islamic-Chinese
cuisine

mustard 70, 147, 151

N

Nanjing 102, 162, 164, 166

Nanking
See Nanjing

Nanking Road 174

Nantou Prefecture 6

Napa cabbage
See vegetable

Ningbo 165, 169

Ningxia 120

nira
See vegetable

noodle
cat's ears 106, 109, 137
hand-pulled noodles 32, 123, 136,
137
knife-cut noodles 88, 106, 109,
123, 124, 135, 137
longevity noodles 32
yi-fu mian 48, 106

white radish
See vegetable

White Sugar Cake
See dim sum/yum cha

wines
See beverage, alcoholic

wintermelon
See vegetable

wonton 47, 74, 99, 151

wonton in red oil
See Sichuan, cuisine

Wuhan 129

Wuxi 161, 162, 165, 170

Wuxi Spareribs
See Jiangzhe, cuisine

X

Xiamen 2

Xian 120

Xiang 97
See also Hunan

Xinjiang 120

Y

Yang, Quanren 115

Yangtze 146, 149, 161, 162, 164, 166, 167, 169, 171

Yangzhou 162, 165, 169
See also Jiangzhe, cuisine

Yangzhou-style Fried Rice
See Jiangzhe, cuisine

yeast 17, 106

yellow nira
See vegetable

Yellow River 102

youtiao 71, 128, 129, 131, 133, 134, 137, 141

yuanyang
See beverage, coffeeshop

yuanyangguo
See Mongolian hotpot

Yuan Dynasty 5, 18, 20, 101, 121, 138

yum cha 67
See also dim sum/yum cha

Yunnan 145
  cuisine 156
    Across the Bridge Rice Noodles 145, 156, 157, 159
    Chicken in a Clay Airport 156, 157, 158, 159, 178

yu choy
See vegetable

Z

Zhejiang 7, 8, 13, 162, 167, 169

Zhenjiang black vinegar 61, 149, 167, 170, 176